The Worship and Love of God

The Worship and Love of God

EMANUEL SWEDENBORG

IN THREE PARTS

Translated by
Alfred H. Stroh and Frank Sewall

**SWEDENBORG
FOUNDATION**
West Chester, Pennsylvania

Originally published in Latin as *De Cultu et Amore Dei,* London, 1745.
First English translation by R. Hindmarsh, London, 1790-1791.
First U.S. edition translated by A. H. Stroh and F. Sewall, Boston, 1914.
Fourth printing, 1997.
Fifth printing with minor modifications, 2020.

Library of Congress Cataloging-in-Publication Data

Names: Swedenborg, Emanuel, 1688-1772, author. | Stroh, Alfred Henry,
    translator. | Sewall, Frank, 1837-1915, translator.
Title: The worship and love of God : in three parts / Emanuel Swedenborg ;
    translated by Alfred H. Stroh and Frank Sewall.
Other titles: De cultu et amore Dei. English
Description: West Chester, Pennsylvania : Swedenborg Foundation, 2020. |
    Summary: "This allegorical retelling of the biblical creation story blends
    science, poetic understanding, and the spiritual revelations of Swedish
    visionary Emanuel Swedenborg (1688-1772). Starting with the creation of
    the earth from the substance of the universe, Swedenborg takes the reader
    through the formation of plants, animals, and finally human beings.
    Swedenborg puts particular emphasis on the spiritual nature of Adam and
    Adam's marriage to Eve. Although not considered one of Swedenborg's
    theological works, this book was written just prior to his visionary period
    and contains the seeds of many of his later ideas. This edition is a reprint of
    a 1914 English translation by Alfred H. Stroh and Frank Sewall"
    -- Provided by publisher.
Identifiers: LCCN 2020006202 | ISBN 9780877852902 (paperback) | ISBN
    9780877857129 (ebook)
Subjects: LCSH: Creation--Early works to 1800. | Adam (Biblical figure) |
    Eve (Biblical figure)
Classification: LCC BX8712 .W7 2020 | DDC 231.7/65--dc23
LC record available at https://lccn.loc.gov/2020006202

Printed in the United States of America

Swedenborg Foundation
320 North Church Street
West Chester, PA 19380
swedenborg.com

CONTENTS

PREFACE OF THE TRANSLATORS

Parts the First and the Second of this work were published in Latin by the author in London in the year 1745. Translations into English of these two parts have been published in 1801, 1816, 1832, 1864, and 1885, but no translation of Part the Third has hitherto appeared. A portion of this Part in print and the remainder in manuscript have been preserved in the Library of the Royal Swedish Academy of Sciences at Stockholm and made accessible to scholars through Vol. VII of the photolithographed manuscripts. From this copy as carefully compared with the original writing itself Alfred H. Stroh has now transcribed this hitherto unpublished portion of the work, and translated it into English for the present edition.

The translation of Parts I and II by the Rev. John Clowes published in 1816, and used without change by the Rev. Thomas Murray Gorman, M.A., in his edition of 1885, has been very thoroughly revised and its omissions supplied with careful reference to the original text by Alfred H. Stroh and Frank Sewall, this work having been undertaken as a result of the interest roused in the work at the meeting of the Swedenborg Scientific Association held in Washington, D.C., in the year 1904. A simultaneous translation from the photolithographed Part III kindly submitted for comparison by the Rev. Alfred Acton, afforded valuable assistance in the effort to find the most accurate rendering of a text in places obscure both in the writing and the meaning. With an edition of the Latin text of the entire work which is now contemplated, it will be possible for scholars to examine these passages for themselves and satisfy themselves as to their most correct rendering into English.

Alfred H. Stroh
Frank Sewall

INTRODUCTION

1. WALKING once alone in a pleasant grove to dispel my disturbing thoughts, and seeing that the trees were shedding their foliage, and that the falling leaves were flying about—for autumn was then taking its turn in the revolution of the year, and dispersing the decorations of summer—from being sad I became serious, while I recollected the delights which that grove, from spring even to this season, had communicated, and so often diffused through my whole mind. But on seeing this change of scene I began to meditate on the vicissitudes of times; and it occurred to me whether all things relating to time do not also pass through similar vicissitudes, namely, whether this is not the case, not only with forests but also with our lives and ages; for it is evident that they, in like manner, commencing from a kind of spring and blossom, and passing through their summer, sink rapidly into their old age, an image of autumn. Nor is this the case only with the periods of men's individual lives, but also with the ages or eons of the world's existence, that is, with the general lives of societies, which from their infancy, integrity, and innocence, were formerly called the golden and silver ages, and which, it is now believed, are about to be succeeded by the last or iron ages, which will shortly moulder away into rust or the dust of clay.

2. For the ancient wise men, whose minds were, so to speak, more remote from their bodies, and thus nearer to heaven [than ours],

in applying themselves most intently to investigate the interior secrets of nature, discovered clearly in the revolutions of their own times, that ages nobler than their own had preceded, and that in the beginning, justice and purity, with their attendant virtues, directed the helm of the kingdoms of the world; wherefore they taught posterity to believe that their deities, descending at that time from their astral abodes to the earth, consociated with mankind in all the friendship of life, so that heaven itself as it were descended from on high to these lower spheres, and poured forth its superior delights upon the inhabitants of air, or of its ultimate region of operation. In compliment to these deities these times were called Saturnian and golden. The earth itself also they conceived to be adorned with the most delightful self-cultivated shrubberies and orchards, and they represented it as entirely converted into a sort of continual garden or paradise; yea, they contracted the four seasons of the year into one, and this they concluded to be a perpetual spring, which breathed its zephyrs continually, so that while it produced this temperature of the atmosphere, it also filled and refreshed the

2 minds of the inhabitants with its blandishments. With such introductory scenery the ancient wise ones (*Sophi*) opened the theatre of the world which we behold, doubtless because in all its sports, or offspring and products, both living and dead, they contemplated an express image of such an order. For there is nothing but what commences its existence from its spring and blossom, and from its infancy and innocence; for particular representations are so many mirrors of things in general, and general representations are so many mirrors of things in particular, which have their allotted places under these general things. From the persuasion wrought by this perpetual authority of nature they conceived, in looking back to former times, that a similar state of spring and of infancy existed in their beginning. Let us also contemplate the face of the universe in the mirrors presented by the singulars of which it is composed, and from them let us evolve the fates of times and of

ages. Nevertheless, without the favor and influence of the Supreme Deity, from whom, as from the only Fountain and Highest Sun of Wisdom, all truths flow down as rays into our understandings, vain would be our inquiry; wherefore, let us with adoration supplicate His presence and His favor.

The Worship and Love of God

PART ONE

which discusses the origin of the earth,
paradise, and the abode of living creatures;
also
the birth, infancy, and love of the
first-born, or Adam

ON THE
WORSHIP AND LOVE OF GOD

Chapter I

Section First
Concerning the Origin of the Earth

3. ROUND about the sun, the centre of this universe, our earthly globe revolves every year in an orbit, and measures the stages of its gyration by the constellations of the zodiac past which it is carried; the time of its circuit, or its return to the same point of its circle, is called its year. While it performs this its gyration or year, it is turned aside, a little obliquely towards the constellation of the seven stars, and downwards in opposition to them, from the great equinoctial circle, and thus in its every least progress, wheresoever it is, it beholds the sun under a varied aspect, whence come its four seasons of the year, namely, spring, summer, autumn, and winter. In this its circumvolution, it turns like a wheel about its axis, which runs from pole to pole through the middle equinoctial circle or equator, and by these revolutions it divides the circumference through which it runs, into parts or degrees, which are called the days of its year. The effect of each of these rotations is, that the sun rises, and from rising gains a meridian altitude, and thence declines,

and at length sets and is hidden. Hence again come the four times of every day, called morning, noon, evening, and night, together with their hours, which, as it were, surround this day, and measure the divisions of the seasons of the year. The four intervals of every day represent themselves in the four intervals of the whole year, as lesser effigies in greater; thus the morning represents itself in the spring, noon in summer, autumn in evening, and winter in night, and so forth.[a]

4. As the terraqueous globe revolves around the sun, as a fluent circumference encompasses its centre, so the moon makes a circuit around the earth, as again her centre; and in like manner cuts the equinoctial circle in two opposite points or nodes, and runs through a kind of zodiac; thus being nearer to one or other of the poles, she changes her situation every moment of her progress, and with her situation her aspect, by which she enlightens her central globe. The revolutions which she makes are so many of her years, to us months; thus again an image nearly similar is represented of her course, seasons, vicissitudes, and other changes, which result from these revolutions as from causes, resembling the image which exists in our earth.

5. Besides these, there are large and ponderous bodies, wandering around our sun, the common fountain of light, within this its universe, which are called wandering stars, popularly planets.

---

[a] For, as was said above in the introduction, general representations are mirrors of things particular, and *vice versa;* thus not only do the diversities of days represent themselves in the diversities of years, but also the least moments of days represent themselves in the same; for whatsoever relates to time has its allotted places under annual spaces, as common subjects; for, in like manner, every period of two hours of every day corresponds to its month; for there are twelve periods of two hours of the day, as there are twelve months of the year, since the periods of two hours in the morning represent so many vernal or spring months, the periods of two hours at noon so many summer months, and the periods of two hours of night so many winter months; in like manner, the warmth of spring or summer may be likened to the sunshine of those hours, and their cold to the shade. If we proceed further, there occur still other similar correspondences in the subdivisions of these times, as of the first minutes of the hour with the [first] quarter of the day, and so forth.

These in like manner perform their gyrations, and, according to their distances from the centre, roll and describe circumferences, which are so many annual times or spaces which they accomplish. These immense masses, in like manner as our terraqueous globe, carry each its axis erect to the poles of the universe, and are urgent in their course according to the flexure of their zodiac, whence they also have springs, summers, autumns, and winters. They have 2 a rotation also like orbits around an axis, by virtue whereof they behold their sun, within each turn of rotation, rising in the morning and setting in the evening, whence they also have moons and nights, with intermediate lights and shades. Moreover also around these globes, which emulate the globe of our earth, there are moving moons, called satellites, which in like manner illuminate the surfaces of those orbs with light borrowed and reflected from the sun. The globe which is rejected to the most remote circumference, and is farthest distant from the sun, lest he wander in a fainter and more doubtful light than the rest enjoy, is encompassed by a large satellite, like a continuous lunar mirror, called his belt. This gathers up the rays of the sun, wearied with their journey, and diffuses them at large, when collected, over the faces of that globe which are turned towards them.

6. Around the great system of the sun, and of its wandering orbs, and of the moons which accompany them, shine innumerable stars, which constitute our starry heaven, divided into twelve signs, according to the sections of the zodiac, and make visible its immensity. All these stars remain fixed, and, as images of the great sun, immovable in their central stations, they also occupy a kind of plane constructed by their rays, which they subject and ascribe to themselves as their own proper universe. There are therefore as many universes as there are stars encompassing and crowning our world, greater and lesser, according to the strength and quantity of light emitted from them. These heavenly circles mutually press 2 and bind each other by contact, and by continual interweavings enfold together a heavenly sphere, and by infinite orbits complete

a form which is the exemplar of all spheres and forms, in which the starry orbs each and all most harmoniously conspire to one and the same end, namely, that they may establish and strengthen each other. By virtue of this union resulting from the perfection of the form, this complex of universes is called the firmament;[b] for in a grand body thus consociated, no member claims anything to itself as its own, unless it be of such a quality that it can inflow from what is general into what concerns itself, and again, as by an orbit, can reflow into what concerns the other universes, or into what is general; on which account also they do not confine their lights and torches to their own sphere, but diffuse them even into the opaque bodies of the solar world, and into our earth, and when the setting sun causes night in the hemisphere they supply his place.

7. In the bounded space of this universe, as was said, immense bodies revolve, which, performing their circuits round the sun as a common centre, grow to their respective ages. The sun, like an

---

b This form, which the stars with their universes determine or co-effect by intermixture and harmony with each other, and which on that account is called celestial, cannot at all be acknowledged as the most perfect of all forms in the world, if we depend only on the view presented to the spectator's eye on this globe of earth; for the eye does not penetrate into the distances of one star from another, but views them as placed in a kind of expanse, one beside another; hence they appear as without order, like a heap without arrangement. Nevertheless, that the form resulting from the connecting series of all the starry universes, is the exemplar and idea of all forms, may appear not only from this, that it serves as the firmament of the whole heaven, but also from this, that the first substances of the world, and the powers of its nature, gave birth to those universes, from which, and their cooperation, nothing but what is most perfect flows forth; this is confirmed also by the distances of the stars from each other, preserved for so many ages, without the least change intervening. Such forms protect themselves by their own proper virtue, for they breathe something perpetual and infinite; nevertheless, they cannot be comprehended as to their quality, except by lower or lowest forms, the knowledge of which we have procured to ourselves from objects which affect the sight of the eye, and further, by continual abstractions of the imperfections under which these forms labor. But let us view these forms in their examples: the lowest form, or the form proper to earthly substances, is that which is determined by mere angular, and at the same time by plane subjects, whatsoever be their figure, provided they flow together into a certain form; this, therefore, is to be called an ANGULAR FORM, the proper object of our geometry. From this form we are enabled to contemplate the next higher form, or the form perpetually angular, which is the

The Worship and Love of God

aged parent, regards these revolving globes no otherwise than as his own offspring that have attained to a considerable maturity in years; for he continually consults their interests general and particular (*singularem*), and although they are distant, he never fails to exercise over them his care and parental protection, since by his rays he is, as it were, present in his provision for them; he cherishes them with the warmth issuing forth from his immense bosom; he

---

same as the CIRCULAR or SPHERICAL FORM; for this latter is more perfect than the other in this respect, that its circumference is, as it were, a perpetual plane, or infinite angle, because totally void of planes and angles; therefore also it is the measure of all angular forms, for we measure angles and planes by sections and sines of a circle. From these 3 considerations we see, that into this latter form something infinite or perpetual has insinuated itself, which does not exist in the former, namely, the circular orbit, whose end and beginning cannot be marked. In the circular or spherical form, again, we are enabled to contemplate a certain higher form, which may be called the perpetually circular, or simply the SPIRAL FORM; for to this form is still further added something perpetual or infinite, which is not in the former, namely, that its diameters are not bounded or terminated in a certain centre, neither are they simple lines, but they terminate in a certain circumference of a circle or surface of a sphere, which serves it as a centre, and that its diameters are bent into a species of a certain curve, by which means this form is the measure of a circular form or forms, as the circular is the measure of the angular. In this spiral form we are 4 enabled to view a still higher kind of form, which may be called the perpetually spiral or VORTICAL FORM, in which again something perpetual or infinite is found which was not in the former; for the former had reference to a circle as to a kind of infinite centre, and from this, by its diameters, to a fixed centre as to its limit or boundary; but the latter has reference to a spiral form as a centre, by lines perpetually circular; this form manifests itself especially in magnetic action, and is the measure of the spiral form for the reason above mentioned concerning inferior forms. In this, lastly, may be viewed the highest form of nature, or the perpetually vortical form, which is the same as the CELESTIAL FORM, in which almost all boundaries are, as it were, erased, as so many imperfections, and still more perpetuities or infinities are put on; wherefore this form is the measure of the vortical form, consequently the exemplar or idea of all inferior forms, from which the inferior descend and derive birth as from their beginning, or from the form of forms. That this is the case with the formations of things will be demonstrated, God willing, in the doctrine of forms, and the doctrine of order and of degrees adjoined to it. From 5 this form those faculties and virtues result, by which one thing regards another as well as itself, nor is there anything but what consults the general strength and concord, for in that form there is not given any fixed centre, but as many centres as there are points, so that all its determinations, taken together, exist from mere centres or representations of a centre, by which means nothing can be respected as proper to it, unless it be of such a quality that from what is general, or from all the centres, which taken together produce

adorns their bodies and members every year with a most beautiful clothing; he nourishes their inhabitants with a perpetual supply of food; he promotes the life of all things, and, moreover, enlightens them with his luminous radiance.[c] Since the sun thus executes all the functions of parental duty, it follows from the connection and tenor of causes, that if we are desirous to unfold the history of the earth from its earliest infancy, and to examine it from its origin, we must have recourse to the sun himself; for every effect is a continuity of causes from the first cause, and the cause by which anything subsists is continued to the cause by which it exists, since subsistence is a kind of perpetual existence.

8. Let us first then contemplate the earth in its birth, or in its egg, and afterwards in its infancy and flower; let us afterwards follow it through its several states and periods. These, if they coincide with those things that are presented to our view in the mirrors of

---

what is general, it may inflow into itself as a similar centre, and may reflow through an orbit for the benefit of all, or into what is general. This indeed must of necessity appear strange at first view, because it is fetched from far beyond the objects of our sight; nevertheless, that the case is so, is clear from a consideration of all phenomena traced up to their causes and their principles; especially from the animate body, where such an arrangement of parts is everywhere to be met with that while each is a centre in itself it is yet related to the terminations of near or remote parts in a kind of circumference, diameter, or axis; the eye presents to us a still more evident idea of these phenomena in the ether modified by rays.

c Let us consider these things more particularly: *that the sun is present by his rays* with all the wandering bodies in his universe, is manifest from his heat and light, for both are contained in his rays, heat in the measure and proportion of his altitude, and according to the density and column of the atmosphere through which the rays pass, also in some degree according to his continuance above the horizon, and the meeting of heat exhaling from the object; and lastly, according to the distance or angle which his wide gaze embraces; for bodies in the extreme limit of his universe are affected with a less power of heat than those which move at a less distance and more immediately under his view; wherefore the sun *cherishes with heat bursting forth from his large bosom,* these bodies which, according to our proposition, have been derived from him. Moreover he also *adorns them with the most beautiful clothing;* for the universal face of the earth, with its fields, shrubberies, and gardens, blossoms at the new breathings of his warmth, namely, in the spring and summer seasons; and all things which clothe that face, though dead, rise again from their tombs to a kind of life; but instantly, when the sun descends from his height, and becomes lower

universal nature, will be so many satisfactory proofs, which, transposed from the place of consequents into the place of antecedents, will conversely confirm the origin itself from its own series.

9. There was, then, a time like no time, when the pregnant sun carried in his womb the gigantic brood of his own universe, and when, being delivered, he emitted them into the regions of air; for if they were derived from the sun, as a parent, it is manifest that they must have burst forth from his fruitful womb. Nevertheless, it was impossible that he could carry in his burning focus, and afterwards bring forth, such heavy and inert productions, and therefore such burdens must have been the ultimate effects of his exhalation, and of the forces thence flowing and efficient. Hence it follows, that the sun was primitively overspread with effluvia excited and hatched by his real irradiation, and flowing together in abundance and from every direction to him, as to an asylum and only harbor of rest; and that from those fluids, condensed in process of time,

---

by the inclination of the plane of the horizon, cold begins to prevail, in consequence of which the subjects of the vegetable kingdom sink to decay, and are consigned to death; thus he *nourishes the inhabitants with perpetual food* excited from the bosom of the earth, and *preserves their life.* Moreover also he *gives times,* which derive from the sun their great- 3 est and least durations, and their vicissitudes; for ages with their years, years with their days, and days with their hours, exist by his alternately changed aspects, and by his risings varying to his settings, and by his settings returning again to risings; and thus they become subjects of number, because subjects of sense. *He presides over annual and diurnal motions;* for as the sun by his rays excites active and living powers in all other things, so also he stirs up and renovates his whole universe with the ethereal atmospheres excited according to the nature of his rays, by a general force corresponding to irradiation, and thus by a kind of animation; without such an origin of motion these great bodies could in no wise be kept in a constant revolution around him, their source. From particular forces there results a general force, as a compound results from the simples of which it is the aggregate. Moreover also he *enlightens those orbs with his luminous radiance;* for, as was said, his rays 4 convey along with them both heat and light, but this according to his elevations above the horizon, and according to distances, also according to columns of air and the time of his continuance in the hemisphere; thus in his rays there are two natures, so distinct, that one exists without the other; as in midwinter, when the sun shines with as great light as in midsummer from the same degree of altitude; to this latter nature of his is opposed shade, but to the other, cold; by his luminous radiance he enlightens those things which he produces by heat, that they may affect our sight.

there existed a surrounding nebulous expanse, or a mass like the white of an egg, which, with the sun included in it, would resemble the GREAT EGG OF THE UNIVERSE; also that the surface of this egg could at length derive a crust, or a kind of shell, in consequence of the rays being intercepted, and the apertures shut up; and this crust, the sun, when the time of parturition was at hand, by his inward heat and agitation would burst and thereby hatch a numerous offspring, equal in number to the globes visible in his universe, which still look up to him as a parent.[d] Something similar to this appears to take place both in the great and smaller subjects within the sphere of his world and of its three kingdoms on the earth, whether they be produced from a womb, from seed, or from an egg, for they are all only types effigied according to the idea of the greatest, and in themselves, although in a small effigy, resemble and emulate a kind of universe.[e]

2 in

10. On the bursting of this immense repository there sprang forth large masses, equal in number to the planets visible in this universe, and resembling our earth, but which being yet without form, and not balanced in any ether, pressed upon the great surface of their parent; for no force was as yet operative to carry them in

---

[d] It is manifest that similar incrustations have also not unfrequently appeared in the starry heavens; for occasionally new stars have been seen, shining exceedingly with a ruddy (*rutile*) effulgence, and presently by degrees growing obscure, yet afterwards either returning to their former splendor, or altogether vanishing; which is a sure proof that those stars, in consequence of a conflux of parts excited by their exhalation, have been covered over with a similar crust, which would either be dissipated, or would altogether hide them, so as to withdraw them from our view. Besides, if we compare the immense magnitude of the sun with the planetary bodies which revolve around him, we may easily be instructed, by a slight calculation, that such a surrounding crust would have sufficed for the production of so many and such large bodies. This egg was the chaos so famous in old time and at this day, consisting, as is supposed, of the accumulated elements of all things, which afterwards being arranged into the most beautiful order, produced our world.

[e] It is a common opinion, that everything is produced from an egg; even the viviparous creatures of the animal kingdom, first in the ovaries, next within the chorion and amnion, which, with their liquid, resemble the shell with the white in the egg. The seeds of vegetables also represent the same thing, being covered with little coats and encompassed

another direction. Thus they lay scattered like suckling masses near the burning bosom of their father, and, as it were, at his teats. But 2 presently when the sun, the folding-doors being unlocked and the gates thrown open to the empty universe, had begun to cast forth fiery exhalations from his now full and swelling mouth, and to distend it with his powers and forces, he first filled the neighboring and presently the more remote distances with auras and thus with spaces.*f* Hence arose ether, which being diffused around the sun, and at the same time also around the masses which encompass him, wrapped the latter, as it were, in swathings or spires, and encompassed them with spheres suited to the mobility of each. In the circumferences of their spheres he placed a vertical point, which he drew into perpetual orbs, and from them produced a central gyration, in which the mass was involved. Hence it came to pass that 3

---

within with a juice resembling that of animals. In all cases there is a similarity, for when the time of birth is at hand, whether in the womb, in a seed, or an egg, there is a bursting of a cover, or coat, or shell. The only difference between these lesser instances of birth, and the greatest in the case of the sun, is, that the cherishing heat or warmth in the former, penetrates from things outermost to things inmost, before it acts from things inmost into things outermost; but in the latter, from things inmost to things outermost, that it may return towards those things which the inmost involve; for the operation of principles is in a manner altogether inverted, in respect to that of the causes or effects existing from those principles; this is continual not only in the moments of birth, but also at other times, as will be illustrated by examples in what follows. In this manner these orbs, as so many offsprings, have gained their birth and existence from the bosom of the sun; for it amounts to the same thing, whether elements have been accumulated immediately from the centre into that immense crust, or from the circumferences excited from the centre, and relapsing to the compass of the centre with the incipient (*inchoamentis*) elements.

f The ether itself, with which the solar universe is filled, and whence spaces and times, in a word, nature herself, as something, exist, could not derive its birth from any other source than from the same principle and fountain; for unless this was the case, all concordance or agreement must perish. And if we examine that ether from its own phenomena, we shall find it to be of no other nature than that of the substances which excite the solar focus itself; nor of any other form than the supreme form in nature, which is called the supra-celestial. But those substances were thus only formed anew in order that they might afterwards receive the rays of their sun and transmit them when received to the most remote limits of the universe; in this beginning of existences, therefore, it is not said that a ray bursts forth from his burning furnace, but an exhalation, that is, his own matter.

those bodies, being as yet fluids, and as it were molten, assumed an orbicular form from the concourse of so many centripetal forces. These now became orbs, and of no weight, as it were, because in centres, and being conveyed and put in rotation by the surrounding ether, they first began to creep and then to walk around the sun, and presently, like little children, to dance and leap, and by quick and short circuits to make a commencement of years, and a rotation of days, and thus to enter upon their periods.

11. When these masses were now carried round the sun into their first periods, and by quick and short circuits accomplished their annual spaces, according to the perpetual gyrations of the heavenly bodies, in the manner of a running spiral or winding line, they also cast themselves outwards into new circumferences, and thus by excursions resembling a spiral, removed themselves from the centre, and at the same time from the very heated and burning bosom of their father, but slowly and by degrees; *g* being thus as 2 it were weaned, they began to move in another direction. There were seven fœtuses brought forth at one birth, equal in number to the planets which revolve in the grand circle of the world; each of these being balanced in its sphere according to the proportion of its mass to its weight, receded by a quicker or slower pace from its natal centre. The brothers being thus separated, every one moved

---

g The spire which the novitiate orbs formed in their excursion from the solar centre, cannot be conceived intellectually unless the supreme forms of nature above mentioned are unfolded in their order; then it will be manifest that the fluxion of the orbs with their spheres round the centre, was like that of a spire round an axis, and afterwards like a projection from its vertical point into a larger curve, of which we shall speak presently. This circumgyration may be especially deduced and confirmed from the solar spots, which are also so many globes wandering proximately around the sun, some of which have quicker periods of revolution, but some slower, altogether according to their distances from the sun as from their centre; the same may also concluded from the orbits of the planets compared with each other. Such gyrations, marked according to superior forms, are in no wise determined without respect to poles and greater circles, the equator and the ecliptic; the very nature of the form involves this. Both the declinations and the inclinations of the magnet, as well as its attractions, which are so many visible effects of the determination of that ether, confirm also the same [conclusion].

The Worship and Love of God

with a velocity resulting from open space, and while flying off into gyrations gradually also gyrated into circumferences stretching out into the ether. Some of them also brought along with them 3 from the palace of their parent little orbs, some more and some fewer, like servants and satellites, received within the spheres that were in gyration around them; but our earth brought as a hand-maid only one, which is called the moon, to reflect into the face of the interposed earth, her mistress, especially in the night time, the luminous effigy of the sun received in herself as in a mirror. Thus whithersoever they went, and in whatsoever direction they turned themselves, they nevertheless acted under the view, and in the presence of their parent.

12. Our globe, therefore, was impelled round its sun in perpetual windings, and in the spires of a continued screw, in order that by quick and repeated revolutions it might turn to him all the points of its tender and as yet naked body, and thus receive into itself by all vicissitudes and degrees, the breathings (*afflatus*) of his heat; for it was not as yet earth, but an uncovered wave, the whole without a shore or slime, and being thus a large fluent heap of the principles of inert nature, operated upon by the rays of a neighboring burn-ing focus, effervesced and boiled from its depths. To the intent, 2 therefore, that these principles or elements of inert and heavier nature might coalesce into secondary and new principles of water, salt, earth, and the like, and in order that from these principles fœtuses of an infinite variety might again finally be hatched, this globe must of necessity have undergone innumerable vicissitudes and changes, which were like so many efficient causes, from whose series, continued in the globe itself, general effects might be pro-duced, which would derive their perfection according to the order of these successive principles, and the perpetual continuations of these causes.

13. For two principles of nature were now come to their birth and luxuriance, namely, active and passive principles, the former of which filled the whole universe, for ether was the atmosphere of

such principles or forces; but the latter, or passive principles, were heaped together into one, and constituted globes suspended and equally balanced in the centres of the circumgyration of the active forces. But these principles were to be joined together, and one was to be given to the other in a kind of marriage, in order that a new and mediating atmosphere might be conceived, which might proximately encompass the orb, and receive the solar fires, and temper them according to the variation of its state, or density and column; when this atmosphere was born it was called air, deriving from its birth this [property], that in all modes of acting it emulates ether, and, moreover, being heavy, presses itself and thereby the earth.[h]

14. After this atmosphere had been hatched from the most attenuated principles exhaled from the bosom of the orb and married to ether, and had thereby begun to temper the heat which flowed from the fiery fountain so near at hand, then our liquid orb began to contract a crust, or to be superinduced with a kind of coat, at first rare or attenuated, but presently denser, which continually increased according to the affluence of the parts emerging from beneath, for as yet it was boiling (*aestuabat*) from its very bottom. Being covered round, and, as it were, clad with this surface, the orb then first assumed the appearance of an earth, and, indeed, a clean and beautiful one; for it was a perpetual plane, without scars (*mendis*), hills, or valleys, one sphere without a boundary, perforated by rivers and streams springing up from hot baths, like warm veins in a new body, and overspread on all sides with a dewy mist which

---

h Air when modified produces sound, as ether produces light; the organ of hearing is allotted to the former, but that of seeing to the latter. That air emulates ether in its modes is evident from its sound, which is propagated by right lines to a considerable distance, like light, and conveyed in every direction from the different centres of motion; also that each in like manner rebounds or is reflected according to the angle of incidence, and presses equally inwards and outwards in the manner of a perpetual circle or sphere. But that air is at the same time a concrete of passive principles, or principles endowed with a *vis inertiæ*, is evident from its manifest gravity, wherein it differs from ether, which, in consequence of its purely active force, whence comes its elasticity, derives this [property], that it is neither light nor heavy.

entered the new-born atmosphere, and, relapsing into the warm bosoms of the earth, cherished it with continual vapor.

15. This virgin and new-born earth, furnished with so becoming an aspect, now represented a kind of new egg, but one laden with as many small eggs, or small seeds, collected at its surface, as were to be of its future triple kingdom, namely, the mineral, the vegetable, and the animal. These seeds or beginnings lay as yet unseparated in their rudiments, one folded up in another, namely, the vegetable kingdom in the mineral kingdom, which was to be the matrix, and the animal kingdom in the vegetable kingdom, which was to serve as a nurse or nourisher; for each was afterwards to come forth distinctly from its covering. Thus the present contained the past, and what was to come lay concealed in each, for one thing involved another in a continual series; by which means this earth, from its continued beginnings (*auspiciis*), was perpetually in a kind of birth, and, as it were, looking to that which was to follow; while it was also in the end, and, as it were, forgetful of what was gone before; and receding from the centre as according to progression in its orbit it continually involved new powers from which uses were to be successively unfolded.

Section Second
Concerning Paradise

16. THE earth, still naked and unadorned, advanced in years, and like a young damsel, as yet undeveloped, hastened to the flower of its first age; for so long as by its interior gyration it grazed the near surface of the sun, its seasons were so rapid, that it passed through ages, which, if measured by the periods of our time, would scarcely equal as many months, inasmuch as every gyration was a year, and every rotation about its axis was a day; but it prolonged these times as it increased its spaces, while running along like a spire, continually enlarging the orbits of its gyrations. Thus there was a time when it moved over the disk of the sun like a spot; and afterwards there was a time when it revolved in the orbit in which the planet revolves which is at this day nearest to the sun; and next in that occupied by the beautiful star which in the morning announces the sun's rising, and in the evening his setting; thus there was no space from the centre to its present circumference, which it did not once occupy and circumscribe.

17. When therefore the earth, by its evolutions, continually extended the circumferences of its orbit and grew in years, it came successively to the first flower of its age, namely, to that goal of its course or first station where its annual gyrations, being neither too much contracted nor too much extended, preserved a kind of mean; when, namely, the four seasons of the year pressed so closely on each other, or succeeded each other so rapidly, that one was quickly

changed into another, like [the sections in the circumference of] a rapidly revolving wheel; or, when the very short summer hastily overtook the short spring, and the quick autumn the summer, and the winter again the autumn, bringing back the year to its spring, so lately left, and not yet driven away. Thus the four seasons, distinct from each other, by the quick blendings (*influxus*) of one into the other coalesced into one season, resembling a PERPETUAL SPRING. For in such contracted spaces of the year, the daystar heat, or the heat of summer, could not enkindle to excess the warmth of spring, nor could the autumn abolish it, still less could the winter disperse it; but one only tempered the other by a pleasing variety and interruption; for it is the tediousness and delay, especially of cold and shade, which induces on things a sorrowful countenance; but a quick return or rapid alternation disperses this and turns it into pleasantness; thus from the union of seasons in contiguity with each other, there resulted a resemblance of a continued vernal brightness, tempered by a delightful effusion of cold.[i] The case was the same also with days, which, like the years, broke the forces of duration by their quick revolutions; for as soon as Aurora unfolded the day, it was not put to flight by noon, but was brought back again by a

---

i That by quick successions of seasons a sort of middle temperature, resembling spring, is induced, may be proven experimentally by a thermometer fixed to a kind of cylinder, and turned at various distances, and with a varied velocity, during a season of intense cold, round a hot fire; for while it is kept in a middle space, and turned round with a middle degree of velocity, the liquor enclosed in the tube neither ascends too high nor descends too low, but occupies the degree of temperate air, since neither the heat can raise it, nor the cold depress it; for elevation and depression are determined by distance and velocity, or by space and time. In like manner also the case would be similar if you were to emulate the lights and shades of day by a lamp tied to a revolving cylinder; for while the cylinder is in quick motion with the lamp the light does not disappear, but is continued round the whole circumference with a kind of middle light or torch, but it is otherwise if the rotation be slow. The case was the same on our earth when its distance from the sun was a middle space, and when its years were scarce equal to months of our time, and its day to two of our hours. The wise ones of antiquity also, and their poets, contracted in like manner the four seasons of the year, and thus introduced that perpetual spring mentioned in their writings, not knowing that it had been so provided that it should follow as an effect in the common course of nature.

rapid declension towards evening, and after a few moments of night, returned again to Aurora. Neither did cold disturb the heat of the day, but only tempered it, and by a pleasing alternation brought it back again to the bosom of Aurora with a kind of usury. Thus all things relating to space and time, both things greatest and things least, conspired [to the end] that our globe might enter into the flower of its age or perpetual spring.

17(a). Nor was this conjoint labor confined to times and spaces, but it extended also to the stars of heaven, to the atmospheres, and to the earth itself, in order that such a springlike temperature should be induced over the globe, while it tarried in this its station; for the *stars of heaven,* by a hasty rising and precipitate setting, took the place of a dubious shade with their lights by night, and enlightened the terrestrial disk by a continual brightness, thus adapting the very atmospheres to receive in a better prepared bosom the warmth of the quickly rising sun. The case was the same also with the *moon,* which being now nearer, received with her large face the countenance of the immense sun, and by an abundance and influx of reflected light prepared the equatorial belt of the earth (*mediam telluris sphæram*), to admit the cherishing warmth of the quickly returning sun. The proximate *atmosphere* itself, or air, breathed the 2 most grateful temperament in consequence of receiving so copious a light and alternate heat, and of being warmed at the same time by fruitful dews exhaled from the bosom of the earth; for as yet there was no furious wind, no Caesias and Boreas to disturb the air with his stormy whirlwind; nor as yet did the smallest cloud intercept the splendor of the sun and of the stars; but the face of everything was serene, and zephyrs only, with their gentle fannings, appeased the murmurs of the winds. The earth herself also, being encompassed with so many blandishments, and gently warmed within from the surface to the centre, did her part in return, and, embracing these vernal delights which flowed into her bosom, poured them back again into the bosoms of her guests. Thus it might be supposed that all heaven had descended to this new-born earth as to its centre, with a kind of perpetual spring, and had conferred upon her all its favors as if she were the only object deserving of them.

18. That the natures of all things in the universe might gather their means and unite their powers to introduce such a spring, it was decreed and provided as an end, before the birth of the sun and the seasons, that is, from eternity, that the virgin earth should not only hatch the seeds and eggs which she carried in her now most chaste womb, but also should nourish and educate every individual of her offspring, born from no other than the common parent of all things; likewise that she should bestow upon every one the vernal season which she herself enjoyed; for everything derived its auspices from a similar spring. There was a time, therefore, when first of all the vegetable offsprings burst forth from the seeds wherein they were reposited; and when the animals themselves, both those which swim and fly, and also those which creep and walk, were unfolded from their first wombs and eggs, and afterwards nourished as from a breast with the sweetest milk emanating from the florid bosom of her who gave them birth, and were brought even to that age when they were able to provide for themselves.[k] This, without the favor of heaven itself, could never have been put into an effect, which was again to be an efficient cause of so many infinite effects, for without that favor the produced off-springs, at their first birth, would have exhaled their new souls. Therefore the Divine Providence so arranged and directed the orders of things, that there was a succession of powers, as of causes, continually joined together, and mutually embracing each other, to perpetuate the effects which they produced.

19. When the earth first entered upon her spring she brought forth most beautiful flowers from those small seeds which lay

---

[k] Something similar takes place in our spring, in which not only are vegetables resuscitated from their seed or root, but animals hatched from little eggs through the mere influence and aspiration of a vernal temperature; this, however, is the case only with those animals which do not prolong their ages beyond the boundaries of our spring or summer.

The Worship and Love of God

nearest to her surface and attained their maturity; these flowers
were variegated by a thousand sand forms and colors, like so many
smiles and delights of nature; for the all-producing earth, like all her
productions, was herself first in a state of spring and of efflorescence,
and this with such a variety of beauty that every flower disputed
with its neighbor the palm of loveliness, inasmuch as that must of
necessity be most perfect, which is produced immediately by the
Creator Himself, the Fountain of all perfection; thus the varieties
of efflorescent beauty were in proportion to the number of the
clods of earth on which the different rays of the sun exerted their
influence. Even the North was luxuriant in flowers; but to express 2
in words and numbers these sports of rejoicing nature would be
to run through the whole boundless globe; for as each bit of turf
produced its own new form, so every step of the advancing spring
kept adding new ones, even some which were never afterwards seen,
namely, which had inscribed on their leaves, and presented to view
in different ways, the series of the fates of the globe and the nature of
the universe. Some, for instance, were marked with stars, or varied
with spots, and thus represented heaven itself with its scattered
constellations; while some again figured the flaming sun with its
rays, and his marriage with the earth; some again represented the
circles of heaven, being distinguished by some color, with its spheres,
above which was placed a crown; for the number of the first-fruits of
spring was proportionate to the number of lucid mirrors of things
in general, and to the number of representations of destinies even
down to this end of the series.$^{/}$ Thus the earth in this its first age, 3

But it was a law binding on the larger animals, that they should be born in a continued
spring, corresponding to the length of their infancy and life, that afterwards they themselves might conceive, hatch, and bring forth their offspring; and thus by continued cherishing and ardent care, might have a resemblance in themselves to that continued and
perpetual spring which had caused these its limitations. Both the one and the other is a
manifest proof of the Divine Providence.

/ This is a common case in generations which arise by successive series, in order that
they may in themselves represent things prior and contain things posterior, as present; for

disporting herself like a new bride, clad in a kind of robe adorned with the most beautiful roses, and wearing a chaplet of the choicest flowers, advanced in her course, while the very flame of all pleasantnesses sparkled in her countenance, so that she might invite to her bedchamber the inhabitants of heaven themselves, and greet them with grateful gifts and frankincense collected from her first-fruits, the delightful product of each bed. Each offspring in this case, like the great parent herself, breathed interiorly a kind of perpetuity, and a spring resembling the great one; but one efflorescent germination in one way, and another in another, thus in a thousand 4 modes. It was [a property] common to all, that each produced new seeds, the hope of a future race, which having conceived from its ultimate strength, and afterwards brought forth, it let down into the great bosom of the parent, near its own, and covered with its own leaves, and when these were fallen into dust, overspread it with new ground, and thus, like a new parent, prepared it to call forth 5 and bring forth its offspring. It was otherwise with others of the offspring; for being quickened again and again with their stock, they either renovated their flowers in a long series, or resuscitated themselves from their own ashes; for the sap, which, being extracted from the mother, they diffused into their veins, was laden with pure principles, and thus was fruitful in innumerable new beginnings of itself; for the whole earth throughout was already a seminary and ovary, and ground at length grew up from the tombs of dead flowers. There was still a difference with other efflorescences, for in every place and every time there was a constant variety. Such was the adornment with which our earth entered upon the theatre of its orb.

---

everything is born to an image of the form of its genetrix, and includes in itself the general destinies of the future offspring as if they were present; wherefore, while these seeds unfolded themselves according to that successive order in which they had birth, they must of necessity effigy their former universe in some aspect and form, which also is presented to view at this day in the case of most things that come to bloom.

20. Whilst the earth was in this efflorescent state, and advancing in her spring, shrubs and young arbute-trees* sprang up in all directions out of the new-born ground, but the forest was at first lowly, adorned as yet only with flowers, or the firstfruits of spring. Afterwards, as the globe took a still wider circle of revolution, trees arose, which struck a deeper root in that pure (*candidam*) earth, increased by the decay of so many flowers, and unfolded their crowned heads in the air. The greatest part, in resemblance of the great spring, contracted also their seasons or ages into one, for they were perpetually in a state of spring, and at the same time perpetually bringing forth fruits; and they concentrated their first forces and powers in their last, after performing a continual gyration. While the flowers, were hatching seeds, they infused into them their very nature or soul.*^m At the same time they also performed the office of a mother in imitation of the great one; for these seeds, deposited in ovaries or receptacles, they encompassed with manifold coats, nourished and matured with overflowing juice, and at length presented them to their great mother, that from them she might raise

---

* The arbute-trees or strawberry-trees (*arbutei fœtus*) here referred to belong to a small genus of trees or shrubs of the heath family (*Ericaceae*), having evergreen leaves, white or rose-colored flowers, and a red berry. (TR.)

m The first generating or plastic force, innate in the very seeds of vegetable fœtuses, may be likened to a soul, for from this, and in resemblance to it, are formed their bodies with their members and muscles, while the stems are continued with their branches, leaves, little tubes, and several other particulars which resemble animal fœtuses; these also, in like manner, pass through their several ages; in their infancy they are efflorescent, then become adolescent, afterwards verge towards old age, and lastly decay, not to mention innumerable other particulars. But such genitures are the first and ultimate forces and powers of nature herself, excited from the conjunction of her most active forms, constituting ether, with the earth's forces of inertia through the mediations of the rays of the sun; from which origin, in their first and ultimate principles, consequently in mediate ones also, they derive an image of primitive and most perfect nature, and, in a certain type, relate to superior or living essences themselves. But what the quality of this seminal force is, cannot be known but by unfolding the forms of prior nature, both those which have reference to active and those which have reference to passive powers, also in what manner the solar rays operate to join them together, to evolve which, from lasts to firsts, would be too vast an undertaking.

up an offspring like her own, with infinite discrimination and yet with one and a most constant law, that each thing might live from its own beginnings, and might perpetuate from itself the birth which it had received.

21. Thus our globe, lifted as it were above its own ground and changed into a most beautiful grove, respired nothing but pleasantness and plenty, and exhaled fragrance from the branch of every shrub and from the pore of every leaf and fruit, and filled the ambient air with these delightful fragrances which were so many fruitfulnesses exuding from the earth by new ways, by the roots, the twigs, and leaves of new-born vegetations. This was the delightful garden called PARADISE, situated and erected in the highest region of the ether, and in the very neighborhood of the sun.[n] Innumerable streams, bursting from their fountains dissected this garden, and, preparing a way for themselves through beds of violets and evergreens, sported in perpetual circuits, whose rivulets, cut into multifarious hidden channels like so many blood-vessels full of warm blood, watered the members of their earth and by winding ways returned to the gentle heads of their fountains as to their hearts. Thus the earth itself, a large body, as it were, not unlike its flowering and fruit-bearing offspring, was luxuriant with its veins, and thus continually nourished the roots of its germinations with a milky moisture pregnant with principles and little eggs. This was the first scene of the theatre of this world, and such were the painted tapestries with which it was adorned.

2

---

[n] There were not wanting some among the ancients who divined that Paradise existed in the higher region of ether, thus nearer to the sun, since at the present distance of the earth they saw it to be impossible that such an effect could flow from any given cause; nor was this divination far from the truth, since the earth at that time performed her annual revolutions in that region which might be called the superior region of ether.

Section Third
Concerning the Abode of Living Creatures in Paradise

22. THE earth at this time, in whatsoever aspect she was viewed, presented herself as a most beautiful theatre of the whole world, for she was adorned with such festive and circumfluent ornaments that it might be said that she singly carried in her bosom dainties and riches which were concentrated from the universal heaven. But all this, which was so beautiful, was void of life, being only a comely and gaudy clothing woven together of this abundant vegetation. For nature, streaming from her fountain, or from the sun, had now exhausted all her powers, since to perfect this most flourishing kingdom she first, in agreement with her own order, called forth the lowest, and afterwards the highest forces conferred upon the seeds of her productions, and sent them forth and transferred them into a kind of new orb of nature. Thus she performed her greatest gyration, and by this she established all other gyrations in resemblance to this.*°* The earth herself also poured forth her forces,

---

o For all and single things in universal nature, and in each of her kingdoms, which flow determinately, perform and accomplish revolutions of this sort, that is, they commence from their first natures, and from them proceed in order to last or lowest things; and when they have there established new principles (*principia*), they return from them in a like order to first or supreme things; so that they descend, and then from newly formed beginnings ascend. This is a constant effect, not only in the vegetable kingdom but also in the animal, which kingdoms, in their most general [principles] have reference to, and

and lavished the fruitfulness she had received in the beginnings of so many fœtuses; nor did she now any longer bring forth new seeds from her own general ovary, but only received what were sown from her own productions and vegetations, and hence resuscitated primitive images; for now the ground and the earth were made.

23. But these magnificent preparations, whence every kind of store abounded, were not for her own sake, for a kingdom was yet to come consisting of animate things only, which was to enjoy these bounties overflowing in such luxuriant abundance; the time also was now at hand when animals were to be introduced to these stores. There was no shrub, nor even leaf, or least effect of nature, which did not in itself respire some use, and this not for itself alone and its own branch, but also specifically for its stock, and a general use besides for the whole earth; yea, a still sublimer one for the kingdom to be inhabited by souls, for the use of which all those uses in their multiplicity were to serve.

24. Thus in every product or effect use ruled in-mostly, like the soul in its body; wherefore in each of the vegetables something was deeply hid, especially in the nature of seeds, which incited them from inmosts to the production of something new, conceived also

---

2 resemble, each other. For nature, taking her birth after an egg, and from an egg, first excited the supreme and most simple auras or atmospheres, then middle ones, and finally the last, or the aerial. These, or their individual forms or substances, which are the most active forces of her universe, she conjoined by the mediation of the sun's rays with the principles of the earth, endowed of themselves with no activity, and thus she conceived new forms, which being enclosed in seeds were to be the most fruitful principles of new

3 fœtuses or productions. But these she hatched in an order inverted from her own, that is, she first principled these forms which were conceived from the ultimate aura, then those which were conceived from the middle aura, and lastly, those which were conceived from the supreme; by which method, as before observed, out of this earth first sprung up flowers, afterwards shrubs, lastly trees, which were prior to the rest in perfection and duration. Thus nature is said to have advanced from her first to her last, and from her last to her first, and to have performed her greatest gyration, the model of similar and lesser subsequent ones; how this greatest revolution was established is clear from the series itself above mentioned. That a similar progression takes place in the animal kingdom throughout, appears manifestly from those continual gyrations which prevail in bodies and produce them, both in general and in particular.

from seed, and to come forth in like manner from an egg, namely, such a production as might not only be endowed with an activity of nature, but also of life, to the interest or advantage of which all this redundance might be subservient. Therefore every vegetable now became as it were pregnant for the purpose of establishing these new ovaries, of replenishing them with a choice juice extracted from the marrow of their seeds, next of exposing them to the sun, and moderating his heat by their leaves;[p] afterwards of raising up and cherishing the hatched offspring, and of supplying him with a soft couch, preparing provision, and nourishing him with the milk of their veins, and with the spirit of their fibres, as it were, not intermitting parental care, until he was grown up, and could leap forth from his couch or nest, and again return to the breast; and, at length, when left by his proper nurse, procure food for himself from his common stock or house. This natural instinct, as it were, was in every plant from its very seed; for inwardly in the generating nature of seeds such an effort and endeavor lay concealed; consequently there was something living in what was not living, or animate in what was inanimate, which at length unfolded and opened itself. For there are two principles perfectly distinct from each other, one 2 natural, in itself dead, the other spiritual, in itself living;[q] this latter acts efficiently, ruling most singly in everything, and universally in all, in order that nature may breathe and intend nothing but uses,

---

[p] For the sun itself no longer reached the earth with its rays, but was checked in its progress by that numerous vegetable offspring, which now covered the earth's surface, into which offspring, as into its new posterity, it began to pour all its influences.

[q] That there are two principles most distinct from each other, one natural, the other spiritual, is concluded and demonstrated of itself in all the subsequent passages in this work; also, that the natural principle derives its birth immediately from the sun of the world, but the spiritual from the Fountain of Life itself, or the Supreme Deity. I wish here only to resume and continue the thread which was begun at no. 6 note *b,* where the *forms of nature* were treated of, and lastly, her supreme form, called *celestial.* These forms, or the atmospheres arising from them as the active forces of nature, are all inanimate, as is everything which derives its origin from the sun, the fountain of natural things. But above this supreme form of nature, or this celestial form, there is a form perpetually celestial or

or be subordinate as a cause to a cause, and that thus the series itself may advance to its effects. Consequently the earth was now efflorescent with both continual effects and continual uses, joined like bodies to their souls, and this with such a pleasantness that if she had been viewed by some mind or superior sight which could view effects and at the same time the uses which they contained, this paradise would have appeared to it so abundant in delights as to seem not terrestrial, but celestial.

25. This seminal nature, animated from inmosts, now impregnated the tender leaves, which began to swell like new seminaries and ovaries, and hatched newborn little eggs, but of another genus.[r] First, therefore, they produced animalcules of a more ignoble stock, and afterwards those of a more illustrious one, exactly in the same order as that in which nature had propagated her vegetable progeny. In the beginning, therefore, and during the progress of the spring, little worms and caterpillars crept forth for the enjoyment of light, foetuses which performed the exercises and offices of their life in a state of greater ignorance than other creatures. These least semblances of life or living types of nature, in like manner concealed in the first forms by which they were animated, a still more interior hidden principle, which unfolded itself after the life of the reptile or worm had ceased. This interior living force changed its worms into nymphs, aurelias, or chrysalises, and so continually

2

SPIRITUAL, containing in it nothing but what is infinite, flowing from the irradiation of the Sun of Life itself, as the other forms flow from the irradiation of the sun of the world; and as this flows immediately from the Infinite, or from God Himself, who alone Is, therefore it lives in itself, and is that which animates the souls of living things for the uses of their life; not that it is a universal soul, but that it animates those things which were born and made for the reception of life; for every soul is a substance by itself, which is perpetually excited to live its own life like natural essences by their auras.

r The vegetables themselves, in imitation of their great mother, were primitively, as it were, mere seminaries and ovaries, but which produced not only after their own kind, but also after a kind different from themselves, for one thing lay so folded up in another, that the other did not come forth until all things which might serve for the exercises and necessities of its life were ready. From the series itself of productions, it may be manifest whence

The Worship and Love of God

protracted and knit together the stamina of the former little body, that presently, shaking off all hindrances, and casting off their exuviæ, they were girded with wings, and being elevated on high from the ground, passed the small remainder of their lives in the delights of their loves, for the sake of perpetuating their kind, and becoming fruitful like mothers. There was no natural function, not even the smallest, in the little orb of their more obscure life which had now elapsed, nor any little artery or fibre in the organic texture of their bodies, which had not a view to this condition of their life, and urged it, as it were, to a kind of goal, that they might reap the fruit of their accomplished labor; thus the life, from which they acted, derived its stamina through the series which contained it, and nature accommodated herself most readily to its purpose. Moreover, in this universal ignoble family, there was no species which did not contribute something to the common stock, if not for the present, still for future ages, although we are not able by any of our senses to discover those utilities, which are myriads in number, since our senses only sip the surfaces of effects, and collect very few uses from them. Thus now by new uses and at the same time new decorations our paradise was exalted in its leasts to still superior splendor; for every leaf carried its living principle, and every flower glittered with the effulgence of its color, elevated by the life of nature with which it was united.

3

---

came the souls of brutes, which are said to have been ingenerated in the seeds of the vegetable kingdom; for as the seeds of vegetables arose from the conjunction of the active powers of nature with the inert powers of the earth, through the medium of the radiation of the sun of the world, so these seeds, which are animated, arose from that form or spiritual essence, which is spiritual and living, infused into the forms or active powers of nature, through the medium of the radiation of the Sun of Life; wherefore these lives went forth in the same subordinate series as those powers of nature themselves which constitute the atmospheres, consequently in the same as the seeds of vegetables themselves, from which they were finally hatched. And since that life from its fountain breathes nothing but uses, and nature is nothing but an effect for the sake of uses, it is evident that it was so foreseen and provided, that uses themselves, as effects, might unfold themselves. He is totally blind and in the grossest darkness who does not discover what is Divine in these things.

26. When now the violet beds and groves of paradise became luxuriant with these new breathings of life, then another progeny, which was to adorn the animal kingdom, began from similar rudiments and matrixes to come forth into their day, namely, the winged tribe, prior indeed by nature, because more noble, but posterior in birth to the above volatile and twice-born progeny. To this winged tribe the earliest arbute-trees,* or the growths of middle spring, pregnant with leaves and juices, gave birth, which afterwards hatched the seeds of their own proper stock, and asserted for themselves the hope of duration, [but now] unlocked their still more interior windings and fibres, and began to put forth these their more noble fruits, namely, partly little eggs with their yolks, and the beginnings of new life, which being laid gently in nests, constructed of twigs conveniently near-by, they committed the remaining care to each parent, namely, to the earth as yet warm, and to the sun about to hatch them with his ray; just as if the leaf-bearing stems acted from 2 intelligence, or from genius resembling science. But nature in all things was compliant with the life, which, acting from inmost principles, excited such effects, in order that from them the uses of that sort of life might exist in act; for use, as was said, is the soul of every effect. Thus the feathered offspring were cherished and hatched by the vernal warmth issuing from the pores of all things, and at length were nourished and educated by the ways of their parents and by the grain which was providently scattered round about, until they balanced themselves by their wings, and, pendent in the new air, attempted to fly. From the nests of these, which were built spontaneously, as many genera and species of the winged tribe flew forth as there were genera and species of shrubs. But the secondary vegetations of this kind, or those which budded forth, not from the seed of the earth, but from their own, ceased to be oviparous as soon as they were born; for the Principle of all principles, whence Life is derived, so arranged together all those first origins before

---

* See translator's note at the beginning of no. 20.

the rise of intermediate causes, providing one from another in a continual series, and thus establishing the orders themselves from inmost or highest principles, in order that one in its proper season might produce and bring forth another. This offspring, proud in its adornments, gave lustre with its celestial and flaming colors to the whole atmosphere and orb; for there were some species which had their heads crowned and crested with gems and diadems, as it were, which hung about the neck like costly necklaces, while stars, auroras, and future rainbows, were distinguishable in their tails, and the sun's rays, turned into purple, adorned the large feathers of their wings; some also bore the marks of paradise itself, or of its grand scenery, in their feathers. At this time the new earth was 3 almost encrusted by a granary heaped together from the fruitfulness of so numerous a progeny. Into this, as into a rich repast provided and prepared for them, this new earth-begotten offspring was, at the proper time, introduced, and then also to that first-born swarm of living things, the insects, in order to lessen their superfluity and keep their increase within moderate bounds. Thus universal Providence directed in things most single what was to be effected and what was effected,[s] in order that as one cause flowed from another to another, so use likewise might flow from one into another by a constant and eternal law.

27. Lastly, quadruped animals, and flocks of cattle and herds, entered into these stores thus enlarged, but not until the low shrubs had produced their vital progeny, or the winged fowl, lest the four-footed animals, which were of later birth, should consume

---

[s] Providence is called universal because it is in things most single; everything universal is known, exists, and is denominated from its presence and power in single things, just as what is general is known, exists, and is denominated from its parts and particulars. What is universal is the complex of all single things, as what is general is the complex of all particular things; unless what is universal be in single things and with single things, or in least things as in greatest, it is not universal; wherefore if we take away Providence in things most single from universal Providence, or separate one from the other, we destroy the very essence of universality.

the vegetations, trample them under foot, and destroy the seed intended for nourishment. These last and proper productions of paradise were in like manner produced from viviparous forests, but from such as had in them a superior nature. These forests, from a like tendency to prolification, at length unfolded their inmost bosoms, and impregnated with seminal juice the soft little eggs hanging from the branches, which being brought down into expanded wombs, and committed at the same time to flowers and herbs, clothed themselves in coats, the Amnion and Chorion, and sealed the entrances with placentas, and the vegetable milks purified therein they drew by means of winding little cords with suction to the liver, where the same underwent purgation, and, like chyle, being married to the blood, were delivered up to the heart and the brains, to be distributed and dispensed for the use of the growing body; nor did the zealous and provident care of the nurse cease until the cattle entered upon the activity of their own proper nature, under the auspices of their own life. The greatest part grew with brawny muscles and ribs, and presented bodies of large bulk, carrying on their foreheads branching horns, so many proofs of their descent from the forest, and of the noble maternal stock raised high above

2 the ground. From the countenance of every one of them the mind (*animus*) was plainly discoverable, nature herself transcribing herself into the figure of the body, at the same time that she transcribed herself into their habits; for bodies in a kind of type represent their souls, since life joined to nature begets a cause, and a cause which contains both produces an effect, which is the complex and image of uses designed from life by nature. In proportion therefore to the number of new faces was the number of dissimilar minds (*Animi*), so that it might be said that all the minds in the universe, joined and disjoined, being clothed with body, united to form this comely terrestrial Olympus, and a government consisting of diverse minds (*Animorum*); for some were fierce and savage, and delighted in nothing but blood; some of them, hating their own light and that of others, were black with gall, and had sullen countenances; some

were spirited (*animosi*) and haughty at beholding their own image; some were boastful and walked with a kind of strut; others were tame and gentle, and indulgently endured the threats and haughtiness of their coeval race; but others were timid and fearful, trembling at the mere sight of fierceness; some were employed only in the pleasures of love, and were continually sportive. Nevertheless, among this 3 tribe, so discordant in their dispositions (*animis*), there prevailed a certain form of government, and a restraint induced by love and fear; for every one knew another from his countenance alone, and read the motions of his nature as if they were written thereon, inasmuch as the senses, which were as guards, and kept perpetual watch, instantly referred the discovery of every one's nature to the soul, the principle of their life, from which conformable motions resulted, and the institutes and determinations of life flowed forth as from an oracle. They were as yet ignorant of their destinies, 4 which were about to unfold themselves at length, after many ages, like threads from their spindles; the horse knew not that his mouth was to be curbed with a bridle, and that his back was to afford a seat for the rider; the sheep knew not that they were to give their wool for clothing; the timid deer were not aware that their flesh was to be accounted a great dainty; and so with the rest of the animals; but there was not one of the number, in which their uses were not determined before times of times; hence came such a variety that nothing was wanting which could be admitted into the number or account of uses.

28. As the earth, when adorned with flowers and shrubs, gave birth to its reptiles, its winged and quadruped animals, so also did the banks and bottoms of streams, clothed with their vegetation, give birth to aquatic animals of every species, and indeed in the same order as the dry earth did, namely, first those which enjoyed more obscure light, as shell-fish and snails which carried on their back their houses, shining with the bright color of gems, and winding in perpetual circles or spires after the manner of the revolving heaven; afterwards fish, which being furnished with oars like those

of a ship, cut their way through their heavy atmosphere, and which, unfolding their still wider sails and wings, made a path through the air; and also the amphibious race, which when they had enjoyed their watery dainties, crept forth to a second meal on beds of earth; finally, the greater monsters, which trod upon the broad bottoms of the waters as on their own firm ground. All things were now filled with animals, or with souls living in bodies; every blade of grass, every shrub and grove, as it were, exulted that it could now open its bosom with dainties, and extend from itself a rich and choice repast for its new inhabitants. Nothing was omitted, for the atmospheres themselves, and also the rivers, received and nourished their own productions, and spontaneously offered to them every abundance of aid which was allowed them. But what elevated still higher the natures and the lives of paradise and its perpetual spring was this, that there was nothing which did not represent in itself the type of a kind of new ovary; the very abode of living creatures (*Vivarium*), in general, specifically and individually, had reference to a kingdom which was to receive perpetual animation from them; the case was the same with every thing in the general garden (*Viridarium*), since it also had reference to every future vegetable which was to spring from it throughout all succeeding ages; altogether in imitation of the great parent or earth, which, as an ovary, contained together and in one complex all the offsprings of its kingdoms, and by means of the fecundating spring hatched one after another in order; thus particular representations were the mirrors of general ones. The earth herself also effigied in herself the grand egg of the solar world; for this latter, as an exemplar and idea of the ovaries existing from itself, carried at the same time, and in one complex, whatsoever was to be produced in process of time in its world, and in its globes, the resemblances of our earth. What then must be the case in the Principle of all principles, or in the Divine and Infinite Mind, before the origin of origins, or before the birth of the sun and the stars, in which mind, both universally and most singly, together and in one complex, must needs be contained and present, not only whatsoever the solar world, but also whatsoever the universe of universes, and the heaven of heavens, brought forth successively from their eggs, without even the least mistake or accident.[t] This was the second scene in the new theatre of the orb, ornamented by so many festive and campestrian sports of living things.

---

[t] We can with sufficient clearness contemplate the idea of a sort of creation as represented in our own minds; for our minds first represent to themselves ends, which are their first and last goals, to which they direct their course; presently they intend means or causes, which being subordinate to each other, may promote ends by effects, that uses may exist; by which method also there are formed, as it were, eggs, which being animated by the mind, and conceived by the love of the end, and presently also cherished and hatched, produce vital offsprings conformable to the pre-conceived idea; in which it appears that the ends themselves and uses are altogether different from the causes and means in their first origin, and are present in the mind howsoever the mediations or series of causes succeed each other, all which existed in the same mind together, and in one complex, even before their birth. And if such a series has place in obscure and most finite minds, what must be the case in the Divine and Infinite Mind!

Chapter II

Section First
Concerning the Birth of the First-Born, or Adam

29. THE earth now being enriched with its living creatures (*Vivariis*), and so amply furnished and adorned with delightful fruits, advancing and wandering through its degrees, at length reached the middle station of its spring, or the mildest temperature, and having now attained its highest degree it overflowed with every advantage. The infant beasts (*feris*) being weaned, droppings of milk flowed plentifully from the fertile and lately pregnant branches, and through new veins flowed back to the roots of the maternal leaves. The grassy bed-chambers acquired a consistency and coherence from the honey dropping from the combs of so many colonies of bees. The silkworms spun their webs, and overspread the face of the earth with threads connected into reels as with cheap merchandise. Every species of animal was kindly led to the employment suitable to its nature, and provided uses and benefits for future time only, and, as it were, for posterity. Everything, according to the nature with which it was endowed, celebrated the festival days, not only of its own spring, but also of the general one at the same time.

30. The globe was now at its height, nor was anything wanting to any sense, by which it might exalt its life, and replenish the soul

itself with joys. For the touch, there was the sweet warmth of the spring, mixed with the moisture of the earth, which by its influence gratified every fibre. For the smell, there were fragrances exhaling from every pore of every leaf, with which the air, being filled, expanded the inmost reticular textures of the lungs, with the little vessels, and thus the breast itself, beyond their common measure. For the taste, there were fruits of the most exquisite savor, and clusters hanging down to the ground from the leafy vine, whose grapes, taken into the mouth, stimulated the repositories of the chyle and of the blood by their essences, which were as it were vivified from an inmost principle. For the hearing, there was a concert and lovely melody of so many chirping and singing birds, which echoed so harmoniously through fields and groves, that the interior recesses of the brain were put into a tremulous and concordant motion. For the sight, there was the whole aspect of the heaven and of the earth, whose greatest objects were so distinctly ornamented by their least

2 that they easily disposed the mind (*animos*) to their pleasures. But there was still wanting a being who could refer these pleasures of the senses to a sort of proper mind (*mentem*), or to his own consciousness and perception, and who, from the faculty of intellect, might decide upon the beauty resulting from all these harmonies, and might also from beauties perceive joys; from joys, grounded in a true origin, might form conclusions concerning goodness; and, lastly, from goodness might comprehend the nature of blessedness; there was wanting, I say, that son of the earth, or that mind under a human form, which from the paradise of earth might look into the paradise of heaven, and from this again into that of earth, and thus from a kind of interior sight embrace and measure both together, and from the conjunction of both be made sensible of pleasures to the full; consequently, who, from a kind of genuine fountain of gladness and of love, could venerate, and adore above everything, the Bestower and Creator of all things. There was no object, not even the least, from which some resemblance of Deity did not shine forth, and consequently none that was not desirous

of offering itself to the enjoyment of such a being as could offer immortal thanks to that Deity for himself and for everything.

31. Nature, according to the Order instituted by the Supreme, which order embraced in itself all orders in the universe, first called forth from the earth her lowest energies (*dotes*), then higher ones, and, lastly, the highest, and thus by degrees raised herself to things more elevated, and to her first principles. In like manner her every production, beginning from its first nature, unfolded itself to its last principle, and from this as from a goal returned to its first. Thus in all cases, what was first, having performed a semi-revolution to its last station, bended itself backward to its beginning.*u* In like manner, that great Order, which, opening and leading all other orders, directed the universe, now by its mediations and the process of causes brought itself to its ultimate, and from its ultimate determined itself to return to its first, or to such a subject of life and of nature as might lead back all and single things universally to the fountain of their derivations, or, to complete the orbit predetermined from eternity, might refer them to the Supreme and Creating Mind. Already everything appertaining to the earth expected this concluding excellence; heaven also viewed this [object] as present, namely, man, who, as being first in the Infinite View (*Intuitione*) of

---

u Whatsoever is born from a seed or egg, and whatsoever is born from a kind of mind, as was shown before in note *o*, is bound to run through this gyre or orbit. Plants, flowers, and trees, from their seed unfold their nature, and grow into trunks or branches as into their bodies and ultimate members, and from these return again to their beginnings, or conceive and hatch seeds; so that all this gyre which they perform, is only a kind of excursion of mediating causes, to the end that they may return to their first principles, and thus bring forth fruits or uses; the case is similar in the animal kingdom. Such an order also existed and was derived from the grand egg of the world; for seeds and ovaries took their beginnings from the first and most perfect nature, and their increments from posterior and more imperfect nature; but by an inverse method they unfolded themselves from ultimate to first principles; in like manner also the fœtuses of the animal kingdom. But that this gyre, by which ultimates were to be conjoined with first principles, or to return to their beginning, might be perfected, the human mind, clothed with a body, was to be introduced into the orb. But this gyre was the grand one of creation; a still greater is at hand, which will be treated of in the series of what follows.

the Deity, was to be the completion, or last ornament of creation; for he was to combine lowest things with highest, or nature with life; and highest things with lowest, or life with nature; not like the animals sent before him into his orb, which do not refer the habits of their life to the first principle of their power, but to something made natural, from which nothing raises itself upwards towards higher things, but instantly rolls itself backward, and bends itself towards the animus and the diverging natures of the body.

32. There was a grove in the most temperate region of the orb, not under the meridian sun, but in a certain middle station between the arctic pole of the zodiac and its greatest curvature from the equator, which was exposed to the rays of the summer sun, not falling directly from the zenith, nor too obliquely from the side, but where they held a kind of middle focus between their heat and cold, or highest ascent, and whence from a kind of centre of his annual rising and setting, the sun could thus temper the subject air with the mildest spring of all. This grove, I say, was a complete orchard, so dense with leaves and branches folded into each other, that by its shade it broke the [violence of] daily heats, and cooled the days, and thus, as it were, induced a new spring under the general one. In this grove also little streams sprang forth, which, diverging [into different channels], beautifully perforated its area, and from which a vapor, drawn up by the rays to the foliage of the trees, and there pendent, cherished the ground continually with a falling dew. This was a PARADISE IN A PARADISE, or the delight and crown of every grove and garden of the earth. It was also the latest in its formation, and crowned this centre of the solar rays. In the midst of it again was a fruit-tree, which bore a small egg, the most precious of all, in which, as in a jewel, nature concealed herself with her highest powers and stores, about to become the initiaments of the most consummate body; therefore this fruit-tree was called the TREE OF LIFE.

33. But this little egg was not yet fecundated, though nature had collected into it, as into a sort of sacred little ark, her most excellent

treasures and valuables, and provided it with such noble furniture as a bride prepares for her bedchamber when she expects the coming of the bridegroom and the offerings of a new covenant. When nature had thus in every respect completed her work, and collected her circumferences, as it were, into this egg, as into a centre, then the Supreme Mind came to meet her, and from itself, as the Sun of Life itself, with concentrated rays, conceived the supercelestial form, or soul, which was life, and capable of containing what is infinite, or the Infinite itself. This form or soul the Supreme Mind infused into this treasure or little egg.[x] This was the first connubial token of [the union of] spiritual essence with the supreme aura of nature, which was effected in order that the fluent orb of causes, conceived by the Infinite in the grand egg of the world, and brought down to this least egg, might be completed within nature, but afterwards, by connection with the Infinite, might be rendered infinite; and

---

[x] What, and of what quality the human soul is, can hardly fall into the first ideas of our understanding by a bare description perceived according to the expressions themselves, for it is a spiritual essence, and therefore is not easily signified and expressed by terms similar to those which express natural essences; but, whereas these terms and formulas must be made use of as aids, therefore, in order that it may be perceived, the ideas must be as it were sublimated by the intellectual faculty itself, which is superior, and the boundaries which attach to natural things withdrawn, and thus its faculties represented to itself in an eminent manner. But how a notion of the soul in some measure distinct may be insinuated into our mind, will be shown in what follows; hence it will be manifest that the soul is the only essence in our body which lives, so that our being (*Esse*) and life (*Vivere*) is of one soul, and all other things, which are supposed to live, pertain to nature, because they are actuated from its life; wherefore it is a substance so real, that by it and from it we proximately exist and subsist, and without it we are not bodies, but stocks; consequently that there is nothing truly substantial in living bodies but the soul; and that other things, as accessories, are called in to its aid, that through the instrumentality of nature ends may be promoted by effects, and in that universal series of effects or causes, continual uses may be produced; for intelligence is a more sublime life, and it is [the property] of intelligence to regard nothing but ends, and by means of nature to arrange effects, which are called uses so far as they conspire to attain the end. By a slight reflection on the operations of our own minds it is clearly enough discovered that to regard, to arrange, and to provide for ends, is a thing altogether different from the causes and effects, which are adjoined that the end may succeed and perfect its gyre through intermediate ends, as causes through mediate causes.

that by such conjunction a terrestrial court might be annexed to a celestial palace. From this continual influx of ends into ends, and of uses into uses, it is clearly evident that everything has come forth from the Supreme Fountain of Intelligence and Wisdom; for it is [the property] only of an Intelligent [Being] to regard ends, and to arrange means into order; and it is [the property] of a Wise [Being] alone to provide, and by his power so to operate, that while all things produce an effect they may also promote an end; it is therefore [the property] of the one Provident [Being] to complete a chain of ends, in which every link, and every ligament of a link, may perform its gyre for the support of the whole; and moreover that this concatenation may flow from perpetual uses, so consociated that every one may be directed to an ultimate, and may flow only from its end into its origin and from its origin into its end, and thus may never cease.

34. This soul, a spark irradiated from the Supreme Mind, as soon as it was first breathed into its little egg, instantly began also with pure ideas to regard ends, and to represent to itself the universe, not only the universe of nature, as the souls of brutes do, but also, at the same time, the universe of heaven, with its stores and intelligences. It began, therefore, to burn inwardly from a kind of sacred fire, and to desire that, being furnished, as it were, with wings, or winged sandals, it might be let down from that highest citadel on which it was seated to the lowest things of the world, or the bottom of the atmosphere, even into paradise itself, the birthplace of its egg; and that after it had imbibed its delights through organic doors, thus through the senses, it might thence be carried upwards and tell in heaven of these delights turned into felicities by virtue of an interior sense, and of the soul itself. While it was revolving in its ideas and taking a most distinct view of these and similar things, it looked around for means and instruments, by the assistance of which it might realize its wishes and prayers; and while it was intent on these things, lo! Nature, with her aids inclosed in the same mansion or little egg with her, was immediately at hand, and

made a tender of herself and of her powers and forces of forces, to be called forth at the least intimation of the soul's purpose, to afford every assistance that might be desired; for they were so ordinately arranged within, that when this animating point from the navel of its egg only intended to produce the ends represented in itself, and contemplated by itself, they, as if they heard what was said, or as if ordered from their principled forms, spontaneously hastened to obey. For nature with the forces of the substances of the world, 3 and the world with the substances of the forces of nature, were so excited, made, and constructed from nothing (*a nihilo*), that they might be subject to intelligences, souls, or spiritual essences, just as these latter were subservient to their Deity or Creator, like ready servants who have no will of their own, but that of pure compliance, and who most obsequiously conform to everything which is agreeable to order; wherefore nature was prepared only for the sake of minds, that she might bring into effect, and thus turn into continual uses, the good pleasure and decrees of the Supreme Mind, or its ends; for all intermediate ends in act and effect are called uses, and they are so far true uses as in their series, consequently in their measure, they lead and conspire to the last, or End of ends.

35. The soul, burning with this desire, as a mind formed to the image of the Supreme Mind, began also to build a kind of little world or microcosm after the effigy of the great world, but not out of nothing, with the eternal purpose of clothing herself with it as with a body, and that she might operate in it as a kind of Deity, administering laws at pleasure by means of the understanding, and so holding the reins of her nature according to her intuitions that she might have only to regard ends, and all things which at any time were woven together in the body from fibres, would hasten to act in conformity and compliance with these ends as readily as if they were not required to do so; by which also she might represent and testify in herself, as in a little universe, the obedience of universal nature to the powerful Creator of all things. Nor did 2 she hesitate a moment; but from the little fountain of her life, as

from a little star, she began to emit her vibrating virtue, like rays, into the apparatus of the egg, and from these rays gyrating into little spheres of a celestial form, she first of all designed a kind of Olympus, or type of heaven, which she allotted for the habitation of intelligences, and of sciences and of experiments, their servants; and from that Olympus, and its little vortices, she brought forth the finest stamina, of the consistence of vapor, and the beginnings of as many fibres as she might need to prepare and weave together the webs of an organic body, and its viscera and members. Thus she began to construct her winged sandals, or rather her stairs, by which she might descend from the supreme watch-towers of nature, where she now resided, to its bottom, and thus into paradise.

36. But as yet there was only an egg, into which she introduced these beginnings, causing it to swell gently as they increased; but in order that from these auspices she might complete this Divine work, she studiously and vehemently sought [to bring] everything into her service, according as its nature was likely to make it serviceable. The tree of life itself unfolded its branch, which bore this golden and vital fruit, into a soft and easy womb, and covering it with a thin bark and soft leaves drew off the nourishing juice from the neighboring leaves, and was solicitous for its life only. The neighboring trees also contributed their juice, by instilling it into the roots of this tree which crowned the centre of the grove, rejoicing that they were allowed to impart from their juice something of life to the same. The sun dared not approach near with his light to this last egg of his world, burning with a spiritual lumen, except by rays, which, passing through lucent fruits, and thus turned as it were into the streaks of a kind of flower, were divested of the more immoderate force of their heat. The air, with its spring and zephyr, indeed breathed, but it was forbidden to invade interiorly, lest it should disturb the web just beginning from highest principles by the influence of its rude and, in ultimate things, active spirit, and should too soon expand the tender lungs which were as yet in their lineaments. The shoots of the surrounding arbute-trees, which were

born for guardianship, extended as it were their arms, that they might sustain the burden of the leafy mother and receive the birth at her delivery; others prepared cradles, and overlaid them with cotton carried through the air from the cotton trees; in a word, the whole neighborhood was skilfully and assiduously employed in exerting every endeavor that nothing might be wanting to the fabrication of this last effigy of the world; for all things were so prepared that they accommodated themselves to the arbitration of the Supreme Mind, and to [the performance of] the duties [which it imposed].

37. Nor was nature alone at hand to guard with all her aids, but Heaven also lent favor by its presence; for its inhabitants, or spiritual minds, were let down for this gracious purpose, that they might second and direct the offices of nature; also that they might guard, lest anything infest this sacred grove; for, the instant any fierce animals overleaped the boundary prescribed by the intelligences, being struck with sudden terror, they fled far away into their forests, or with a faltering step fell down on their knees as if to worship their Prince and Lord; part also kept watch, and guarded the passage itself at a distance. For pure spiritual essences, by virtue of the power and force alone which issue from them, so move and daunt minds (*animos*) enslaved to nature, that they ignorantly and impotently rush into actions not their own.

38. All things were now prepared; the parturient branch, according to the times of gestation, inclining itself by degrees towards the ground, at length deposited its burden commodiously on the couch spread beneath. The heavenly beings (*Vitæ*), clothed with a bright cloud, also stood by, and found that nothing had been neglected, but that all things were prepared obsequiously by nature in conformity to their provisions. Hence when the months were completed, at that time so many years, the fœtus, perfectly conscious of what was decreed, himself broke through the bands and bars of his enclosure, and raised himself by his own effort into this world and its paradise, desired from the first moments of his life; and he immediately drew in with his nostrils and breast the air, which

he saluted with a light kiss and which pressed in by its force as a new vital guest and spirit, for which the approaches and interior chambers had been previously provided,[y] and opening by its aid a field for exertions, he excited to their offices all the powers of his body, which were already in potency and endeavor, to exercise

2 themselves. The choicest flowers, encompassing this couch, now exhaled their odors from their deepest pores, that by them, infused into the attracted air, they might penetrate and exhilarate with rich and delicious gifts all the blood of the infant, flowing from the heart and now meeting the air. Whatever was in the kingdoms of nature, as if conscious and excited by a kind of festivity, favored, and in its own manner, greeted this birthday; for all celestial stores at this moment were effulgent, and by their influx, as it were, announced it. Choirs of the heavenly ones concluded this scene, which was the third, with the delicate vibrations of their lights, as so many tokens of gladness and favor.

---

y That by the vital spirit infused into Adam (Gen. ii. 7), was not meant the soul, so far as by soul is to be understood the spiritual mind, but only the air, by which respiration is effected and the life of the body preserved in activity, is very clear, not only from the words themselves, but also from parallel passages of the Sacred Scripture; for the words are these: *When Jehovah God had formed man out of the dust of the earth, He breathed into his nostrils the vital spirit, by which man was made animate.* It is evident, as well from inspiration on the reception of air through the nostrils, as from animation or the respiration thence arising, that the life of his body was opened by means of that spirit. Moreover that the wind and aerial atmosphere which the lungs respire, is called divine spirit more than once in the Sacred Scriptures, may be manifest, as was said, from parallel passages and the interpreters of this, as from Gen. chap. vi. 17, chap. vii. 15; Psalm civ. 29, 30. To quote here only Gen. vii. 22: *All things whatsoever on the earth, which drew in vital spirit with the nostrils, died.* Also Exod. xv. 8, 10: *At the blast of Thy nostrils the waters were heaped together; by Thee, when Thy spirit blew, they were overwhelmed in the sea.* 2 Sam. xxii. 16: *At the blast and spirit of Thy nostrils the whirlpools of the sea were discovered.* Job xxvii. 3: *So long as breath shall remain in me, and I shall have divine spirit in my nostrils,* etc., etc.

Section Second

Concerning the Infancy
of the First-Born, or Adam

39. IT was midnight, and the constellations of heaven also, as if about to applaud, did not now shine with brightness only, but glittered with a kind of flaming splendor; they burned to delay their setting, but Aurora, hastening to her rising, dimmed their lustre, and instantly opened the day for the sun. The inhabitants of heaven, as was said, stood around, and by their little flames prevented the rays of any other lumen from kindling the first spark of the light of his life; gladdened also at the sight of an infant, the first-born and hope of the whole human race, lying with his breast and face upward, and his tender hands folded and lifted up to heaven, moving also his little lips, as if he would venerate the Supreme Builder, and his Parent, not in mind only, but also by a certain posture and correspondent gesture of the body, showing purest thanksgiving that the workmanship of the world was now completed in himself.

40. He was naked, but encompassed with the mildest spring, as with a bath; so fair, and of a countenance so beautiful, as if he were a god not born to mortal life. Innocence itself, with its brightness and purity, beamed from his face, for it was so entirely effigied according to the idea of his mind or soul, that every fibre represented some ray of it shining, and at the same time delineated in itself, so that the mind appeared under a human form. He acted

also wholly under its auspices and government, for according to the reason of his existence he subsisted from the same, and this in such a manner, that while it inwardly delighted itself with his body, the countenance, instantly smiling, effigied the gladness of the soul, which also much increased his beauty. Thus now the soul, like a sort of active force governing its powers, incited its little body to all things which were to be done, and taught it how to incline itself to the breasts, many of which were extended by the maternal branch; to press them with its fingers; to suck the milk with its mouth; to roll it about with the tongue and palate; to lie down again after taking a proper quantity; and very many other 'things, which were inspired into this infant alone, born without a nurse, into the very order of life and nature, and educated under the protection of heavenly beings; for, if not even the smallest action of this infant could be concealed from the omniscience of the Great Creator before the birth of the world, so not even the smallest could escape His Providence.

41. Those godlike essences, or heavenly images, to whom the care of this little infant, as of the world's treasure, was committed, and who ministered to him, as to the little son of the Supreme Governor, were providently and attentively circumspect to see that nothing was omitted of the supplies to be presented to him by nature; nor did nature intermit her spontaneous labor until the infant pupil, under the guidance of his own mind, seemed able to provide for himself. Moreover, the heavenly guards, to the intent that the little body might sooner be initiated into this compliance, accelerated it by breathing into him their strength and directing to him their power; nor were they only like idle spectators standing about him, but they also infused themselves into his little body and its recesses, as yet folded up in delicate membranes. For heavenly [beings], because they are spiritual essences, have a power of penetrating even into inmosts, since nothing which is of nature opposes; for as they are in supreme things so also they are in inmosts, yea, they

even enter into a certain kind of society and discourse with the soul and mind itself. When therefore they had saluted this soul or mind, they explored the single things which were organically woven in it, especially those which encompassed its inmost shrines, namely, its Olympus shadowed in the crown of the head, which was the habitation about to be allotted to intelligences and sciences,[z] being much delighted at finding it formed to be a living and exact effigy of the great or heavenly Olympus; into which, therefore, under the influence of this delight, they invited each other, and inaugurated it by a kind of sacred rite and vow, rejoicing also at this, that every intelligence had his assigned abode and that all things were so

---

[z] As to where this Olympus, or heaven of intelligences, is, or to speak more clearly, where our intellectual mind resides, there is no other medium of investigation given than to follow the fibres themselves even to their ultimate and first boundary; for all our sensation passes to its inmost sense, and thence to the understanding, according to the fibres which are called sensory (*Sensoriae*), thus from the sight of the eye through the fibres of the optic nerve; from the smell of the nostrils through the olfactory fibres; from the hearing through the hard and soft fibres allotted to that sense, and so forth. In order, therefore, that their first and last boundary may be found, the brain (*Cerebrum*) must be thoroughly of the fibres. In the brain thus explored, there occur little spheres, wonderfully formed like gyres, which are commonly called the cortical glands, where, inasmuch as the fibres there terminate and commence, our mind must needs act, and nowhere else, if it acts from the beginnings of all the fibres; for to them, as ultimate ends, it deduces and collects the modes and radii of all its senses, and there emits them into a spacious and interior circus of perception and understanding. For all fibres, howsoever numerous, are born and [2] produced from these substances, wherefore here is our common sensory, consequently also our inmost, or intellectory, which from its senses perceives, from what it perceives thinks, from what it thinks judges, and from what it judges chooses, from what it chooses desires, and, lastly, from what it desires determines into act the things which it wills; here, therefore, is the supreme sphere of our bodies, and as it were our Olympus or heaven, for hence, as from centres, or from inmost or supreme things, other things are seen and provided for as in circumferences or beneath. That these substances, called cortical, taken together, constitute this our heaven, is also confirmed by the light of experience, for when they are affected, the universal appendix of the fibres, that is, the brain and the body, is affected and decays; and indeed according to the degree and mode in which those substances are affected, the powers of imagination grow dull, those of thought languish, the memory decays, the determinations of the will hesitate, the desires are vacillating, and the sensations grow numb.

beautifully arranged into a representation of the starry heaven,[a] that you would suppose the great heaven, which had designed the least according to [its own form], had been brought into its smallest concentrated type. They observed also the grand egg of the world portrayed in a kind of effigy,[b] whereby, according to two axes, it transmitted and poured forth its fibres, like rays brought forth from the very palaces and habitations of the intelligences, into the inferior regions of his world, or body. Finally, they discovered that the soul itself, like a deity, chose its seat in inmost and supreme things, in order that it might view and govern everything as placed without and beneath it; not to mention many other particulars which were noted, the ultimate texture of which they saw clearly as if already effected, from first principles, and also from ends, discoverable from the series of connections consequent on each other.

42. After they had so cheerfully indulged themselves in these joys, they decreed, with unanimous consent, to institute a festival in celebration of this last day of creation, and the first of the human race, wherefore they devised a new kind of sport, called paradisiacal, never before sported in the heavens. This sport did not consist in tripping and dancing, such as terrestrial nymphs employ in their amusements, but it was like that in which heavenly intelligences indulge when they wish to return into a state of innocence and, as it were, childhood; for they so began it by gyres and, as it were, mutual inflowings into itself from its borders, that from innumerable sports they formed one which was perpetual and continued. This

---

a In another place it will be shown that those little spheres, called cortical—which are the beginnings of the fibres, consequently also of the cerebrum at large, or together with the cerebellum, the medulla oblongata, and spinal cord—are so arranged and formed into spires, yea, are also furnished with their greater circles, poles, and axes, so as altogether to resemble the form of the celestial sphere.

b Namely, the cerebrum, which is not only likened to an egg, but also first receives into itself all the fibres derived from the above-mentioned principles, and presently transmits them, and finally brings them down in every direction into the provinces of the body by the medulla oblongata and spinal cord, in this case also corroborated and collected into nerves.

The Worship and Love of God

result was secured by circular spheres and spiral windings, to our sight like so many labyrinths, but still most distinct in themselves, so that not even one number in the rhythms gave an ambiguous harmony; for they insinuated themselves from the circumferences by continual circuits and involutions towards the centre, by a rapid but continual flexure, that all concentrated themselves by ways so succeeding each other and so united, that there was not even one which did not see itself, as it were, placed in the very centre. Thus by employing the harmony and form alone, from being discrete they could unite together in one continual sport. Nor was 2 this sufficient, for being thence only enticed and incited to a still more delicious continuation of their sport, commencing from this centre, as it were a common one, because diffused equally among all, this crown of heavenly beings, from more interior goals, and a more universal gyre, thus still more perfectly, began new orbs, which in like manner concentrated themselves, that they might again, from the former unity continued distinctly into one and all of them, introduce themselves into a more intimate and thus a prior concentration; which same sport the chorus also triplicated, until they so insinuated themselves into each other, that they no longer emulated what is perpetual, but what is infinite, and beheld themselves so very closely conjoined to the idea of super-celestial harmony, and, as it were, initiated into it, that they had a sensible perception that they were no longer many, but as it were one, and in the inmosts of centres; for in like manner as they united themselves, they united also their minds and their minds' delights. By these 3 windings they translated also along with themselves the mind of our infant, from the ultimate gyre in which he was placed, towards inmosts, and being thus united with it, they solemnly presented him conjointly as one and a divine spirit from unanimity itself, to the Supreme Deity, Who, being delighted with the end of His works, both first and last, as represented in him, hailed his coming with grace and favor. Then bursting forth [under the influence of] this divine honor, from this inmost recess of centres, they again extricated and unfolded themselves by similar circuits and concentrated orbs, but now gyring backwards in the same order towards the circumferences, and unfolding themselves from one again into 4 several, they placed the infant again in his ultimate circle. The very delights of his soul, which were excited by this sport, sparkled with such lucidity from his mouth and eyes, that his soul appeared, as it were, to have leaped forth from inmost principles into the outermost forms of his countenance; and while they were with him in inmosts they observed him so animated with the pleasantness of all delights, or the concentrated joys of happiness, that his lungs forgot to reciprocate the attractions of their air, in consequence of the festive stupor and lovely swoon of the spirits in the fibres, and when he was conveyed back to his circumferences those lobes beat with so quick, so frequent, and rapid reciprocations, that by their little motions they emulated the ultimate rhythms of the sport. By this sport, and others like it, they so excited the tender body to compliance with its soul, which was thus called forth into its ultimates, that the court of his mind seemed to act from its inmost nature.

43. From these and similar excitements, our firstborn, from the first time of his birth into the light of his world, acted like a delightful imitator, under the view and full control of the soul itself from which he was formed, and although ignorant of it as to the body, he nevertheless effigied and gesticulated, although with a weakness of action, her pleasure and decrees; in this respect being altogether exempt from the lot of his posterity, and impotence of action, in 2 their most tender [years].*c* Thus lived wholly and entirely the soul,

---

c Brute animals, which are born into a full obedience to their soul from the first moment of their nativity, have also control over their limbs and muscles, stand upon their feet and walk, and skilfully perform the proper functions of their nature still more wonderful than these; and from the same moment they enjoy in full keenness the external senses. But it is otherwise with the human race in their most tender infancy. The reason is,

under the image of an infant clothed with body; for the soul saw the beauties of paradise shine through, as it were, her own eyes, not his, and delighted herself not from the harmonies of effects, but from the joy of uses, and of the goodness contemplated in them. According to his delights also, the pupils and eyelashes of his little eyes had a fiery brightness; for the use of no object is concealed from the soul, inasmuch as it contemplates all things from an end, and from the principles of nature, and therefore perpetually acts in her body from the most secret and inmost principles of causes and of sciences; on this account from her new sight she instantly perceived what was profitable or what was injurious to the body, and its connection with herself; she therefore moved her imitator at pleasure, as a force acting upon a wheel, bent him at her will, and directed his joints and muscles to effects, as she directed herself to ends; wherefore, at the first twinkling of his sight, the little infant crept from his couch, and with his fingers laid hold of whatever came in his way, but only on such things as were suitable, and brought them to his little lips, and again crept back to his couch. Sometimes 3

---

because we enjoy a certain proper mind, which is called intellectual and rational, from which, as from its fountain, the will proceeds; this our mind is what governs the muscles and sensories of the body; wherefore also the actions, which are determined by means of the muscles, belong to it, and are called *voluntary,* which are so far rational as they descend from the purer and more sublime intellect of that mind. This our mind, which, as was said, presides over the muscles and organs of sense, is not born together with the body, but is opened, grows, and is perfected in process of time by the help of the senses; and this is the reason why we are born into such impotence of acting and feeling. It was altogether 2 otherwise in our first-born, whose rational or intellectual mind was not to be instructed and perfected in a similar manner, or from the bodily senses, but from the soul itself, while the sensories of the body only administered and were subservient. For he was born into a state of the greatest integrity, and into perfections themselves; wherefore from the first moments of life, full power must of necessity have been given to his soul, enabling it to operate upon the muscles and sensories of the body, without the mediation of this secondary mind and its will; but that the case is otherwise in his posterity, is a most evident sign of imperfection. Nevertheless without a clear perception of what the soul is, and what the intellectual mind is, and how one is joined to the other, and one distinct from the other, it is not allowed clearly to discern rational truth on this subject; wherefore we shall endeavor to elucidate it in the series of what follows.

also the ruling mind laid him on his back, where drops of milk fell straight into his little mouth. Wheresoever also fragrant flowers grew, thither he extended his hands, and moved them to his nostrils, that he might excite his organ of smelling. In like manner he pricked up his ears at the singing of birds; nor was anything pleasing to any of his senses which was not conducive to the development of his body. After repeating these operations occasionally in the course of the day, she laid him asleep again, possibly also with a whisper and oscillatory motion inwardly excited; and when he was disposed to view again the utilities of paradise, she awoke him. This was the constant habit, that when he was asleep, she lifted up the hands, closely folded together, towards heaven. But all these things were done under the influence of the Supreme Deity providing, yea acting, who in all and single things is the sole Agent, because the sole living Being; for from Him, because from His life, we live, and living, act.

44. Although the soul transcribed herself into the form of the body, and to accomplish her ends formed a type of herself, as a kind of perpetual plane of uses, from fibres radiating from herself, and infused fluid and heavier essences into its continuous little channels and pores, winding in perpetual circles, which essences pressed downwards by their weight this its effigy, and, as it were, fixed it to the earth to be its inhabitant,[d] yet she herself, residing in her supreme and inmost principles, and thus in a heavenly palace, while in her own, was always endeavoring to elevate her type, or little machine, to herself, and thus towards things superior, and was continually inspiring all the fibres of the tender body, drawn

---

d The very form itself of the body, viewed in its fibres, is from the soul alone; for there is nothing therein which is not composed of fibres, whether they be blood-vessels or even bones; it is a collection of fibres which alone gives birth to the inferior and corporeal forms, and renders them manifest, and arranges them into forms, so as to perform each its particular use, and no other. Every fibre whatsoever, which is in the body, has been brought forth from the soul and from no other principle, except what was first formed from the soul. But that a body may exist and appear, which by the force of its gravity may

The Worship and Love of God

downwards by the accessory forces of inertia, to take a direction upwards. For the infant as yet crept, and differed nothing from the wild beasts in his manner of moving, which being observed with deep indignation by the soul, she strenuously labored to lift him up on high, and to set him erect upon his feet. While she was intent upon this end, means could not be wanting for its accomplishment, for it is from the centres and recesses of all the arts and sciences that she conceives the beginnings of her operations, and thus arranges the works of nature to provide for the necessities of all ends. Hence she contrived various, but at the same time lovely tricks; for she bended his eyes to the most beautiful fruits hanging from branches aloft, and instilled a desire to lay hold of them with his fingers, adding also strength to his muscles; in like manner she enkindled also a desire to feed on clusters of grapes, which grew high on their vines, but bending downwards, that clinging to the branches he might lift himself upwards; by these and similar incitements, and as it were playthings, she allured him to raise his countenance upwards from the ground. The heavenly 2 genii also adjoined their divine skill to these incitements, and by devised enticements encircled and sported with him; for at one time above his eyes they represented a floating paradise, girded and wreathed with garlands and nosegays, delightful to his nature; at another time they induced him to believe that he saw infants, as so many little brothers, flying rapidly and winged, and directing their course towards him, for the sake of playing with him, but presently raising themselves on high; and when he endeavored to follow them, they led him to suppose that he also was furnished

---

tend downwards or towards the earth, terrestrial elements, endowed with the force of inertia, are called into aid, and these are infused into the humors, especially the blood, which pervade the vessels and little canals fabricated by those fibres. By means of these, and at the same time the composition of fibres, our body is rendered heavy, and is furnished with the force of acting in these ultimates of the world; whence it is clear that the blood was called into aid especially for this reason, because from the blood is principally derived this effigy of the soul called body and flesh.

with similar wings, on which to balance himself.[e] For the inhabitants of heaven, before pure eyes and minds free from earthly loves, are able to represent anything, and at the same time to enkindle in those minds any ardor and attention they please. By these sportive blandishments, and pleasing witcheries, our infant, in the space of a few days, being set upon his feet, walked erect with his countenance directed upwards to the stars and heaven; nor was he willing to let it down again, except when he desired to refresh himself with the food, prepared on all the tables of the earth, solely for the sake of recruiting his body.

45. But these things were only preludes, and, by the loves of his nature, inaugurations of the muscles into their active and motor forces, and of the organs into the modes of their sensation; especially into favor and obedience to the vicarious and subordinate mind, which being about to become rational, was to be adorned with understanding and will, and to which the soul was to deliver up the reins of its body, while she herself ruled the orders of his nature. For already, for his provided advent, from the first stamen, she marked that Olympus, and in it, as in a sacred temple, she furnished three interior chambers, the inmost of which, called the sanctuary, the soul herself, as the goddess of her little world, and an inhabitant of each heaven, reserved for herself; but the second,

---

[e] There are some loves of the nature of the body itself, which manifest themselves first of all in new-born children, namely, a desire for those things which contribute to the establishment and reestablishment of the union of the parts and forms of the body, as a suitable nourishment, such as milk and the like; the very wants of nature, which express themselves by hunger and thirst, and by desire and delight thereto annexed, excite this love, not only towards the means themselves, but also towards mediating and ministering causes, as towards nurses. This is especially rendered manifest by a kind of hatred joined to indignation, as it were, of envy, which is an affection contrary to that love, when infants like themselves are also adopted and taken to the bosom of the mother or nurse. To the loves of nature is also to be referred the love towards little infants like themselves, for they view and perceive themselves, as it were, in them, and thus discover a kind of union; for love is an affection of union, and such love results from the life of the soul diffused throughout the very nature of the body, where the soul herself, by means of her fibres, is omnipresent.

named the sacristy, she dedicated to the intelligences united into *one mind,* to be as their own; but the third, as a court, she granted to the sciences with their verities. She also established this law, 2 before the gates were opened, that the sciences, as servants, should observe every inclination of the intelligences, but the intelligences, bound by a kind of religion, should yield obedience to their soul as their chief ruler, and, in the performance of their duties, should provide also for her safety. Such was the design, previous to their birth, which looked to their being introduced, as they grew up, as brides into these their inmost marriage-chambers. For the soul herself, sitting alone with the key of her own kingdom, without a vicarious administration by this mind, could will nothing except from the necessity of a governing end; thus she was bound to compliance with that end, but the end was not under her government; when she viewed through the eyes of her infant the most pleasant theatres of paradise, she did not view the harmonies except through their utilities, nor these except as inwardly involved in their ultimate end and at the same time as conducing to the welfare of her body; but when she elevated herself towards heaven, becoming almost forgetful of her body, she grew negligent about it and her own nature. Sometimes also she strove to be elevated upwards, while 3 the body was carried downwards, and to separate from herself all her earthly encumbrances, but the necessity of the end opposed. When the soul perceived this opposition in herself, although not from herself, but from the Supreme Deity, she desired nothing more than to introduce into her consecrated Olympus a kind of mind, which, from the affection of good might comprehend truth, and from the understanding of truth might desire good, and which might conjoin things celestial with things terrestrial, and in herself might rightly balance both as in a pair of scales.

46. With a view of exciting this mind to be her vicegerent in the kingdom of her body, the soul, like a schoolmistress, prepared the eye, through which nature might flow in with rays of her modified light; therefore she turned it to beautiful forms, and such as allured the

sight. While the infant was as yet living in the shadow of his life, creeping like a worm of the earth, then the soul, elevating the forehead and the eyebrows, poured forth his full vision into splendid and pleasant gardens, that at once, and by one draught, she might induce the most general idea of the parts. Afterwards she directed the eyeballs to peculiar kinds of flowers, concealing all other things by the interposition, as it were, of veils, lest the sight should wander into things more common; and at length she concentrated it, fixing it upon some individual flowers, and at the same time also she inspired the pleasantness of their beauty, by the sweetness of the odor which issued from them, so that he might examine them more closely by taking them into his hands and applying them to his

2 nostrils. Thus she began to build that new mind, which was to become intellectual, altogether according to the idea of creation, so that she might quickly cast all things in a complex as into an egg, in which she might distinguish, and afterwards unfold, all other things successively insinuated by a series. But when she had raised her little child from that low life, or from his creeping state, and set him on his feet, then, in like manner, she presented to his view the whole garden of paradise, in its lofty aspect, even to its highest boughs; and by degrees, little clumps of trees, and at length each individual tree, as objects of his attention; and lastly she fixed him in the tree of his own life, and in the branch of it which as yet yielded

3 milk. Afterwards she introduced animals to his view; for there was nothing which did not comply with the wishes of the soul, as with so many decrees of the ruling end, that is, of the Supreme Mind, from which proceeded the government of all ends [and their operation] in causes. The animals, with their young, being called from their forest and sylvan haunts, and rushing by troops into the grove by a new impetus of nature, spontaneously so arranged themselves into companies and legions, according to their genera and species, that they were presented to his view as one herd; but afterwards being distributed into species, and by degrees discriminated, they departed singly, each looking to the ground in token of respect. The

inhabitants of heaven also, by their skilful representations, made flowers to spring from seed before his eyes, which seed, after it had put forth its stems and germs into leaves, produced new seeds by the release and concentration of the juices into their first powers; not to mention several other kinds of forms, full of fruitful joy, and of joyful intelligence, by the sight of which the ardency of the eyes was awakened, and transmitted them as new objects of vision through fibres, even into the inmost chambers of the future mind.

47. The soul, from the sanctuaries or centres of her Olympus, that she might continually meet those beautiful forms which insinuated themselves, like new guests, through the doors and chambers of vision, dimmed by degrees her most splendid light, and girded herself with a less shining mantle, and at length descending to the lowest door,^{f} clothed herself in a shadowy but still pellucid robe, adding also gems, but crystalline ones; thus she always compounded herself anew, even to the meeting of those images, which borrow their form from the rays of the solar light. When she had seen the images, she received them with friendly kisses and embraces at the very threshold and around the last step of her ladder. But these images, when they had returned the salutation, instantly felt themselves formed anew, so that when they looked at each other, they could no longer distinguish themselves as sisters; for that goddess or queen infused life into them from her own life by her kiss and embrace, so that they no longer appeared as images, but as ideas. She also turned their very harmonies into beauties and changed into delights and joys whatever at its admission smoothed and soothed

---

f The form itself of the body, in its fibres, from which are derived each and all of its structures, is from the soul alone, as was shown above; for the fibres are its productions, the first of which are more properly called its eradiations, or their determinations, than productions. In order, therefore, that it might be in lasts as well as in firsts, or in lowest things as in highest, it so again and again compounded the fibres, into which it transcribed its own essence, and furnished the compositions with blood-vessels, formed also from its fibres, that they might appear under the form of an organic body, and at the same time might perform the uses which, from the first stamen, she had intended as ends. For

the hinge of the door. In like manner all the modifications of that light, by the mere breathing of her life, were changed into sensa-
2 tions; this first door they called their *eye*. This most excellent queen led down these strangers with her right hand even to the first court of her palace, where very many lodgings were constructed in the most perfect arrangement, and she assigned an abode to each one of them, so that they might dwell in it as in a recess withdrawn from herself, until being called forth thence into her view, they might be admitted into the interiors of her palace; this place was called the *memory*. But presently putting off her assumed and shadowy ceremonies, she compounded herself again, and invited the strangers into higher chambers, or sacristies, in becoming order, and so animated them again with the breath of new and purer life, that while they again viewed each other they were lost, as it were, to each other's view, and still less recollected each other than when they were beneath in the threshold, so resplendent were they made by her light; for what were before seen under an effigy as ideas, now perceived themselves, by mutual consociations, transformed into *reasons,* which yet, being surnamed from their prior form, were called *rational* or *intellectual ideas,* the beauties of those ideas, which were formerly harmonies, being now renovated into goodnesses, and their delights and joys flowing out of beauty, into gladness and
3 happiness, thus altogether into celestial forms.[g] But these again being distributed into most becoming orders, she furnished with

---

nothing lives in the body but the soul, to which appertains all that life which is in the senses, because in the fibres, which being modified, instantly acquire a sensation according to the form of their composition; wherefore the soul is said to have descended from its sanctuary, or highest abode, by the steps, as it were, of a ladder in coming down from her highest form to the lowest. For the soul is so real a substance, that all the substances of the body, which enjoy active life, are from it, and are called substances, but compounded ones, since every compound is only an aggregate of its simple substances, nor is anything truly a substance but the supreme substance, which is therefore called a simple substance.

  g The expressions which suit one form do not suit another, for the accidents and modes of a prior form, like substances themselves, change themselves; therefore what are called goodnesses in a superior sphere, are called beauties in an inferior one, and harmonies in

members and organs, that they might emulate corporeal forms, and then she no longer called them rational ideas, but truths. These, so conformed and of simple elegance, she sent back into the first chambers of her court, or memory, with the command that they should be most ready to fly forth into the sacristy at the first beck and token of their being wanted. From these, at length, she begat intelligences, which, in order that they might live in unanimity, she called *understanding.*

48. This mind, or soul, took to her chaste breasts these intelligences, her daughters, whom she brought forth by the connubial torch of life and of nature, after they had been conceived from truths, and from the moment they began to use their light; and she instilled into them, with her milk, not only life, but also the purest love; for as in the lumen of nature there is not only the splendor of light, but also heat, so also in spiritual lumen, there is not only life, but also love. This spiritual fire, as well inborn as given by the milk, she so transfused, as a kind of blood, through the nature of their body, that from it they became effulgent with a flame of pleasantness, like that of the morning at the first appearance of Aurora. Every moment they increased in the power of growing wise, as in active strength and beauty; for the intelligences themselves, or the understanding, have their infancies and progressions in wisdom. From their first stamen, as also from their milk, from this vital 2 ardor, they so intensely loved their mother, that with difficulty they suffered themselves to be plucked from her embrace, and although removed, they still remained in her view, that they might obtain by sight what they could not secure by grasp; for love is an affection of union, and in its purest state is such that one sees

---

the lowest; or what amounts to the same, what in a superior sphere is gladness and happiness, in an inferior one is delight and joy, and so in other cases. There remains only a kind of image, and by it of correspondence, for an inferior form must be altogether resolved, that a superior one may exist; and *vice versa,* a superior one must be compounded into a new one, that an inferior may exist, with its proper predicates and adjuncts.

himself altogether in another, separated indeed in nature, but not in mind. These infantile genii, refusing the milk to which they had been accustomed, were so overcharged, and, as it were, overflowing with gladness, in consequence of the excitations of that love, that everything seemed to them to exult and sport, especially at the sight of the harmonies, which were re-formed into beauties, 3 and at length into goodnesses. They were also made sensible in themselves of felicity resulting from their gladness, but as yet they knew not that they were felicities, conceiving them only to be pure gladnesses; but afterwards, when they became more intelligent, they began both to think and perceive that gladness and felicity flowed forth from love, as from their fountain; yea, they also saw clearly from their light, that truth, goodness, and felicity had continual reference to love from love, as by a kind of revolution, wherefore they sought nothing more ardently than the embrace of that love. Thus they began to look at love as the end, and all other things as means leading to it; which also they loved for the sake of the end; for in the means they beheld the end, as it were, present. On perceiving these things the pious mother, exulting as it were with all gladnesses, began to take the highest delight in her infants, as in images of herself, because from desire they both willed and regarded ends, and, between her kisses, she saluted them no longer as her intelligences, but as *wisdoms*.

49. At length this mother seemed to herself most happy, and having called together her daughters, and at the same time, out of the chambers of the court, their slaves and servants, who arranged themselves about the wisdoms, now their mistresses, into the form of a most beautiful crown. And while she fixed her gaze upon all and each of them in the assembly, she thus began to speak: My most beloved daughters! the time is at hand that we must depart, you to your sacristies, I into my sanctuary. Remember, little daughters! that I am your parent, and that the life which you derive from mine is so devoted to you by love itself, that by mind I am in you; thus although we part, still ye can do nothing but under my auspices.

The light, by which ye view ends, is from mine, because by me; 2
yours is only to be circumspect, and to arrange means, that our
ends may exist in effect and use.[h] I have adorned you not only with
understanding, but with will; and thus I have subjected my ends
to your decision. But again and again I pray and beseech you, not
to look at and covet any other end than the best, that is, the love

---

[h] The activities of this new mind consist in thinking, judging, concluding, choosing,
and willing, consequently both understanding and will pertain to it. All these operations
or activities are mere variations of form, which being regarded as forces are called changes
of state; for as the soul itself is a real substance, so also these forms, the first and supreme of
its organic ones; for whether we speak of forms or substances, it amounts to the same
thing, since no substance produced from God is without a form, whence it derives its
faculties of acting, and its qualities. But what is the quality of the variations of forms, 2
or changes of state, we do not well perceive, except from the forms or organs subject to
our sight, each and all of which are constructed and fabricated so as to have the power of
varying their forms in ways innumerable; the muscles never act but by a variation of their
forms determined by the motor fibres. Nor do the viscera of the whole body perform any
operations except by similar changes. But in proportion as the substances are prior or
superior, in the same proportion they are able to vary their forms, or change their states,
not only more alertly, but by modes, if I may use the expression, more infinite, so that in
the supreme substances there is such a power of varying them, that they exceed all calculation, and all series of all calculations; for their very perfection, because their activity,
consists in the variability of their form. That this variation may be comprehended by some 3
idea, let the circular form be taken for an example, which allows itself to be varied into
every possible kind of ellipsis, of cycloids, and of curves; the ellipsis itself allows itself to be
varied into infinite kinds like and unlike itself; but the form perpetually circular or spiral,
which is a superior form, is variable into still more kinds, because it does not immediately
respect a single centre, as fixed, but a kind of entire circle, or another curve of the family of circulars, instead of a centre; hence this its power increases still more to a kind of
infinity: and this is always the case even more in forms still superior. They are therefore 4
real activities which produce our ideas, and indeed so real, that they may be demonstrated
to the apprehension, yea, to the sight; consequently the understanding flows from the
activity of its forms, as sight from the activities of its eye, and motion from those of its
muscle; wherefore it is not improperly called interior sight. These variations cannot exist
in our first infancy, for we are to be inaugurated into them by the influx of our sensations,
which is effected according to the fibres, into the very beginnings of the fibres, where the
understanding itself resides. The determinations of the will into acts are also variations
or changes in the same beginnings of the organs, but not such as are perceptions, imagi-
nations, and thoughts; for there are given variations of dimensions, or expansions and
constrictions of form, since by these, as the blood is forced from its heart into the arteries,
so the animal spirit is forced from its little hearts or cortical substances into the fibres, to
excite the muscles; that this is the case is confirmed by all experience and science.

of the Supreme, breathed into you with life and with milk, for He is the End of Ends, the First of the Last, and the Last of the First: from Him are all things, because He is the All of All; hence your happiness and its felicity; from your love ye are loved, and from His love ye love; hence the light of your intuitions, and the sacred warmth of your actions; for the rays of His light are so many truths,

3 and the fires of His rays are so many goodnesses. For the sake of His and your love I abdicate my kingdom, and I deliver up the key to your care, for my great concern is only about you; behold me therefore no longer as your lawful mother but your companion and minister. But I entreat you, my most beloved, and most dear, with the most earnest prayer, remember my salvation, while you remember your own, for my salvation and happiness are at your disposal, since I have delivered up to you my soul. At these words tears flowed from the mother and her daughters; they sank into each other's bosoms, and remained in close embrace.

50. But after a short pause of silence, she resumed again her discourse which had been interrupted with tears, and addressing her children, thus expressed her pious wishes: Behold, the kingdom which I have submitted to you, furnished by me so as best to promote your happiness It is, as you see, a little type of the universe, a copy of the greatest, so formed, that nature herself, unless she were blind, might in it distinguish herself, and the effigy of her own world; but I have adorned it with natures (*naturis*) or powers and forces exempt from those of her world, namely, proper to itself, yet according to her pattern, to the intent that it may comply, not with her but with your endeavors and determinations; wherefore I dare not give her more authority in your world, than only to secure and

2 support its orders and states by general aid.[i] I have also woven it of

---

i That our animal world, which is also called a microcosm, is ruled by natures, or powers and forces proper to it, may be manifest from many things, for the blood flows with as great rapidity upwards as downwards in its vessels; in like manner the rest of the humors; and also the aliments in the stomach and intestines; no gravity or centripetency is

mere centres, arranged into such an order that these may jointly effigy the circumferences, these the axes, and these the diameters, namely, that all things, as mere equilibriums, may comply with your good pleasure in the most favorable manner, and that none of the

---

induced, except by its own proper active forces; wherefore its nature is altogether exempt from the nature of the circumfluent world; this nature is what our soul governs. Thus to attribute anything immediately to nature is to derogate from the government of our soul, as we should derogate from the will of our mind if we were to ascribe actions to nature. Now because our living microcosm, in consequence of possessing its own proper nature, departs from the jurisdiction of the grand or circumambient world, let us consider what it derives from that world and what from itself. I. The atmospheres of the circumfluent world are incumbent on the animal microcosm, press its single [parts] with force and weight according to their activity and column, and thus hold together in inseparable connection whatsoever belongs to it; but the microcosm itself reacts against these forces, gravities, and incumbencies, with similar ones of its own, so that the balance stands even, and action is equal to reaction. The case is similar when the atmosphere flows into the lungs, and inspires the body and its members with motor forces. II. The atmospheres also, especially the ethereal or prior ones, urge its single parts, consequently the whole, to their centre of gravity, so that we, being pressed to the bottom of the atmospheres, may walk on the clods of the subject earth, and may there construct our habitations and take up our abodes. In other respects we ourselves take the reins of our body, and direct it as we please, governing the kingdom by our own laws of administration. III. Moreover the atmospheres, by the rest of their properties (*naturas*), administer to and serve us, as by modifications, whereby they flow into the organs of our senses, and present and represent objects, notwithstanding their distance, as present, and, as it were, contiguous. These objects we apprehend by our sensories of hearing and seeing; we consider them as proper to us, we endow them with life and turn them into sensations. The case is the same also with the substances endowed with the *vis inertiæ*, and which attain to a purer touch in the organs of the smell and taste. IV. The atmospheres also share with us the changes of their states, as seasonsof heat and cold, varying temperatures, conditions of dryness and moisture, the motions of parts of their volume, storms, and several things besides. We, on the other hand, oppose to them the states of our body and changes, flowing from inmost principles, as ardors, states of cold, temperatures, and variously affected dispositions (*animos*), in order to prevent the outer conditions from entering clandestinely and penetrating more deeply than our nature thinks allowable for us to be affected by them. V. The atmospheres also nourish, refresh, and continually renew our blood and spirit, by elements sublimed from a saline matrix, which are thus invisible (*occultis*); especially by aliments insinuated through the circumambient skin and the pulmonary vessels. In like manner also the earth [furnishes aliments] from its triple kingdom, but through open orifices and tubes, into the viscera of the chyle and blood. We, on the other hand, having enjoyed these aliments and gifts extended and attracted towards us, cast out through the pores into the field of the universe, and also unload through the alvine gates, the obsolete

powers may dare, even in the least instance, to resist your will.[k] I have also induced upon the members, held together by bonds at once hard and yielding, a kind of society, that none may cultivate itself more than another, except for the sake of itself and of all; thus also I have inspired them with love derived from my own. Take now into your hands the reins of this kingdom; all things are obedient to you; let it only be reserved for me to govern its nature, for I am aware that the acts of your will tend continually to effect a change of the natural state; sometimes, also, if your minds are enkindled with ardor, to disturb the orders themselves; therefore I will constantly be upon the watch, especially during the night, when ye repose your cares upon my bosom, that I may recruit whatsoever has fallen to decay in the daytime, so that it may be ready to comply with your new purposes when you awake. Thus I shall studiously and diligently attend to your necessities and conveniences while ye are at rest. Behold what I commit to your charge! the whole compass of this body, with its muscular, brawny parts and joints, for it is covered around by muscular fibres as with a coat of mail; at the same time also I give you charge over the organs of sense, which keep watch like so many guards stationed round about. But the things which are within this compass, or all interior things, with

3

---

things which have performed wtheir office and are useless, and which might pollute the habitations. VI. The terraqueous and atmospheric orb ultimately receives into its bosom, buries in tombs, and claims again what had been borrowed from it, thus again dispersing this corporeal world, nourished by, and composed of, its elements, when it has now closed its life. But the soul and supreme mind of that body, not dust, but a part of heavenly nature, whose life that corporeal orb has lived, when it divests itself of its habitation, and bids farewell to the microcosm formerly its own, betakes itself inwardly into its own superior sphere of which it is an inhabitant. From these things it appears what we derive from the circumambient world and what from ourselves, namely, that that world, by its general aid, only sustains the orders and states of our body, and gives a faculty whereby we can enjoy our proper powers and natures.

k That it consists of mere centres, may at first view appear as a paradox, but only to him who is ignorant of the determinations of those essential principles from which superior forms arise; but that it really is so, may be manifest from a particular examination of the subject.

The Worship and Love of God

their viscera, I would have committed to my care;[^1] for I know that you, by the intuition of your mind, take account of those things that are without, and of the universe which encompasses us, and of the innumerable varieties of heaven and of the earthly paradise (*Cæli et Telluris Paradisi*); in the meantime, in order that all things within may be properly performed, I will provide for and favor your endeavors by my counsel (*mente*). I will also by your leave, 4 withdraw from your direction that lower sport, which is called the palestra of the exercises of Venus, lest, excited perhaps by your nymphs (turning her eyes towards the slaves, who stood around transformed into ideas), ye extinguish, by too great an indulgence of that love, the tinder of your bodily life, and exhaust the forces of our kingdom; but, as ye show your good disposition towards me by obedience, I also will season your prayers and pleasures by means of these blandishments. I grant also to you half the custody 5 of the lungs, that ye may have something of rule and jurisdiction in the government of the nature of our body; for to the lungs, as to a general mart, I have committed all the blood, which partakes of life from me in the lowest degree; the lungs also are the instruments which excite all our organic operations, and direct them to their offices. Moreover, I have created for you an ample palace, 6 and have divided it into hemispheres, according to the idea of a celestial court; and all its great and lesser circles I have tied to poles; and have besides guarded it about with walls of bone; there is your throne and tribunal; this is called the *cerebrum.* But lest I should interrupt you in your occupations, I have selected for myself a kind of little court with its little cells, where the secrets of the kingdom

[^1]: All the muscles which are excited by our will are situated on the surface and limbs of the body, as the muscles of the face, of the breast, of the abdomen, of the loins, of the arms, etc. The actions produced from these are therefore called voluntary; but no muscles inside of this surface are subject to the will, but to the soul, which governs the nature of all the viscera—as in the thorax, the heart itself; in the abdomen, the liver, the pancreas, the spleen, the stomach, the intestines, the kidneys, the bladder; furthermore, also, the organs in both sexes dedicated to generation.

are concealed beneath your feet and borders, distinct from your magnificent palace, not as a throne, but as a bench, which therefore I have called *cerebellum*. Thus ye see, my daughters, with what anxious care I have provided for you. But it was time for them to recede from each other, and for the intelligences to take into their hands the reins committed to them; the sun also began to rise with his upper border, and the sensations began to awake.

51. These wise intelligences, separated from the embrace of their mother, with joined hands and quickened pace betook themselves to their court, where they beheld divine and superb furniture, and a magnificent throne, rising even to the ceiling of the roof, with a sceptre and the insignia of royalty deposited on an ivory chair, which they eagerly examined, with both eyes and hands, deriving thence serenity. In the midst was a hearth on which the flame, divided into several tapers, immediately on their passing over the threshold, thundered deeply; the hearth itself, constructed of adamantine circles and wreaths of wrought gold, and, as it were, molten by flaming fire into adamantine gold, gleamed; hence innumerable colors gave forth their radiance according to the position of every one's eye; which also appeared in every intelligence, for in like manner they glittered by its reflection and became efflorescent.[m] On seeing these things, being struck with divine amazement, not knowing whether they were freed from the shackles of their body or carried aloft, they prepared themselves to begin their government, but not until, inspired by what they had seen, they had performed sacred rites.

52. Our first-born, not now an infant, but a youth, in that most quiet state of first awaking, for it was morning, distinctly overheard

---

[m] What is meant by fire with its flame, what by the hearth with adamant and gold, and what by each in the gleaming of that fire, which was, as it were, molten into adamantine gold; also what by the colors, which gave thence their radiations, with the splendor varied by reflection in each intelligence, according to its position, with several other things, will be explained below.

The Worship and Love of God

the very sweet discourse of the parent soul with her daughters, as if whispered within himself; he himself also hung upon her mouth that he might read all her words; and at the same time he was attentive to what the virgins saw and did in the court of their Olympus; wherefore he hastened to meet them as they came towards him, and embracing each of them upon the highest degree, he thus accosted them with a smiling countenance:[n] My Intelligences! do not suppose that the smallest expression of the discourse which our parent poured forth into your bosoms from her most pious lips escaped my ears, and that I did not behold your entrance into the court, also the sacred hearth itself, and your libations, with my attentive eyes; for nothing of what ye think is concealed from me, since ye are in my Olympus, which my mother and yours has committed to you, and which ye have consecrated. Be it ratified; I also venerate 2

---

[n] There are two ways or methods of teaching and of learning, one is called the synthetic, the other the analytic; the former, or synthetic, commences, or enters upon a view of things from inmosts, and proceeds in order to outmosts, or from ends themselves or the principles of causes to effects, lastly to ultimates; or what is the same thing, according to the received method of speaking, from what is prior to things posterior, or from reason, by the philosophy of mind, to those things which are confirmed by the experience of the senses. But the other, or the analytic way, is the inverse of the former, for it begins from 2 outmosts, and, according to an order natural to us, leads itself back or inwards to interior things, namely, from effects to causes, and thus finally to principles and ends themselves, which is called [a process] from what is posterior to things prior, or from the experience of the senses by the philosophy of the mind, even to first causes and reasons. By the synthetic way, or from ends, and thus from principles to causes and effects, all spiritual minds proceed, for they are in the very first and supreme principles, and view, beneath them, as it were, those things which follow in their order to ultimates. According to the same order also proceeds all formation, as of plants from their seed; for this adapts and unfolds itself from its principles, even to the extreme effect, and from this afterwards betakes itself to its prior principles, or to seeds; according to the same order also, the soul builds its body; consequently according to the same order she formed and informed this rational and intellectual mind, already in her first-born. By a similar order the world was created from the Divine or Supreme Mind. Hence it appears that the intellectual mind of Adam, 4 while all things were excited from their first auspices to things posterior, was instructed by the synthetic way, by the soul first, and afterwards by the senses; wherefore now he is said to have met his understanding, or the intelligences who were coming to him. The case is otherwise in his posterity, in whom the rational mind, which had altogether no existence

and confirm her commands and decrees as sacred; in that Olympus let your habitations be fixed, let us unite also and dwell together in the same chambers, for it is my intention to pass my life with you. Nothing shall be sweeter to me than to derive from your minds the maxims and the reasons of my life, for I am indebted to my mother for the one, and to you for the other. It is owing to her that I live and respire, but to you that I am wise and act with reason; consequently I have to thank you that I am a man, for that alone is human which flows from the understanding and will of

3 your mind. Moreover, I dare not claim and arrogate anything to myself as my own, except what is conveyed from your bosom into mine; for what ye deliver to me to be possessed as a possession from yourselves, that alone I hold as my own and claim to myself; for it is mine, because I not only perceive it, but also feel it, being affected by it; and inasmuch as it is mine, whatsoever flows from the sight and endeavor of your mind is rightfully attributed to me. But I am not my own, unless I be yours; all other things in us, which we do not seem to possess, belong to our common mother, who being bound by the hard, but now golden chain of necessity, governs the nature of the kingdom for the purpose of serving us; but she also communicates to us her pleasantnesses, for whatever she meets which is delightful and pleasing she reflects into you, and causes us to enjoy her delights, with which she imbues and charms our minds and wills before she disperses them into her own nature; thus also she teaches us to know goodnesses themselves by a sense of exquisite

4 pleasantness. And from that liberty, which I enjoy through you, I derive the faculty of self-possession; with the help of your minds I am enabled so to elevate my views as to raise them into the palaces

---

in infancy, is first, as it were, to be constructed, or opened from the senses, before it can be instructed; for it is perfected by age, by the help of experience, which is of the senses, and afterwards of the sciences, conceived and brought forth from the experience of the senses; and by like degrees the soul, with its spiritual light (*lumine*), goes to meet it, and infuses power, whereby we are enabled to think, to judge, to choose, and to will. This, as was said above, is a manifest sign of the imperfection of our state.

The Worship and Love of God

of heaven, and introduce them into association with its god-like inhabitants. I remember how I was lifted up, as out of a deep sleep, by a paradisiacal sport conducted by a chorus of celestials, even into the sanctuary, and, as a pledge of union, was presented to our Supreme; on the other hand also, by means of your minds, it is allowed me to descend with the animus into the intermediate joys of the earth and paradise, and thus to look upwards or downwards as I please, and to choose and embrace whatsoever loves present themselves. But, my comrades! give attention to what our mother 5 said, that there is only one only Love, which is the beginning and end of all loves, for they are infinite in number. Let us only enjoy these, but in such a manner, that they may lead us to that single One, for of themselves, as far as I have seen, they thither point. Wherefore, while we fix our eyes on them, let us fix our minds on this One; for it is by virtue of It that we are ourselves capable of enjoying, as our own, the felicities flowing from that Love, and that the Supreme sees, as it were, Himself, because His own grace, in us by mutual love. Wherefore, since we are confederated by so many and so great considerations, let us be united by an indissoluble bond, by virtue whereof I may cultivate and embrace you, although ye are several, no longer as several, but as one, and may call you my mind, my understanding, and my will.*o* I will also introduce 6 new intelligences and wisdoms into your palace, and thus by new associations will fill up the measure of your delights. When he had spoken these words, one of the chorus, who stood next to the sacred hearth, lifted up the insignia of the kingdom and the sceptre from the ivory seat, and with a graceful bow extended them to the youth; she also conducted him with her right hand to the throne,

---

o All these things, and those besides which follow in this chapter, are proper to the human race, for they become proper because they proceed from the rational mind, and its liberty of choosing goodnesses, consequently loves. This is not granted to brute animals, because they lack the understanding, by which they may take a view of what is good and what is best, as of the degrees and differences of natural, moral, and spiritual goodnesses.

while the others, taking in their hands his robe and purple, arrayed him in it; and thus they venerated him as their prince and king.

53. Our acute and discerning youth exulted with joy, not because he was adorned with a crown and sceptre, but because he was exalted to the first rank in the assembly of wisdoms and intelligences, and was by them venerated as king; wherefore he did not demand of them, but entreated them to continually assist him with their counsels; and first of all he invited them to the sport of his paradise, which he called the sport of wisdom, by kissing his hand and beckoning them. Surrounded, therefore, by their company, when he had descended by the steps from the court to the threshold, he walked into the midst of a grove under the covering of a shady tree, not far from his maternal tree, where was seen a circus, constructed in the form of an amphitheatre, with native porticos, the best contrived couches, and, as it were, benches. Here, having so arranged his damsels, as he called them, in a most beautiful order, according to the genius and talent of each, that he might view all at once and each successively from a kind of elevated seat, he thus again began to speak: *p* Behold, my companions! how many pleasing beauties smile around you, and around me who am yours, and how many sweet melodies resound from the tops of our trees; and how many delights and charms endeavor to captivate my senses by open allurements; but I wish you to be persuaded and to believe me, that these forms do not allure my senses, but my mind. I see also and read in your eyes, that the gladnesses exhaled from them do not remain fixed in your senses, but in your minds; for I do

---

p By his discoursing with his intelligences is to be understood that he discoursed with himself, or with his understanding, that is, that he thought; for thought is a certain kind of discourse with a man's self; for since the operations of our mind are real activities, or changes of state by variations of form, it follows that they also constitute a kind of interior speech; for our speech itself is in like manner affected by variations of the form of its larynx, glottis, palate, tongue, and mouth; and in place of the air, whence sound from the mouth is derived, in the mind is the most pure air, which is called ether, and which agrees in all its nature with air, but is more perfect; so that there is no other difference
2 between them than that of the perfection of the acting substances and principles. Unless

not fix my attention upon their delusory and fading beauties, but taking a deeper and more penetrating view, I behold only that which is stored up in the marrow of them, namely, what they have in them of good, and what of usefulness; I do not look at leaves, but at fruits and their seeds, nor do I relish shells, but kernels; for their goodness and usefulness delight me more than their most ornamental forms. For while I yield up myself no longer to the impressions of ocular vision, but examine those things by the rays of two lights, I am affected by a kind of inmost harmony, sparkling, as it were, from their very harmonies. I believe that you, my 3

---

this were the case, and the same also in respect to vision, it would be impossible for us to perceive what we think, still less to discourse with ourselves, and to utter the same and transcribe it into articulate sounds, or words, altogether according to the ideas of thought; from endeavor alone no action arises, as from rest no motion. Since, therefore, thought is real speech, but more perfect than our speech by the larynx, and involves in it more things both at once and successively, it follows that it is heard and understood by heavenly minds, which are called angels, as well, yea, infinitely more perfectly than oral speech is heard and understood by our companions and those we converse with. Let us not then, I pray, immerse our rational views in empty sophisms, or rather in mere shades, and play at chess in the city of literature, now exalted to its highest pinnacle, by asking whether our minds and souls are material, or whether they are extended so as to fill spaces, and whether their activities are to be measured by times or the velocities of times, and the like. For matter is only an expression whose attributes and predicates must be defined absolutely to every sense and apprehension, before it can be demonstrated according to what understanding those [mental] forms and their activities are to be perceived. It is sufficient that they are 3 substances, and actually exist and subsist, and that their activities are real activities, for they alone are, and act, in our body; therefore they are in space and in time, when in their body and in the world, for they belong to our body, not to the body of another, and they are in it and emit their views even into heaven, as the eye emits its sight into the world; but out of their body, after separation, as they betake themselves upwards or inwards within nature, so the idea of space and time perishes with them. But in order that their 4 state may be understood, the states of the active superior forms must first be understood, especially of the celestial and spiritual, which put off the properties and adjuncts of natural bodies, and put on, as was shown above, many more perpetuities and infinities. Let us, however, pass by those shady sophisms [which were referred to above], since they are not real, but purely verbal, flowing only from an ignorance of forms and of their elevation, for we are persuaded that those [higher substances and forms] exist and subsist, and at the same time live, more than any material substance, as will be shown below, and alone give us the faculty of perceiving, and of feeling and being affected according to perceptions, and thus of enjoying pleasantnesses which flow from the perception of goodness.

wisdoms, insinuate this into me, as a kind of inmost sense of sweetness, which gratifies my mind, and disperses itself thence through the animus and into the breast; and this with a variety altogether according to the nature and excellence of every goodness. This, from my inmost sense, flows into my understanding, and quickly pours itself forth into the will, illustrating the former as with the most gladsome illumination, and kindling the latter with a kind of fuel of love; and thus goodnesses, related to joy, are revealed to me by a kind of sense and consent.[q] From goodness afterwards, as from an inmost goal or centre, I contemplate all other things; for I see clearly, as through glasses, that everything has reference to goodnesses. My understanding calls them truths, and the things which again tend to these truths she calls sciences and experiences. But all these things I see clearly from goodness itself, for they are fitted to it as members to a kind of body; therefore, truths seem to me to be formed from a progressive series of goodnesses. The uses which tend to the fruition of goodnesses, are like souls, or ends in the soul, which from nature call forth stores to themselves, whereby

4

---

q That our first-born was able to know what is good, or goodnesses, from an internal sense, is sufficiently evident from the formation of his mind, and from causes which follow in their series; for the minds of those who live in the love of the Supreme not only see, but also feel, the affections of its goodnesses, and consequently have their understanding clearly enlightened by truths; wherefore from a sense of goodness the knowledge (*cognitio*) of all truths flows; for that we are bound to investigate truths by experience of the senses and by sciences, is merely to the intent that by them we may finally explore goodnesses, or good as to its quality, whether it be truly good, or apparently, or falsely good, or evil under the shape of good, what is better, and lastly, what is best, thus what we ought to choose. To this end we are gifted with understanding; but he who comprehends superior goodnesses by an inmost sense, has no need to run over that spacious plain of investigation, or to make his way through masses of truths, because he is in the knowledge of goodness itself, or, as it were, at the goal, from whence he can widely view and freely contemplate his whole field; so true it is, as was said, that all truths concentrate in goodness, consequently expand themselves, as it were, into circumferences from goodness, as from a centre. After the inversion of the human state, of which we shall speak below, by the fall, this sensation of goodnesses, such as it was in the firstborn, must of necessity have ceased; nevertheless a similar sense is connate with our external senses, yet not of moral and spiritual goodnesses, but only of certain natural ones; for the ear, howsoever untaught, apprehends,

2

3

they effigy to themselves a kind of body, by which they may prepare and expand themselves and their uses in order that there may be effects. For they are not in their uses until they are in effects; therefore when they are in these, they are in themselves as in their own forms; so that effects are only uses thus unfolded and brought forth into the gyre of nature. Wherefore these flowering ornaments are nothing but external representations of uses, which therefore charm by their harmonies the external senses of our body and their entrances, even for this use, that they may penetrate our minds by an easy passage. But while they penetrate my mind they appear to me as naked without clothing, thus most beautiful, because they sparkle from the effulgence of good and the brightness of truth. Hence I already observe that the discriminations of uses alone are 5 what sport together through so many varieties, and through so many genera and species, and that each of them performs its own gyre,

---

and is sensible of the numbers, harmonies, and melodies of musical sounds, inasmuch as the animus is instantly and agreeably affected; the eye, in like manner, of itself, apprehends and is sensible of the beauties of nature, together with the elegant and harmonious connections of different objects; the same is true of the tongue, in regard to the luxuries of food and nectar; and of the nostrils, in respect to fragrance; for this results from the soul, to which all sensation flows, because it flows forth into all things by its fibres, but not from any other principle, nor from the understanding, because we are affected in like manner before as after its perfection; for in the soul there is order itself, because it has excited and governs the nature of its body, wherefore it is sensible of what is agreeable to order, and in general points it out. But this, which is thus connate, is only an affection of natural good- 4 nesses, which are so gross that they fall into our external senses, wherefore they are called joys or sweetnesses. Moreover, animals themselves apprehend from the senses alone what is agreeable to the blood and life of their body; for they discover this agreement from the mere smell and taste; yea, also, they discern from the hearing and sight what other animals are their enemies or their friends; they are acquainted besides with infinite things which we are under the necessity of procuring to ourselves by sciences, as plainly appears from the government, the collecting of honey, and the honeycombs of bees; from the webs of spiders, the cones of silkworms, the nests of birds, the habitations of beavers, etc., all which things they do, because they refer their sensations, not to any mind inquisitive of truths before they investigate goodnesses, but immediately to their soul, which reflects it into the animus and thence into their natures, and in this way reveals to them natural goodnesses. What then must have been the case with the first-born, who was born into all perfections, not only natural, but also spiritual.

and has a kind of perpetuity; since they flow from a certain first principle, through mediums to the ultimate, and from this again to their first; for I have not as yet seen a single point of the series which is not from use, by use, and for use. From this single view, while I examine all things from single things and single things in all, I discover that no knowledge of anything escapes me, but that general things, with their particulars, from their very sanctuaries, flow in into my mind; hence particular representations are to me so many mirrors of things general, and single representations are

6 mirrors of things universal, and *vice versa*. But what has principally exalted the inmost sense of my delights, even almost above itself, is the consideration, that all the goodnesses and uses of the universe have reference to higher goodnesses and uses, and at length to the Supreme, in a certain order distinguished by degrees, from which they seem to me to be distant, according to the excellence of the series, in which they are by nature; for one thing is continually for the sake of another, and all things finally for the sake of One, or our GOD, the fountain of all goodnesses and uses. Behold, my wisdoms! that Divinity (*Divinum*) which I view in all things, and which flows in from single things, not into our eyes, but into our minds; for it is [the property] of an infinitely Wise [Being] alone to induce such an order into the things of the universe, and to construct, from mere uses, such continued chains, from things continuous in Himself, and out of Himself, and to draw them

7 together in their connection even to Himself. I seem therefore to myself, being introduced into these enjoyments of uses, and into these goodnesses, as if I alone celebrate His glory for them all, thus in their stead, because they are dumb and void of reason, and yet it seems as if they did so from themselves while I pour forth my vows and thanksgivings. As he spoke these words and folded his hands, looking around, he saw himself encompassed with a bright cloud, streaked with purple and flame-colored tints, like the Aurora; he was in the midst of a choir of heavenly beings, who guarded the tree near which they were seated, lest he should gather, any of its fruits;

hence observing that the apple was sacred, he called that tree the tree of the knowledge of good, being as yet ignorant what evil was.

54. Not far from the area of this circus there appeared an elevated seat, after the manner of a theatre, covered with a carpet of interwoven flowers and surrounded with curtains naturally produced; for the leaves of a strawberry-tree were so bound and inserted with vine leaves intermixed and with creeping ivy that by their circuits they designed such a space, and together represented birthday scenes. Hither he introduced his nymphs, not unwilling, as to their school, or sport of wisdom, which he instituted by questions and answers, as in the case of oracles unfolding destiny. To the conquerors he offered rewards, according to the worth of the reply, and the unfolding of what was more than ordinarily obscure; but he did not promise palms, laurels, or leaves, but entire kingdoms, and the provinces of nature, and moreover, purple and diadems, as insignia worthy of the honor. For he called the whole orb his empire, and he called kingdom that which his mother constructed and established for herself as a type of the grand kingdom, whose walls and gates only, having been delivered to him, and opening into his empire and her kingdom by two ways, he was to guard in such a manner, that what happened in his universe, he might learn from the guards there appointed, and might refer it to his court and to the councils of wisdoms. And when, on the conclu- 2 sion of the sport, he had seen all his wisdoms and intelligences in possession of authority, and, as it were, queens, still from their answers he could not yet learn whence goodnesses and utilities, not introduced by truths, inflowed into his Olympus, which he now called Helicon. This he perceived, that they insinuated themselves, not through the doors of the senses, but through a most secret way, from a certain sanctuary, through what was maternal; and that there was something which involved his Helicon in such appearances and forms as distinctly excited, by affecting from their inmosts, a sort of sense of senses, and by it ideas of goodness. I am not, said he, made sensible of this from myself, because I know it not

from means which are mine. And while he doubtfully fixed his mind (*animum*) on these things, and they so affected the hinges of his mind as almost to disturb the habitations of the nymphs who dwelt there, lo! he presently had a full view of his wisdoms in the very bosom of the Supreme Love, and of his intelligences in the consort of holy beings (*Divorum*) proximately encompassing that

3 Love, discoursing together in a friendly and familiar manner. On seeing them, as if awakening from a dream, he almost cried aloud to himself: Behold now what I ask and seek; this is that sanctuary from which the heats and lights of that exquisite sense flow, the rays of which, by their inmost sweets, reveal to me the natures of goodnesses and utilities. Hence being cheered with gladness, as with a most serene aura, he very quickly called his nymphs to him, and with a countenance bright as the day when every cloud is dispersed, he thus accosted them: Why have ye concealed from me, and from my inquiries, the origin of the influx of the most pleasant streams of goodnesses into my Helicon? Did I not say, that ye are the beings who insinuate them into me? Ye have delighted me with your delicious sportive deceits, for it is my wish to be thus imposed upon with more of the same kind, since in this manner ye convert my sport into a true sport of wisdom; for I have seen you with my eyes wide open, in the bosom of Love Itself, and I have seen you in the company of that Love's holy beings; hence ye derive those very goodnesses which ye inspire and infuse into me; for streams flow only from their fountain, and goodnesses flow only from the Best of the good; hence I derive the sensation of all things, and the knowledge (*cognitio*) of all things; I call you to witness, my graces, that hitherto I have cherished you, but now I dearly love you; for while I embrace you with love, and ye embrace the Supreme, I also embrace the Supreme by you; deign also to favor me with your love, for while He embraces you, and ye embrace me as yours, He also embraces me with His Love: let us therefore be again united, and let us strive unswervingly that our former bonds may be altogether inseparable.

55. Having uttered these words both with his mouth and from his bosom, he burned with a vehement desire to know what his native nymphs had heard from the holy intelligences; and when they looked on each other in profound silence, in consequence of increased ardor, and at the same time a stronger love now inspired by his wisdoms, he felt himself, as it were, carried out of himself; but when he endeavored to compose himself, lo! he saw himself in the midst of the bosom of Love, and at the same time in the midst of a choir of holy beings; and when he first strove in vain to prostrate himself on the ground, he heard these words spoken within himself: My son, I love both thy wisdoms and thee; between love and love there is not a closer nor a sweeter bond than wisdom. My ears have told me, for I hear whatsoever thou speakest, how 2 vehemently thou desirest to know whence are the goodnesses of which thou art sensible, whence they flow into the sphere of thy mind. This I will teach thee from my own bosom. Dost thou not know that all the happiness of life flows from love, and that that only is sweet which is loved? What is pleasant grows and rises into what is gratifying, and what is gratifying into what is happy, according to the degree and essence of love. My son, there is only one Love; from this one Love, the First and Supreme of all, thou hadst thy birth and existence, and hence came all the happinesses which are perceptible to the senses. I have just now felt, from the 3 embrace of essential Love Itself, what happiness is, and whence goodness is derived. Do not any longer inquire after the fountain, now that thou sittest at its very heart. Perceive now that the love, with which thou embracest me, is from mine; I make thee feel it in thyself, and make thee perceive that it is from mine, and thus mine from thine; consequently I enable thee at the same time to see both my parent and thine; by me thou art his resemblance and image; and because we are thus both of us from the same parent, thou shalt not be my son, but brother. Fill now and feed thy mind with goodnesses, which flow from that source; but take heed, my little brother, lest thou draw anything from the fountain of the love

of thyself; for from my goodnesses, which are given to thee, new ones are continually born, since whatever thou possessest from me is fruitful and prolific, and like seed, which, when it has performed its gyre in nature, again produces not seed, but seeds. It is necessary that these involve what is mine, for that which is best is stored up in things inmost.[r] Those seeds are goodnesses sown in thy mind, and I entreat thee to gather them from mine, not from thine resown, unless thine shall have been introduced by me to mine, otherwise they will not lead thee to me, but to thyself, as to their only love. I will grant, indeed, that thou mayest discern my goodnesses from thy own, but not that thou mayest feel them; but from mine thou mayest both feel and perceive both thine and mine. I will cause thee also to distinguish them, for I will fill mine not only with delights, but also with happinesses. And that thou mayest remember these things, I have set a tree in the midst of thy paradise, not far from thy maternal tree, which stands in the inmost and veriest centre of the grove, which also I have given to be guarded by my intelligences; while thou lookest upon this tree, let my sayings be

4

5

---

r All formations, as was observed above, agree in things most general, and especially in this, that inmost or purest principles, which are essences themselves, or essentials, when they have unfolded themselves into suitable forms, even to ultimates, by wonderful insertions betake themselves to inmost things; as seeds, when they have put themselves forth into leafy trees, afterwards concentrate the purest essences of their juices again in new seeds. In what manner they betake themselves towards inmost principles is presented to view in the fruits themselves; for in the inmost parts of the fruits they form to themselves repositories, and encompass these and themselves in foldings and membranes; in these lie concealed the veriest seminal powers themselves, which do not burst forth until the foldings are laid open. The case is similar in the animal body, in which the first and purest fibres, which are the essential determinations themselves, or from which the organic forms are designed, when they have performed their common gyre, even to ultimates, or to the blood-vessels themselves, return again by them to their beginnings the cortical glands, and by wonderful insertions involve themselves in those their beginnings and unite with them, where they are adopted, and, as it were, introduced, by the purest fibres; for compound things cannot inflow into simple things, but simple things inflow into their compounds, such, and no other, being the order which prevails in universal nature, because no other is possible. In like manner, the viscera, members, muscles, nerves, etc., of our body, together with their smallest parts, or units, encompass themselves, as they multiply, with coats or coverings

2

3

4

recollected; its fruits have reference to goodnesses; its first root was indeed from a seed out of heaven, but now it is from its own and proper root; it now also performs its ultimate gyre, whence are its fruits; do not feed on them, but enjoy the rich feast and food let down to thee from me. That thou mayest know the difference 6 between them, behold! I will open heaven to thee, and I will fold the rays of thy vision in mine. Instantly, having opened his eyes, Behold, said she, my paradise! Stretch out thy sight far and wide, and tell me whether thou seest here any limits and boundaries, as in thine; whether any rising and setting. All is perpetual in its rising, its light, and its life. What is in my paradise also appears in thine;[s] but only as a shade, and that opaque, and in every point of it a boundary and end. Look now at the fountains of the goodnesses

---

more and more general in their order, to which, from the single parts, ligaments or bands are emitted, which insert and tie themselves to coverings, and at length to the most general coverings, as their band; for things general arise from their parts, but not parts from their generals. This is the case with all other things of which form or substance can be 5 predicated. The formation of our minds is similar, but instead of seeds there are goodnesses which insinuate themselves through the doors of the senses; from these, variously connected, arise series of goodnesses, which are called truths, and are, as it were, germinations from their roots; from truths thus hatched, are again conceived and born new goodnesses, which in like manner disseminate themselves altogether like a tree or body; therefore, such as is the quality of the goodnesses, such is the quality of the truths produced from them, and such the quality of the goodnesses again conceived from these truths; for all truths regard goodnesses as their first and last objects; therefore, in order that truths may flower, all things seem to sport in their infancy. The goodnesses, which are hatched by our truths, derive their nature from the objects of the world, wherefore what is above nature cannot be at all perceived or felt; for this betakes itself to inmost principles, as in seeds, nor is it thence unfolded, unless these coverings are first broken in pieces and reduced to nothing, in which case the inmost principle first bursts forth and produces a new germ. But in all the first-born [men] everything was born in an order the inverse of this our natural order. All other things may be concluded from comparison with what has been said above.

s It is said that the heavenly paradise is opened, and that whatsoever is in it is shadowed in the earthly one; consequently that one is represented in the other, as will be seen confirmed more clearly in what follows; for such is the established correspondence, that we are introduced by natural and moral truths, by only transposing the expressions that signify natural things, into spiritual truths, and *vice versa,* and thus, as it were, from one paradise into another. By way of illustration, let one or two examples suffice; as first: *Light* 2

of which thou art sensible; but look at that Only One from which they all flow; from thine thou mayest enter into mine, wherefore I will now dismiss thee. When these words were ended, a kind of very thin veil being drawn over the sight of the first-born, he felt himself brought back into the place of his school; but his sight was dizzy, as when we pass from a most serene light into one which is uncertain and shady.

56. After some time, when he again beheld his grove, continuing, as it were, in suspense, he began to revolve in his mind what all this meant, that he should seem thus to be carried out of himself; Is not this, said he, the very place where I lately was? Are not these the same flowers, the same fruits, the same clusters, which I just now saw? I have not been removed from the place; but where have I been? And where now is that Love in whose bosom I was held? Where is that Heaven which was opened to me in so great a light? Am I fallen down or am I deluded? And when he was most intent on these inquiries, so that the intention itself made his bosom beat, he said: Tell me, my wisdoms! I entreat you by God, where I have been; rescue me from this darkness; his prayers also were accompanied by tears. Then said one of his wisdoms: Believe not, my lord, that thou hast been carried on high from this place, and art thence fallen down again; here we are, and here we have been; but thou art not

---

reveals the quality of its object, but the quality of the object appears according to the state of the light, wherefore the object is not always such as it appears; as in the case of beautiful things, if they be objects viewed in varied light. Now if instead of light we take intelligence, the quality of whose object is the truth of a thing; since intelligence is admitted by all to be spiritual light, this conclusion follows: *Intelligence discovers the truth of a thing, but the truth of a thing appears according to the state of the intelligence; wherefore that is not always true which is supposed to be true.* In like manner, if instead of intelligence wisdom be called into correspondence, the object of which is good, [it then follows:] *Wisdom manifests goodness, but the goodness of a thing appears according to the state of the wisdom; wherefore that is not always good which is believed to be good.* To take yet another example, for correspondences of this sort, as of all things, are infinite: *Harmony flowing from the union of natural entities is not given without a principle of harmony from a superior union in nature, which conjoins single things universally, and the universe singly.* If instead of harmony we say concord, and instead of union, love, and instead of natural entities, human minds, then this

The Worship and Love of God

with us alone: thou remainest yet in His bosom where He holds thee inmostly, as I see with mine eyes, and as thou also feelest; it is only the shade of thy sight which obstructs thy view. If that veil, which I see in thee to be a very thin one, be a little withdrawn, He will again appear; for He is in our inmost principles, and also in the highest, Himself and His heaven being in the former and the latter. All inmost principles are full of His rays, and where His rays are, there is His sight from the highest, or His throne, consequently His presence, for rays continue objects to the sight. The sight of thine 3 eye was willing to confirm what I said, that there were ladders and steps, as it were, by which He might descend from His Highests to our inmosts; but I smiled at its ludicrous hallucinations, and often said to it: Thou art deceived, but suffer thyself to be taught by thy mind, that descent is not from highests to inmosts, but from highests to lower things, and from inmosts to exteriors, where thou residest; be not so uncertain and dull in giving credit to what I say, for we see more than thou because we are actually there. Our soul, which is in the inmosts of thy body, from its supreme principles both sees and feels also the most minute things which are being done in its kingdom;[t] but when it descends to thee, or to its sight,

---

truth results: *There is no concord flowing from the love of human minds without a principle of concord in superior love, which may consociate single minds universally, and their universal society singly.* Or, if instead of harmony, we adopt the terms satisfaction or happiness; and instead of union, the term love, as before, but speak of souls instead of minds, then the following canon results: *There is no happiness flowing from the mutual love of souls, without a beginning of love in heaven, or in God Himself, who unites single souls universally, and the universal society of souls singly.* But if instead of this love we take another, it will instantly 4 appear what kind of union thence results, for as the quality of the love is, such is the union. From these and an infinity of similar cases, we see how there may be a transition from an earthly paradise into a heavenly one, and how from the one we may be instructed concerning the goodnesses and truths of the other; but from propositions not true result falsities, and thus we are not introduced into paradises. These things, however, will become still more evident from the series of the things which follow.

   [t] It is clear from all the phenomena of our bodies, that the soul has so organically formed its body as to be conscious of whatsoever happens in its extreme parts, in the outer-most or hollow parts of the viscera, and in their windings and pores, so that from the first

THE INFANCY OF THE FIRST-BORN, OR ADAM   85

that thou also mayest see, it descends as by ladders and steps; what then must be the case with Him who is in its inmost principles? But He is also in outmost principles; nevertheless, unless our mind, like a door, is opened inward, He does not appear; for nature is opaque nor is He transparent by His own light itself, unless the 4 hinge be turned. This now is the reason why, when thou retiredst interiorly within thyself, thou wast led to suppose thyself to be rapt above or out of thyself. But heaven, which is also called the kingdom of God, is interiorly within us. Our minds are such as to be capable of turning two ways, as upon hinges, namely, inwards and outwards, or upwards and downwards; for there are, as it 5 were, two ways of entrance, or places of reception. Into our minds also two lights flow in, one which is called spiritual, from the Supreme and His Love; the other natural, from the sun of our world and its heat. These lights meet together in our minds, and from their meeting together they become as centres of the whole universe, namely, of heaven and of the world; hence from them, as from centres, it is allowable to wander forth with new vision into all the circumferences of the universe, and to examine each paradise, as

---

moment of its life it keeps all and single things under its auspices, and arranges them according to circumstances. That the sense of all things inflows to the soul, is evident from the harmonies of modes, of which our mind is made sensible alike before and after the perfection of its understanding, as was observed above; and from the changes of state of all the viscera altogether according to every turn of circumstances, which is rendered manifest in the stomach, the intestines, the liver, the kidneys, and the rest of the viscera; moreover, also, from her fibres, which design the whole organic texture; they are her rays; wherefore, wheresoever they are, she herself also is present, or she sees and feels from her supreme principle: for in those principles she resides in her most simple form, that from them, as centres, she may behold and govern her whole kingdom and its continuous cir-
2 cumferences. That every fibre, or ray, is an actual substance, formed after the image of its principle from which it flows, will be clearly demonstrated below. When therefore the soul is made sensible of anything from her most simple fibres, she is then made sensible from inmost principles; but when she is made sensible from forms produced out of herself, or her fibre, she is then made sensible, not from inmost principles, but from those forms which are out of or beneath herself. For all compound forms are substances by themselves, and have their proper predicates, the inmost principles of which are nevertheless occupied by the soul; in this manner she is said to go forth to her sight, or to descend.

The Worship and Love of God

it were, with two sets of eyes. In this way the Love of the Supreme has introduced thee to Himself. He only lifted up the little shade, and filled thee with His own Love, in consequence of which thou sawest thyself in inmost principles. But understand also the reason 6 of this, namely, that thus he might accomplish the grand gyre of creation, and might draw together to Himself the gyres of universal nature, so as to be the Last of them all, as He is the First; for by our minds universal nature is introduced to her Supreme; wherefore thou art, or thy mind is, the bond and medium of union, by love, of all things which have been created; thus now heavenly things are joined with earthly, and earthly with heavenly. Thou askedst also 7 just now, what was the subject of the discourse between us and the holy intelligences. I will now tell thee; they were ordered, that as often as they descended into thy paradise, they should first always enter thy two-doored Helicon, as a temple or sacred edifice, and not visit the earth until they had saluted us; and when they return, that they should introduce thy intelligences to us. They call us their daughters, their images, but now their sisters: we will unbar the gate. But behold! they approach even now. Before, however, he could lift himself up to meet them, they were at hand. Thus was closed this scene, which was the fourth in order.

Section Third
Concerning the Love
of the First-Born

57. WHILE our first-born was about to raise himself from his couch, he was drawn back by a kind of spontaneous force; nor could he yet see those holy strangers who had been announced, for his sight still wandered in ambiguous light and shade. But presently, having, as it were, wiped his eyes, he beheld himself surrounded by innumerable infant girls, beginning a kind of sport by winding dances. They had all of them beautiful countenances, and were like the images of laughter seen in paintings. Their hair was fastened in knots with golden ornaments; their foreheads were ornamented with bright gems; otherwise they were clad, not in a transient, but in a native garb, for they were naked. They were indeed divided into groups like winding garlands, the borders of which touched each other, thus they really were conjoined and not divided. Their sport was directed into perpetual orbits, by which, like Euripuses,* they inflowed to their goals. The form itself determined the goal, 2 which sometimes was interior, concentrating itself, as it were, but sometimes more elevated, being prominent, like the figure of an obelisk or pillar; into these goals they wound themselves by circuits and spirals, as it were, both inwards and upwards, always with a

---

* Euripus was a narrow sea between Bœotia and Eubœa, which ebbed and flowed seven times in twenty-four hours. (TR.)

forward glide; and thus again and again, until at length they entered by orderly influx to the very couch itself, where the first-born was sitting; and what was wonderful to see, they then suddenly became effulgent like lights or little constellations, the rays of which, shooting forth from each as centres towards the circumferences, formed a kind of luminous and glittering circuit, like a girdle, around this globe or spiral ring; and then they all embraced each other at the same moment. Sometimes also they seemed to separate from their numbers some of their company, and when our youth was indignant at this, and wished to restore them again to their harmony, they flowed back into order of themselves, without his direction; and that he might not indulge too eagerly in these sights, lo! instantly all was at an end; and when in vain he would recall them to sight, and became anxious, he questioned his wisdoms, when he had called them to him, with a quick and tremulous voice, whether they had beheld these infantile sports, entreating them to explain to him, whether anything lay more deeply concealed under this pleasing exhibition than what immediately struck the sight. To this the first of the wisdoms, with a smile, thus replied: Those were the heavenly wisdoms and intelligences whose coming we announced, under the appearance of infants; for they put on whatsoever forms they please, and initiate all actions, representing thereby whatever we express by the words of discourse; for the discourses of holy beings (*Divorum*) are merely representations, as are also the discourses of our minds; thus they interweave all things (*singula*) with delights, and with life, and make them adhere permanently and clearly to our minds;*u*

---

u The discourses of all heavenly intelligences are mere representations by means of images which actually exist before them, and are so contrived that hence every truth may plainly and clearly shine forth before our pure eyes; he who understands those representations understands also the discourse of heavenly beings, or heavenly discourse. Similar also are the representations of our minds by means of their ideas; for that it is not by word and their ambiguities that we think, or conceive and bring forth the principles of things, is sufficiently evident from a slight reflection on the purer modes of the operation of our minds; for we can conceive, think, conclude, in a moment of time, more things than it is

The Worship and Love of God

nor do they give forth the least sign, or stir a step, in which there is not concealed something sublime and mysterious. We have beheld this, not with our eyes, but with our minds; wherefore to remove all anxious doubt from thy mind, I will explain to thee the above sport. Every one of us, as thou sawest, with a glad and handsome face, under the appearance of a love, represented some goodness; for there are as many goodnesses, because sweetnesses, as we have loves. The gold which thou sawest fastened our hair into a knot, is a badge of goodness and innocence, wherefore the first of ages, or our infancy, is called golden. The sport itself of the loves or good- 4 nesses had reference to the truths, which are born from a series of progressive goodnesses; the gems, with which the foreheads were adorned, are also badges of truth. The garlands which they mutually laid hold of, and by which they were, as it were, chained together, were the bands which bind together, and thus connect the forms of truths. The pleasantnesses flowing from the sport itself, or from the harmony of form, are happinesses or felicities, consequently new goodnesses, which thence finally arise. The windings to a kind of goal, inwards towards a centre, or upwards towards a summit, was the unanimous agreement of all truths directed towards one good, or to the Best of goods; and the reason why they were suddenly resplendent when they approached to thy couch, was from the Love Itself of the Supreme, or the Best, in whose bosom we saw thee sitting. The rays flowing forth from each into the circuit, are the 5 common bond which connects each universally, and the universal

---

possible to utter and express by words of speech, or by writing, in the space of a whole day. Words are only of aid when we are disposed to utter, by speech, the things which 2 have thus been born; the veriest life of our intelligence is in representations of this sort, wherefore in these things our minds are like the minds of heavenly beings. But the reason why we cannot so distinctly perceive these things in ourselves, is, because we draw upon our imagination more frequently and with more preference than we do upon our thought, for expressions are represented in the imagination under the appearance of ideas, and *vice versa*. Nor could our first-born enjoy any other discourse, since he was yet alone, nor had he any one to converse with; consequently as yet he had a pure mind like that of heavenly beings, but clothed with a heavy body, that he might be an inhabitant of the earth.

chorus singly; for such is the determination and connection of every form which is in nature;^x wherefore also they embraced each other at the same moment. But the reason why some of their company were separated from the rest, and returned again of themselves into harmony, while thou wast indignant, and wast endeavoring to recall them to harmony, was, that thou thyself mightest discern clearly that nothing flows from thee, but that all things flow together from the Supreme and His Love, into their order and union. He excited a certain kind of indignation or grief, to the intent that thou mightest learn, that nothing is thine which thou supposest to be thine, for we are powers, or organs, and instruments of life, and thus mediations, by which the last goes and returns to the first and the first to the last; consequently, that all things which are created flow to him through thee, and thus subsist perpetually as they were made; for subsistence is perpetual existence, and conservation is perpetual creation; this was the very end of that sport.

58. While he, as it were, immersed his eager mind in these sayings, being struck with the last remark, that nothing was his own which he supposed to be his own, he began to consider with himself, and to ask: Was this merely said in sport? Is it not my own, that I perceive, that I feel, that I distinguish goodnesses, that I prefer one to another? Do not I belong to myself when yet I seem to belong to myself? If these things are not mine, they are all vain names, and like flying feathers, nor would there be any difference between my
2 life and a shadow, or nothing. While he thus became inflated with

---

x All forms, whatsoever be their nature, agree in this, that from their single essences or essentials, which determine the form, bonds flow to the circumference or circuit, and there constitute a kind of common bond; therefore the part which is not connected by that bond, is no longer a part of that form or body, but is rejected as spurious; that this is the case is clear in our own body, and in its single members, or organic forms; in like manner in the forms of truth and good; and also in every society, particular and general, which relates to a similar form; but instead of a common bond we must substitute those things which correspond. Thus from natural forms we may be perfectly instructed concerning all things in all other forms.

The Worship and Love of God

his thoughts, he moved himself nearer to his wisdom, and taking
her by the hand, he said: What is this that thou hast told me, that
nothing is my own which I suppose to be my own, and that I am
only a power? Are you disposed thus to entertain me with a jest?
Do not I speak with thee from myself? And when he began to
grow warm, the wisdom, to calm his increasing ardor, begged his
pardon, and said; I would not dare to jest with thee, my lord; but
again I repeat that nothing is thine own which thou supposest to
be thine own. Thou art only a power, which from itself, or from its
own, never performs any action. But thou art a power more noble
than all created powers. Thou art a kind of jewel, yea, thou art the
delight of heaven itself; thou bearest its treasures, and leadest its
triumphs. But, my lord, do not press my hand so much, for pos- 3
sibly, when thou hast heard all, thou wilt [feel inclined to] release
it. Dost thou not know, that no force excites powers, except that
which inflows extrinsically? Both heaven and earth inflow into thee
with their precious things and goods, but they are outside of
thee; thou receivest those things, and actest as from borrowed forces.
Does thine ear hear anything, unless the modulated air brings in
sounds? Hence is the force which causes hearing. Dost thou taste
anything, unless food be brought to thy tongue? Hast thou any
smell, unless the volatile particles floating in the air touch the fibres
of that organ? Are the organs of thy body, or the viscera, enabled to
perform their functions unless the influent air alternately expands
thy lungs? All those things are only organs and instruments, or are
powers which have no activity without a force acting upon them
extrinsically.*y* Consider only the eye, how it sees nothing unless 4

---

y If we examine the organs and viscera of our bodies, the greater and the lesser, or as
many as can be viewed and discovered by the eye or the microscope, it will appear, that
no one of them can act or operate, unless something from without inflows, which gives
it the power of acting; for whatever inflows, from the motion of its influx, leads in and
imparts that active force. The heart cannot be excited to its systoles and diastoles, except
by the blood of the vena cava, which is poured into its right auricle, and by the pulmonary
blood, which is poured into the left auricle; the liver is not excited to its operations, except

it be illuminated; close it with its lids and thou wilt perceive that the light itself is that active force which enables thee to discern its discriminations, or images and objects. But this latter light is of the sun, whereas the other light, which has life in it, is that from which thou hast intelligence and thy very mind, some parts of whose function thou believest belong to thee. Do not however suppose that this light is in thee as thine own, and that it is not conveyed into thine understanding as the other light is conveyed into thine eyes. Whence are the goodnesses which thou feelest and discernest? Are they from thyself or from heaven? That light is not thine, neither are the other things thine, which are thence formed, as from their beginnings, for one thing is derived by a continuous series from another; He who gives and rules the one, gives and rules the other, for He causes thee to feel that which is brought from heaven. I will give thee a demonstration of this; I will intercept that light which inflows through thy mother, or our soul, and thou wilt perceive whence thy understanding and will

5 are. And presently she seemed, as it were, to retire, whereupon, his

---

2 by the blood, which is first infused into the portal vein. Nor is the stomach excited to its modes of digestion and trituration, except by aliments with which it is loaded through the gullet; also by the spirit, which is infused continually from the cerebellum into its fibres. Our muscles themselves derive motion from a similar spirit infused into the motor fibres, thus not from themselves, but from a force applied extrinsically; it is said extrinsically, whether it inflows from what is superior, or from what is inferior, also from what is interior, thus it is not self-inherent; but when this force is joined or adapted to a power, and the latter is thus acted upon, then it appears as if the power alone acted from itself, for the active force, as a principal cause, being joined to the passive force as an instrumental cause, they both constitute one efficient cause, because they act together; nevertheless that they are separate, and capable of being separated, appears from all that

3 has been said. Wherefore all our viscera and organs in themselves are denuded powers, that is, *have the power of acting, but not from themselves,* for they must either admit, or invite, their force from outside of themselves; and if they invite, there is another force outside of that, which gives them the ability to invite, as the action of the lungs or respiration, or other similar cases; for one thing hangs from another, as a chain from its links, and all things from their first principle; nor is anything else moved by itself, not even fire, as will be demonstrated below. But that all powers may be excited suitably to their forms, as many active forces are created as may correspond to these powers, which are passive.

The Worship and Love of God

whole mind being overshadowed, he wished to cry out: Whither art thou gone, my wisdom? But his voice was stifled in his lips, and he would have fallen down in astonishment, as in a swoon, unless suddenly she had appeared again. Perceive now, said she, what is thine own, and how far thou differest from the nature of a stock; but I did not remove myself; I only prayed that our mother, from the necessity of changing the state, which is an effect of that light, might withdraw some of it; hence came the darkness which blinded thy mind. Hast thou not heard her saying to us that thou livest under her auspices, and that that light which inflows into thee, is from her, because through her? There is only One who lives, and inasmuch as we live from Him, we also act from the Same; and if we live and act from Him we are in Him.

59. On hearing these words, being somewhat tranquilized, with his finger on his knitted brow he considered with himself, and, as it were, looked into himself, for in order to give greater liberty to his mind he removed the light from his eyes. When he had collected his reasons, having let the light into his eye once more and relaxed his brow, he addressed his wisdom cheerfully and courteously: I discover, said he, that I have rashly claimed both kinds of sight to myself as my own, for it must of necessity be that I live and subsist from the Being (*Esse*) of Him, from whom I am and have existed, otherwise connection would be broken, and communication intercepted; nevertheless I seem to myself to be able to will all that which involves any act in mind and body; has He not attributed that to me as my own, which by His force is communicated to my power? This appears to be acquired, inasmuch as it recurs as often as I am pleased to excite it. Still, I perceive that the thread is not yet quite unravelled; give me quickly, I pray, the clue to it, as thou hast begun. Then his wisdom, fixing by her 2 gaze his sight upon herself, said: Thou seemest to be able to reflect on what is communicated to thee, and to recall it, but it does not thence follow that it is thine; dost thou not intend and perform every action from some end? Does not that end rule the cause, and

the cause the effect? Our ends in all cases are loves, or the goods which we love; our sportive infants therefore represented goodnesses under the appearance of loves. Didst thou not observe lately a ring-dove on the tops of our trees, and how violently he beat the air with his wings? He beheld his consort dove, and the nest which contained her young. This was the cause of his so rapid flight. It seemed also to him that he himself vibrated his wings, and chose the shortest way home; but in reality his loves, his fledged young, and his mistress, excited his mind, and his mind moved his wings. That, therefore, which rules the cause, this also rules the effect, for

3 the cause of the cause itself is also the cause of the effect. The case is similar in ourselves; our loves, whatever their number, hold the reins and excite and govern our minds; by them we are drawn, and them we follow; and inasmuch as we follow we seem to act, because we vibrate the wings of our mind accordingly, and exercise the winged sandals of our body. We also run the shortest way, nor do we turn aside unless something opposes, in consequence of which opposition the shortest way is sometimes turned into a circuitous way. Nothing but love excites that which is communicated to our minds. If another love also inflows, we are balanced between the two, and because our reflection is directed to that, which in such case determines our compliance with one or the other, we suppose

4 the decision to be our own. Love is, as it were, the charioteer, who holds the reins and governs us as horsemen do horses, and darkens our minds, and persuades us that we sit as princes or leaders in the chariot; or if love, like a girded attendant, runs before, he hurries us along with him by reins, like biped steeds. These reins are our desires, which are nothing but love continued, for, like bands, they conjoin us to it continuously. But love not only draws us, it also impels; for in universal nature, wheresoever there is attraction there is also impulsion, whence come all equilibriums.[z] Fear is behind,

---

z That equilibriums result from action and reaction, and that impulsion is everywhere where there is attraction, is very manifest from the phenomena of the nature of the

which is urgent to prevent our falling away from love's aspect and favor; for in proportion to the happiness and goodness which we experience in love is the unhappiness and misfortune which we feel in its privation, and which we fear according to the essence and degree of love. Hence we are bound and chained before and behind in the middle, and only act as we are acted upon. Tell me now, what is yours, or what will is yours?

60. On hearing what she had said, *when we are balanced between two loves,* he could hardly contain his spirit to the end of her discourse, being deeply agitated and therefore anxious to inquire what those two loves were; and scarcely had she finished speaking when he interrupted her, and with great eagerness asked her to tell him what that other love was. I am acquainted, said he, with one Only Love, to which all the rest, which are called goodnesses, lead up. I never remain suspended between two, nor between one goodness and another, for one instantly appears to me more beautiful and delicious, in proportion as it is nearer to our Only One. To this the wisdom, drawing a deep breath of gladness from her breast, replied: How I wish, said she, that thou mightest never understand more than the Only Love, and that the other had been forever banished to the remotest distance from our Helicon! In this case we would continue ever to return to thee an exchange of the love with which

---

universe, and also from the phenomena of animal nature; for whatsoever we attract or suck in with the mouth, the palate, the tongue, and the jaws, this, in like manner, is impelled by the activity of the organs. The air, which is drawn in by the nostrils and the lungs, is also forced in by its own column, and the pressure thence arising. The chyle is enticed into its veins and into the lacteal vessels by a kind of suction, but the active forces corresponding to it are also continually pressing upon it. The blood is invited into all the 2 viscera from its great trunks and branches, according to every necessity and use, but there is in the very vessels and arteries a propulsive force, or a force incitative of the same thing, which is infused into their fibres. So in all other cases, not only in quantities, but also in every quality, which results from the disposition and composition of quantities. From this it follows, that they are mere equilibriums, the various changes of which produce various effects and uses. For unless there were two forces, active and passive, and these were joined to each other, nothing would ever be balanced, still less would any effect result from cooperation, by the change and renewal of the equilibrium.

thou lately didst ask us, with so much sweetness, to favor thee; but allow me first to describe what is the quality of our Love; for nothing which lies concealed in shadow can be made to appear, unless it be shown in the daytime or in the light; afterwards, if you please, I will proceed to speak of what is our own, what is freedom, and what is freewill (*Arbitrium*).

61. Emerging, as it were, out of a mist, into a clear atmosphere, Describe, says he, and if you are able, depict this Love before mine eyes. I wish that that very thin veil, which you said obstructed my sight, were rent asunder; hence, I am a little angry with myself, and am envious towards you, because you see that Love clearly without me; how does your mind see more deeply than mine? Blandly regarding him, his wisdom thus replied: We wisdoms, as to our minds, are near thy mother or soul, but as to our bodies, we are in thy Helicon, or near thee; she is not with thee in an earthly paradise, but with the holy intelligences in a heavenly one; hence she draws the knowledges of goodnesses which she reflects 2 into thy mind through us and the forces of our body.[a] As often

---

a It is said that the very minds of wisdoms are in a sanctuary near the soul; and that their bodies are in sacristies, or in the mind, which is called rational or intellectual; but to explain this more clearly, it is to be known that the operations, or if you prefer, the activities of our rational mind, are only the general activities of our soul in its beginnings, which also are the beginnings of the fibres, or where the supreme sphere of our body is, and, as it were, the Olympus or heaven of other spheres. For it is known that all forms are essential determinations, or that they are determined by those things which are called essences or the essentials of form; these essentials not only design and produce the form, but also enable it to enjoy its proper natures and forces, and to act from them, into which those essentials or essences inflow, as principles or reasons into their causes. The activities, therefore, of the form thus compounded or determined, are called the activities or general operations of a prior principle, and thus may be likened to the forces of any body, which flow, as in us, from the determinations of its own mind or soul. Such also are our minds with respect to the soul; whence it may be concluded what is the quality of the natural 2 influx of the one into the other. But it is important that this also should be explained. Those very essentials, which are determinant, always weave the form, which they construct for the reception of activities or forces similar to their own, or if you choose, of similar modes, and thus, as parents, they adapt them for becoming powers of receiving forces similar to their own, consequently their general forces; for no form conceives and produces another, except according to the type of its own nature. But whereas all

as anything inflows through the doors of thy senses, she tells thee
what she sees and perceives in heaven conformable to it; then, as
like excites like, the idea excites its type, and afterwards the type its
idea; one thing flows into another in order, and arranges itself, and
elevates itself by degrees to those things which correspond; hence
it comes to pass, that, as thou saidst, thou discernest not beauties
with thine eyes, but their goodnesses and utilities with thy mind;
they are actually represented to thy soul, partly also immediately to
thy mind; for no other things than those which actually are, can be
sensated; from that which has no being (*Esse*) nothing can ever exist,
and from nothing not anything can come, still less be perceived by
the senses; and do not believe that the lights alone which inflow
produce this effect, for by their virtue thou only beholdest what is
presented (*objicitur*) to the two kinds of sight; for by the benefit of
light thou seest the forms themselves which exist, whence comes
sensation and at length the knowledges of goodnesses. Didst thou 3
not hear Love Himself telling thee, that in thy Paradise there are
the same things as in His, although not in life and in light, but
in shade; and that thou art able to enter His paradise from thine
own; wherefore also he has sent thee back to thine own paradise.
Therefore, if thou wishest, thou mayest not only contemplate His
paradise, but also Himself. On hearing these words, exulting with
joy, and, as it were, forgetting himself on account of love, he said:
Grant, O my wisdom, that my mind may be thine, and that thus I

---

active forces, which initiated that power into its acts, inflow from without; and whereas
those forces inflow either by a prior or superior way, that is, by the way of the soul, or by
a posterior or inferior way, that is, by the way of the senses, in all the first-born [men],
consequently in Adam, they entered by the way of the soul, or by the superior way, in
their order; whereas in us, his posterity, they enter by the way of the senses, or the inferior
way. Hence is the reason of the difference [between the first-born men and ourselves],
that we do not know and discern goodnesses from our earliest age, or, as it is commonly
expressed, that our ideas are not connate. Still by the prior way, or that of the soul, those
active forces inflow into almost all brute animals; but they are only the forces of superior
nature; wherefore the brute animals, from their very birth, know whatever may be agreeable to their nature; and they are born into all the sciences profitable to their love, which
is not the case with us men; these things will be further treated in the following pages.

may enjoy the pleasure of contemplating Love Himself. Continuing, the wisdom replied: Thou shalt contemplate both Love Himsel and heaven, for there is nothing in the universe which does not represent them; I will proceed to unfold this truth, but do not interrupt me again.

62. If we unfold, as from swathings, thine infant paradise, we shall behold, said she, as in a mirror, another paradise, from which it derives its birth, or which it overshadows. Thou art not ignorant that the visible things of the world, and that highly cultivated nature, which by its sports fascinates our senses, derived its first birth, and all its other births in continuation, and perpetually derives them, from that great sun which we view with our eyes; for we subsist from that from which we existed, and we are renewed by that which first made us new. That this is the case, is evident from his own light; for if he were again to hide his countenance in a crust or covering, or to dissipate his fires into the universe, or otherwise to extinguish his torches, would it not be all over with this world and the productions of nature? Would not this paradise be dissolved? Would not thy body also, which thou carriest about with thee, fall apart, but not dispersed into the auras (*auras*), because there would be no air (*Aer*) to receive the powder and dust? The earth also and its orbit would know neither centre nor circumference. These tokens of the fate of the earth call to our minds its seasons of night and of winter, for in the night all things fall into shade, and in winter into cold. But to return; all these things demonstrate that everything in this world derives its nature from the sun, as from a parent; and if the sun be a parent, it follows that his offspring, or products, resemble him in some kind of type. His rays themselves, which glance before our eyes, are so many, and, as it were, continuous suns;[b] if you concentrate them, you will both see and feel him, and at the same

_b_ That the sun's rays are so many images of him is plain not only from the effect, but also from all the other phenomena which likewise affect our sight; for the images of all objects, with their forms, fall under our view, or are continued to it by the rays of his light,

time his fire, in a very small image; wherefore he is present where his ray is, and therefore we are under his auspices while we are in his rays. From these rays exist all things whatsoever our eyes behold, for if they have their birth from him, they doubtless have their birth from those things by which he exhibits himself as present to us. But what is within his rays? Is it not light and at the same time 3 heat? These are distinct from each other, since he may be present with one, and not in like manner with the other; his light appears as serene and clear in midwinter as in midsummer, but heat is then not present in the bosom of his rays; yet he is still with us, and in like manner illuminates our sight; but since there is no heat in his rays, the vegetations of the earth grow torpid, and end their days; but as soon as he rises again with his fire, as in the time of spring and summer, all things become renovated, returning into their bloom and recollecting their former days. Seeds strike root, roots put forth shoots, these produce branches and leaves, and at length beget new seeds and continue in themselves the very web of creation, and thus in their small gyres effigy the great gyre of the universe. For in like manner they rise and set, and in like manner they circumscribe the courses of their life, reckon their spaces and times, and by their ages transcribe themselves, as it were, into the sun's summer and winter, or, if you prefer, into his day and shade; in a word, all things are like small effigies of his great one. But these things, as was said, are not the effects of his light, except together with his heat.

---

consequently also the sun himself, from whom, as from their fountain, those rays flow; but do not believe that the rays are not real continuations, or essential determinations; for common sense dictates that nothing can be continued by what is empty or a vacuum; but they are the smallest or purest forms, which receive discretely the activities or active forces of the sun, and convey them even to the ultimate boundaries of the universe. These small forms or substances, taken together, constitute that aura which is called ether; and from the most perfect excellence of their elasticity they derive the faculty of communicating whatsoever force they receive to neighboring or contiguous objects, so that they destroy nothing which is received by them, this being the nature of pure elasticity. These powers, 2

63. But let us cover the sight of our eyes with a kind of veil, and let us for a time leave this paradise with its beauties, in the brightness of its light, while we examine the other or heavenly paradise with a purer vision, and thus with another light. Those two lights also spontaneously and mutually remove and hide themselves from sight, and one places the other, as it were, in a shade. Hast not thou thyself experienced, while thou passest from one into the other, that the eye itself, as if conscious of it, deprives itself of its own sight, or that the mind abstracts and withdraws itself from the view of its objects, so that that very light of the great sun is involved, as it were, in darkness? On the other hand also this light, when thou descendest to the eye and the objects of its sight, obscures the heavenly light and its objects; nor does the former return to its native opacity until the gate being, as it were, opened, the lightning of heaven glances 2 upon the interior chamber (*cameram*) of thy sight. This indicates and clearly demonstrates, that there are two lights altogether distinct from each other and differing in their natures; and that one does not easily enter the chamber (*cubile*) of the other. It declares also, that heaven borrows nothing from the light of the sun to increase its lustre, but only from its own sun, whence it derives its all. And if the lights are distinct, so must also their effects be, for effects make one

---

which arise from the substances of the sun himself, and are exhaled, as was shown above, from his great ocean, must of necessity act, while they are acted upon, according to the modes or proportions (*rationes*) of his activity; wherefore they are, as it were, the smallest mirrors, and, as it were, receptacles of his forces, when they are actuated; and thus they not only receive him in themselves, while in their forms, but also convey him to our eyes, almost without an idea of space or time. For unless the substances were actual, objects could not be continued to the sight; nor could the organ of sight, or the eye, be formed to exist according to the nature of its modification, as the ear is formed to exist according to the nature of the modification of the air; still less could a ray be concentrated and divided by optical lenses; neither could it be reflected according to the angles of incidence, and be refracted according to rules; still less could those things become heated, on which it strikes; indeed, the ray itself so convulses by its touch the organs of smell as to excite it to a kind of convulsion or sneezing; in a word, unless a ray were a real continuation of the sun through forms, there would not anything exist which yet is perceived by the very senses to exist from these forms.

with their causes, and conjointly weave together their [properties]. Heavenly light does not give thee the faculty of seeing forms such as the eye transmits, but such as are their uses and goodnesses; for these are the ends, designed for the sake of those forms, not in earth, but in heaven. The rays of that light are in like manner continuous and discrete suns,[c] or continued streams of their fountain; and since we are rendered more intelligent and wise the more that we suffer ourselves to be more enlightened by it, hence it follows that that light flows only from the Sun of Intelligence and Wisdom itself, or from our Supreme; also that all things, which thence derive their origins, worship Him as their parent, in like manner as those which are derived from solar light resemble types and images of the sun. From the solar rays we are also instructed, what is likewise within 3 the rays of this latter sun, namely, both light and heat, but that the light is spiritual, whence is intellectual sight, or the understanding of truth, and that the heat is spiritual, or that it is love, whence is the sensation of good. We learn moreover, that in like manner one can be within and be infolded in the other, namely, light in heat, and heat in light, in different ways and in different degrees; for we understand truth, and from this we discern good, but to feel this good, or to be affected by it, is not of light, but of love; without the presence of love that light is like the light of the sun in its winter, and falls into its shade; but the instant that it is warmed by love it is transcribed, as it were, into its spring, and passes into its day; the proportion of both is quite similar. Our mind is that soil, or 4 that ground, into which those rays inflow with their light and love;

---

[c] That those rays are real essences from their fountain, or from the Supreme Himself, our Deity, as also are the rays from the soul in our body, which rays are real fibres, and essential determinations of the whole, is evidently manifest both from all phenomena, and from all effects; for unless they were real, and the very essences of things, there would truly be nothing real in the universe, since all things thence exist and subsist. Hence alone our ability to live, perceive, and feel derives its essence. But these things are so clear to those, who view them in this light, that they think it vain to confirm them by shadows of arguments borrowed from the light of nature.

seeds are the goodnesses, which we perceive with joyous sense; roots are their first effects, and are called the beginnings of truths and of the other goodnesses; for all things derive from them, as from roots, their secondary birth; for hence arise our truths, as germs, which put forth branches, twigs, and leaves, and blossom after the manner of a tree; hence come new fruits, or seeds, or goodnesses, sprouting forth from the truths of that understanding; hence again new roots, new blossoms, and new seeds; and as these become fruitful according to the cultivation of that ground they raise and build up, not trees, but a large forest, yea, a certain kind of paradise; these are the effects, as was said, not of light, but at the same time

5 of heat, that is, of love. From these things it is now evident what is the quality of the one paradise, and what of the other. Every goodness, which thou perceivest, is inseminated in thy mind; it is a certain love, for thou lovest that which thou feelest to be good; nor does anything enter the sphere of thy mind except through a sense;[d] and since every truth bears in itself the image of the Best, in like manner every goodness bears the image of the Love of that Best, for the ray, which is the continued image of the sun, bears forth that Love from its bosom. From these loves, as from so many seeds, thy mind was conceived and born; for nothing blossomed in it, except what thence derived its root; from which it follows, that

---

[d] Nothing enters the sphere of our mind except by a kind of sensation; and the things which first enter excite and inaugurate into the faculty of acting the organic forms of our mind, which are the beginnings of all the other forms, as also of the fibres themselves, and thus clothe them, as it were, with proper forces of acting. But hence we are clothed only with active powers, which are afterwards excited to their very act, into which they are inaugurated by forces which inflow extrinsically. Those forces either inflow through the doors of the senses, or from the reservoir of images or ideas, that is, from the memory; whether they flow in from the latter or from the former, they nevertheless inflow extrinsically, for the proper activity of the memory is imagination, but not thought. Hence it appears that our minds are formed from without and from within, only by those things which fall into some sense, and this in the first-born by a prior or superior way, but in us by a posterior or inferior way; hence comes the difference that we ascend by a sense of earthly goodnesses to a sense of heavenly goodnesses, and this indeed slowly andtardily, but he descended, by a sense of heavenly goodnesses, to a sense of earthly goodnesses, by degrees.

The Worship and Love of God

thou carriest in thyself an effigy of Him, or that thou art an image of the Supreme Himself by Love.[e]

64. But although these two lights and luminaries, together with their two heats, are so distinct from, and so unlike each other, that they, as it were, shun and put each other to flight, still they do not disagree, but come together and unite in a friendly manner with each other, since one is for the sake of the other. But it may be expedient to examine the covenants of their union or marriage, for hence, as in light, will appear the reasons of disagreement; to discover which reasons, I wish to recall, to thy memory, how the soul, our mother, conceived and formed thy mind from its first stamen, for I saw this with mine eyes, and still see it as present, since it inheres as if it were infixed in me. On that occasion, she first let herself down from her sanctuary to the *eye*, now thine eye, for the sake of taking in and receiving the images or beautiful appearances of paradise, so many effects of that reflected light. I remember, because I am the first-born of wisdoms, that in the instant that those images touched the thresholds of that door, they themselves wondered at seeing themselves changed into appearances of ideas from the mere touch and breathing of our mother, feeling that she infused into them something of her own life. Presently she transported those reformed images or ideas even into the court of thy Helicon, which is called the *memory;* afterwards she took them up into our sacristy, or Olympus, after calling them forth with a new kiss and embrace. And I recollect, for I could scarce restrain myself from laughter, that those ideas themselves, while they looked at each other and their companions, could not again recognize themselves, perceiving themselves transformed into ideas of a superior nature, called rational and intellectual. From these ideas at length, when joined by society into one body, as it were,

2

---

e As our first-born might contemplate his love from goodnesses and the truths arising thence, so every one may contemplate his love from his [goodnesses and the truths], concerning which below.

new forms existed, called truths, from which, as parents, were produced intelligences, and when these grew up, and were made wisdoms, they were adjoined to myself as sisters; out of them thy mind was formed, which is called intellectual, and which grows

3 wise. Hence I was enabled to conclude in what manner those two lights, and these two heats of the lights were consociated, and, as it were, married together, and how one altogether acceded to the conditions and compacts of the other, for I see that both are now eager for one and the same thing, namely,[f] that our mother might infuse into the images produced from the light and shade of the sun, and afterwards turned into ideas, life from her own life, which, as I said, she derived from heaven; and afterwards might clothe them by mutual appositions, or by epigenesis, with a kind of body, and might gift them with a kind of nature; thus she transcribed them

---

[f] It appears clearly, as before the sight itself, that the images, which are insinuated through the eye, emerge upwards to a kind of sensory set in a more elevated place, or in the cerebrum, and insinuate themselves into the sphere of the understanding. It appears also that the senses of words in discourse change themselves into similar appearances or images, and being thus re-formed, introduce themselves into the same sphere; for every word involves some idea, or part of an idea. In like manner, it is evident, that those images, whether born or made, resembling visual [objects], store themselves up in a kind of memory; and when they are called forth from that memory into the mind, they come forth under the appearance of ideas, but of such as from their first cradles, while as yet they are as it were infants or immature, have the name of material, because

2 they are similar to visual [objects]. At length being made more sublime, they put on as it were a spiritual appearance or form, for the limits or boundaries with which they were before circumscribed are as it were removed and they begin to shun their own mind itself, howsoever purified; they are then called intellectual and immaterial; for they are more universal than to be capable of falling under one complex of intuition. By this method our ideas approach nearer and nearer to spiritual nature or essence, and subject themselves to its government. That to these ideas, in an imperceptible manner, are associated ideas which are purely spiritual, and look only to ends, is clear, if we take a more distinct view of the interiors of these ideas; for in the mind they are no longer employed as ideas, but as ends in those ideas; thus what is spiritual enters into marriage with what is natural, or

3 one joins the other to itself, as a kind of consort. But it is asked, from what source this spiritual principle inflows into this marriage-chamber of the mind? It is very clear that it does not inflow through the doors of the sight, or by the way of images, for these are only appearances of solar light, which contain in them nothing of spiritual light, but being enlightened and excited by their own light are elevated so as to meet and be conjoined

The Worship and Love of God

into intelligences and wisdoms, and this from the forms themselves which the light and heat of the sun brought forth and reflected by their rays; for she, as it were, borrowed these things, and transferred them into fibres and muscles, whence come members and their tender limbs, and hence our bodies, in which she herself acts as a soul; and since by her, through heavenly or spiritual light, and its heat or love, we live our life, thou thyself mayest behold this in me. Be pleased only to look at my bosom, my breasts, my countenance, and mine eyes, with which I am also looking at thee; dost thou not see how consentaneous, or how single is the agreement of all things, which we derive from the nature of the world, and from the life of heaven. One light does not here diminish or overshadow the other, neither does one heat deaden and extinguish the other, but makes one altogether with the other, as also in thy whole body.

---

with spiritual light. This also is clear, that this spiritual principle is not conceived in the memory, and hatched by it, for until the images are first transformed by the mind into intellectual ideas they are not remitted into the storehouse of the memory. It is also very clear, that our mind itself is not of itself born spiritual, for in the time of its infancy it is no mind, but grows and becomes adolescent with years and age; hence now it follows that its origin is not to be sought after in these paths or byways, but that we must rise within or above this mind, which is called rational or intellectual, and there inquire where and whence that spiritual principle descends with its ends. When therefore we rise 4 a little above this sphere, which is our intelligible sphere, there presents itself to us the first or supreme substance of the body, which is called the soul, which is not only the soul of the body, but also the soul of this mind itself, to which, as was said, our ideas ascend. The essence and form of this substance is spiritual, which alone lives in its universal body, and by which everything of the body exerts the activity of its life, each thing according to its form, for which reason it may be called, the form of forms of its body. Since therefore this substance, whose essence is spiritual, or the soul, resides in the supreme and inmost things of its kingdom, it follows, that through this, as if it was from it, that spiritual principle inflows, which meets the natural principle, entering by the way of the senses, receives it with kisses in the body's guest-chamber, the chamber and lodging-place being that of the understanding itself. From this it now appears in what manner those two lights, namely, 5 the natural and the spiritual, inflow by different ways, and after a sacred conjunction conceive such an illustrious offspring, which are so many intuitions of ends associated with their mediating causes. But I know that a kind of thick darkness can overspread our minds, consequently inject a scruple about the manner in which the rays alone of lights can produce effects so real, when those radiations from objects are nothing but modifications of the interfluent aura; but this scruple easily vanishes when those forms are

4 Life and nature in us are so concordant, that we live, as it were one and the same; from this union our faces, inasmuch as we are the inhabitants of Helicon, appear, as I believe, like beauties, and our acts as joys, which thou once whisperedst in my ear; but our mother, or soul, inasmuch as she does not regard bodies, but our

---

known to us into which they inflow, namely, when it is known to us that they are real organic forms; for they creep inward by real fibres, as is well known from the eye and the rest of the sensories; which forms being the first or beginnings of the organic forms, are taught by those modifications, and afterwards excited to change their states, or to vary their forms, whence arise the real activities of substances, nearly in the same manner as the modification of air falling into the ear, and other modifications falling into their

6 sensories. The modifications of the auras are themselves real active forces, which excite suitable organic forms by their activities; as in outmost things, so also in inmost, with a difference only of perfections.—But what is life? Does not living consist in viewing ends? And since this is [the property] of an intelligent being, it follows, that a life of intelligence is a view and representation of ends; this cannot be the faculty of a natural being (*Entis*), but of a spiritual one; wherefore spiritual things are alive, and the Fountain of spiritual things is the Life of all things that live, and of all lives. But in order that these ends may be brought into effects, and that uses may exist, there is need of instrumental causes which in themselves are not alive, or from themselves do not view an end, but merely comply and are subservient to life and intelligence, consequently in their nature are dead. This clearly appears in our very actions, which are influenced by both principles; for action itself, without its life, is merely a motion of the muscles, as of a machine, but it is called action from the end regarded, or from life, and is the more sublime in proportion as it is influenced by more of life, or more of wisdom; wherefore action is not regarded from its motion, or from its figure and countenance, but from the intention and will, that is, from

7 the end, from which the action emanates. From these considerations it is evident that natural things were made to serve spiritual, as an instrumental or organic cause; in like manner, that this whole universe, which is subject to the sun of the world, was created by the Supreme Fountain of Life, to serve as a medium for arriving at ultimate ends. In our mind itself also some type of a similar creation is represented, while it embraces some ultimate end with means; for then it intends causes, by which it may promote its con-templated ends; and for this purpose it calls forth nature to its aid, and by it tends to its goal; thus it first constructs to itself a mind or orb, to be the complex of causes and effects, which may convey and bring forth those ends; from little things, by way of comparison,

8 it is allowed to comprehend greater. That those lights also are distinct, is also plain from our minds, which, when the sun of our world is absent, as in the night, and in the case of those who are born blind or become so, are alike vigorous in intelligence, yea, with a purer and more excellent intelligence, in proportion as they are less disturbed by the light of the world. Among the ancients also mention is made of wise men (*Sophi*), who are said purposely to have made themselves blind, so as to extinguish the light of the eye, in order that they might be more at liberty to cultivate spiritual light.

The Worship and Love of God

minds, calls those beauties goodnesses and those joys happinesses, for she says that nothing is truly beautiful which is not good, and nothing is truly joyous which is not happy; and that I may believe this, she appeals also to our parents, or truths; she also adds the further confirmation, that nothing can be truly good and happy which does not resemble the Best Himself in effigy and in act; she therefore calls us His images (*icones*). That it may still more clearly appear how very closely life is united to nature, or how this latter is taken into the marriage-chamber of heaven itself,[g] let me call your attention to love itself; it renders itself manifest, and comes forth actually by heat, and its very desire, which is the continuous

---

g There is nothing in universal nature which does not derive its form, and thus an appearance of body, from a certain soul, and this is the case not only with the subjects of the animal kingdom, but also of the vegetable; the souls of these latter are uses, designed by heaven itself as ends; in conformity to those uses they are generated and grow; for, as was above observed, effects are only uses unfolded and sent forth into the gyre of nature; but in our minds uses are called ends, because they are intended by us and thus live; according therefore to the number of ends is the number of the parts of the soul's intuition, each of which, in order to become uses in effect, must put on an appearance of a kind of body; for unless ends, as souls, by a clothing of body, are emitted into the gyre of nature, they cannot be exhibited and actually represented as uses. This now is the reason why nothing ever 2 exists in nature which does not in a type resemble its origin, or soul; and as this origin is from heaven, for all uses, as was said, are ends designed by heaven, therefore things natural and things heavenly must of necessity agree with each other, according to the order first induced, or the most perfect order; and this to such a degree that it is allowable to take a view of one from the other; for if we unfold natural things, and in their place transcribe heavenly or spiritual things, congruous truths result, as may be seen confirmed by two examples above, to which one may also be added here; for instance: *The sun is the fountain of all light and heat in his world, nor is he the cause of shade and of cold; but shade is the privation of his light, and cold is the privation of his heat; the sun is never deprived of light and heat, but earthly objects, in consequence of not being capable of being penetrated by his light and heat; then also the directions of his rays produce this effect, whence come darkness and cold.* This sentence, by a change in the form of expression, reads thus in a spiritual sense: *God is the Fountain of all Intelligence and Love in His own heaven, nor is He the cause of folly and enmity, but folly is the privation of His Intelligence, and enmity is the privation of His Love; God is never deprived of Intelligence and Love, but human minds, which do not suffer themselves to be ruled by the light of His Intelligence, and by the rays of His Love, also the determinations of His rays, that is of truths and goodnesses, produce this effect, whence come all folly and hatred.*

[principle] of love by ardor. Wherefore also by the expressions of our speech we salute and signify love itself by fire, and its cupidity by fervor or flame; the marriage itself by flambeaux and torches; by corporeal sense also we perceive its delight in heat. These therefore are connubials of life and of nature, of heaven and of the world, that is, the covenants of each paradise by love, of which covenants we wisdoms are the hostages and hymens.

66.* Hence it is as clear as light, that life has ordained nature to be a consort with itself; but since they are thus entwined, we must unfold the manner by which one inflows into the other, or what is the order, and what are laws according to order: for the Founder of laws and of rights never acts in any case but from the wisest order. That one inflows into the other, is plainly declared by existence itself, from which we ought to judge concerning subsistence; for as we exist so also we subsist. But although this is evident from the generation of all things, and especially from our own, it behooves me in order to place the truth in its own light to unravel a little the web, just now woven, from its ultimate threads. The soul has received the images themselves which are the forms of nature and of her light, entering in by the way of the eye, and having breathed her life into them, has conducted them into the chambers of the memory, and has suitably assigned to each its abode there; and at the same time, has forbidden them to rush into our Olympus or sacristy, without our permission or order. These she has afterwards arranged so harmoniously, according to the genius and nature of each, when called forth, that at length she constructed from them, as from members, a kind of society or body. Hence we intelligences and wisdoms were born in that form of beauty which thou beholdest; what therefore we derive from nature, and what from life, thou clearly distinguishest with thine eyes. Our soul herself seems indeed to have produced this effect, and on that

---

* A mistake here occurs in the numbering of the paragraphs, number 65 being omitted in the original. (TR.)

The Worship and Love of God

account we acknowledge and venerate her as a pious mother; nevertheless, she herself does not live from herself, being only a power which lives and acts from another. The life itself, as her soul, inflows 3 into her from the Fountain of all things that live, or of all lives, and thus through her into us, her offspring; therefore we are heavenly in our origin, and therefore we are called wisdoms. It was that life, which, by the instrumentality of our soul, went to meet the lights and shades, or forms of nature, and when she had converted them into ideas, through the little cells of the memory, arranged them into classes and tribes, according to genera and species; it was the same life which afterwards called them forth into thy Helicon, whence we derive our birth. Such now was order; and such the influx of life into nature; according to the same we exist, as I said, and according to the same we subsist, or live and act. From this it 4 is now clear, that nature durst not at all, without command or summons, introduce herself into the chambers of our life, but that the Supreme and His Love, according to the intuition of ends, that is, according to His own decision, adopted nature, and adapted her forms altogether to those uses which he intended. This therefore is the order from which all our laws and decrees of nature flow, and from which comes our fate; all these things are derivative veins from that one single Fountain. Supreme things therefore, or things superior in order, inflow into inferior things, and these into ultimate things, but not *vice versa;* hence inferior things derive their powers and perfections, or hence flow all the abilities and powers of inferior things.[h] When this order is established, then there is nothing so 5 complicated and abstruse which is not explained and unfolded,

---

[h] We cannot easily discover from the light alone of our nature, which does not possess ordinate life, what is the quality of this order; for all things in us appear so complex, and so folded into each other, that we are unable to distinguish one thing from another, and thus to view them distinctly; for the veriest vital light itself remains so entirely enfolded in the reasons of the understanding, or in the ideas of our thought, and these latter in the ideas of the imagination, and these again in the images of sight, that we have a very indistinct and obscure view in them of things superior and things inferior. But the cause of this obscurity 2

for it is Light itself which sees, and Living Force itself which acts. By this order follies themselves are reformed into intelligences, and insanities into wisdoms; slime is changed into the brightest gem, and dust into shining gold; the innate darkness of nature is resplendent as in light; our acts become pieties and virtues; and moreover all things succeed according to our wish and sentiment. But it is altogether otherwise if this order be inverted, that is, if license be given to nature to break in, without leave, into the higher and sacred recesses of life; for in this case all things spontaneously involve themselves in shades, the torches of life and of love, hating that light, shun it, and as it were vanish, for the laws of order itself, and the established principles of life, are rescinded, and everything takes a form from the blow, becoming an object of contention and of doubt. If you please, let us make the experiment, but let us make it prudently; let us open the doors of the court, and let us suffer our handmaids, or ideas, to inflow into this palace, from their own

6

---

is only an inversion of our state, on account of which things prior must be unfolded and viewed from things posterior, and thus finally wisdom be attained; for in things posterior things prior lie concealed, as causes and principles in effects, consequently they are deeply concealed as in a shade. But in order that one thing may come forth from another, and that we may view it distinctly, it is necessary that we view it from what is prior, or from light itself, whether inspired or revealed, and thus by that order which is treated of in this article; for it is allowable from a superior principle to contemplate things inferior, but not *vice versa;* consequently intellectual light is, as it were, to be separated from the light of nature, in which there is more of shade than of light; and thus the mind is to be removed from, and, as it were, to keep watch over the animus and the grosser objects of the senses. But what is the quality of that order, and what the nature of influx according to that order, must be drawn from the doctrines of order and of degrees, also from the doctrines of influxes, which must be cultivated. But in order to give a sketch of the quality of that order, and of the quality of influx, it is to be noted, that prior things are altogether distinct from posterior things, or superior things from inferior, as forms themselves, of which one begets another, That which begets, or is the parent, is called prior or superior, but that which is begotten, posterior or inferior. Or if instead of forms you say substances, the case is precisely similar: the supreme form we called spiritual, the next to it which follows in order, celestial; hence, by like generation, there arise inferior forms, even to the last, which is called angular, properly earthly, corporeal, and material, which in like manner is arranged into superior and inferior [forms] in the degree that they are active, concerning which below. Such now is the order of substances, and according to this order the

3

The Worship and Love of God

imaginary order and instinct, and we shall see with our eyes, from that order inverted, their unruly attempts and acts. On saying these words the bars were removed, and leave was given to the ideas to rush from their chambers into Olympus, just as they pleased. Instantly snatching the lamps down from the ceiling, and with their hair uncombed, they rushed in crowds into the court itself, in a graceful manner, as it seemed to their natures (*animos*); and presently, as they entered, they began to search with their lamps for their mistresses, the wisdoms, for by that light they could not discern them; and when they had sought them in vain,[i] seeming to themselves as if they were alone, and left to their own genius, they began to dispute briskly with each other, and, as it were, to

---

organism of our body is instituted; wherefore the soul is said to be in the first and highest [principles] of its kingdom, where it is of a spiritual form; from this form are derived the rest, which, by successive generations of one from the other, put on the quality of the following forms, which are therefore also called inferior or posterior. According to the order in which the forms succeed each other, are also the perfections of all qualities and faculties; for those which are superior in themselves and their own nature, are infinitely more perfect than those which are inferior in themselves and their nature, which every one may understand from generation alone. But it is now asked: What is the quality of influx? One form by itself does not inflow into another, for the prior or parent acts only as the reason of the cause of another, or bestows upon it a nature, or gives the power of acting in this or that manner, according to the influx of active forces; but all active forces, which ought to excite these forms as bare powers, inflow extrinsically; just as Life itself, which is the living force of all things, inflows into our own first form or soul; in like manner into the other, but mediately by the Divine Spirit; for there are as many active forces as there are powers or passive forces in us, of which, God willing, we shall treat in their order. These forces are what inflow, the order of whose influx ought to be altogether according to the order of our faculties, namely, from highest things to lower, but not *vice versa*. We may indeed in some measure conceive the influx of the soul into the rational mind, from a similar influx, or the influx of that mind into the muscles, for the muscles are forms excited according to the idea of their mind, as the mind is according to the idea of its soul. This is a sketch of the subject, but its parts will be considered singly in what follows, that hence a clearer idea may be presented both of order and of influx through degrees.

    i What is the quality of the mind's crew, if the ideas rush in uninvited, is sufficiently evident from our own speech, for what we speak flows down from the mind. From our speech is manifested the state of the mind, namely, whether it acts from a view of natural ends, or of spiritual; if only of natural ends, it is a proof that those ideas have invaded the palace, and hold the key.

contest in a legal manner, as it seemed to them, whether this were
7 the habitation of their wisdoms. Some affirmed, others denied, and
several agreeing together wanted, in an arbitrary and imperious
manner, to pronounce sentence like the supreme intelligences. They
said: Those wisdoms are nowhere to be found, let us occupy these
empty seats; possibly they are spectres, which at the first sight of
our light, fly away into the air; let us enjoy our choice, for we are
free. But what, they added, is wisdom? What is the soul of which
they say they are begotten? Yea, what is life? And what is that Love,
which, by their account, is everything? Where is that sacred fire,
of which we were told, but which does not appear in this court?
Let us light up still more lamps, and examine: but as a result of this
an altercation arose, and when the combat was verging to sedition,
the soul being excited from her sanctuary, for a kind of vertigo
began to seize her eyes, burst into the sacristy, and, notwithstanding
their murmurings, thrust down that disorderly crew by force and
by threats into its dens; for not being able to bear the brightness
of her light, they even sunk down of themselves, as if deprived of
8 all power and animation. At the close of this transaction, the wisdom, turning to her prince, said to him: You see how deformed
they appeared, and how wild was their carriage, with their dishev-
elled hair on their shoulders, like furies, and with bloody and at
the same time ghastly countenances, and yet they seem to themselves
as images of the highest beauty. You see likewise, how great a confu-
sion arose, and how great a one must arise, if that order be not
observed, which requires that superior things should have the
command over inferior, or life itself over nature; for the Supreme
is the order of all orders; from Him flow ends, and thence the uses
of ends, and the effects of uses. When this order is established, first
principles steadily proceed in a right manner to their ultimates,
and ultimates return to their first principles. Let us therefore keep
this order in view, because we bear it in our inmost parts (*medullis*);
by this, life was begotten in us, because by this, love was begotten;
in a word, nothing is more holy because nothing is more venerable,

and nothing ought to be more venerable because nothing is more holy. When therefore nature in us is invited and conjoined in a partnership of life by this order, we wisdoms behold, as from a high summit, all things which are beneath, and widely spread out before our eyes; and we see, as from the highest light, in what manner those inferior lives wander in shades, while they walk in their own light; they, on the other hand, do not look at us, and we are to them like shades and spectres. I saw that thou couldst not refrain from laughter, when those scullions, or our slaves, sought us in the court in vain by their lights; and how they would have fallen head-long into the sacred fire, and thus have perished and been burned to death, unless it had been fenced about and guarded; but we saw clearly all their wandering and ludicrous acts, together with them-selves, not as ideas, still less as intelligences, which they wished to represent, but as insanities.

67. Since therefore our bodies are only the repositories and recipients of life, let us endeavor to behold from the life of our minds, what the life itself is, which we live. Let us also be taught by nature, which makes one and the same thing, as was said, with life, and thus let us contemplate the idea in its type; but that rea-sons may cohere, and we may view truth from its own light, let the life itself now call forth ideas, nor, as of late, let us open the door to our slaves to rush in of their own accord; but let us dictate to them this order, and establish it as an eternal law, according to which they may conformably, and thus uniformly, enter into our sacred temple, from their own small dwellings and cottages. For we have above seen that our minds resemble a kind of paradise, but formed from the rays of the Sun of Life, or of Intelligence and Wisdom; wherefore for the sake of convenience, let us contem-plate the one from the other. It is sufficiently evident to every one 2 of us, that the orchards and rose-gardens of our earthly paradise, without the heat of their light, wither away, as under a wintry sun, while the leaves of their trees and flowers grow yellow, and the branches are stripped of their honors; the fruits themselves fall off

and everything returns to its dust; but presently, on the return of spring, with its new fire, all things rise again out of their tombs into life, and commence and run the career of their pristine ages, from another seed, but from the same life: from which we learn, that all these things are the effects of heat, and not of light alone. Let us pass now from vegetations to animals, or from this paradise of our sight, to the superior paradise of our minds, and in the place of one light, let us only substitute another, or intelligence; and in the place of the one heat, let us substitute another, or love, so far as they exactly correspond to each other, according to what has been

3 said. Our minds, in exact agreement with those fruit and flower gardens, being similarly enlightened by spiritual light alone, yet not warmed by love, in like manner become torpid, their leaves also grow yellow, the branches are deprived of their honors, and the fruits themselves fall off; yea, all things are in such a state of decay, that they no longer appear like minds; for their forces grow cold, and their powers become dulled, as if paralyzed, inasmuch as the understanding itself falls into a shade like that of night, and the will into cold like that of winter, the former being darkened, and the latter remaining undetermined, so that the proportion of both is similar; but as soon as love, or spiritual heat, arises again, all things are heated again into their new life, and the things which have grown rigid, being again excited, as if a flame were applied to their inmost parts, grow soft again, and return into the flower of their ages, for minds instantly begin to desire, and impulses (*Animi*) to lust, and thus again to live; for where there are no desires, and no cupidities, there are also no excitements, or no kindlers of life, since if there be no love, we neither desire or lust after anything.

4 Yea, all our states of life depend solely on the state of the love; for as soon as we indulge our love, the mind is instantly revisited by its life, and we are urged on by a sort of unusual alacrity, whence come our gladness, laughter, and exultation; yea, from the same source are derived the favors and courtesies which we show to each other; but if our love be assaulted by threats or force, we instantly become

inflamed with anger, and attack those who assault us, like foes in battle-array, whence comes our indignation, our anger, and fury, for, according to the danger with which our love is threatened, our bosoms beat, our hearts palpitate, a cold tremor runs through our bones, and the mind, as if overwhelmed with darkness, is half deprived of its life, whence come our fears, terrors, sadnesses, sorrows, and griefs; but presently, while we view, as through a window, the accession or return of our love from afar, the mind again returns, and the life of the mind, and the sight itself sparkles with a kind of joy, whence comes hope, with which we are wont to be suckled: in a word, all the states of our life, as was said, depend upon the state of our love, and we are never affected with anything but what touches our love; nor is this the case only with that love which is lord or primate, but also with all its servants and attendants, which are infinite: [k] for they cohere like one chain, from which if you take a single link, the whole is moved, together with the weight hanging to it. This is the fire of our life, the derivatives from which vibrate like flames; hence it is discoverable as in clear light, that without love there is no life, and that the life is such as

---

[k] That every one may know his own love in himself, or in his thoughts, desires, words, and actions, and indeed in the single exertions of his own life, is sufficiently clear; and although he has learned to put on another countenance, not his own, both in his face and actions, still it is sufficiently evident to himself, and to all who are wiser than to pay any attention to such a countenance and assumed form. Those loves in general are but two, namely, the supreme love, or the love of the Best, and the lowest love, or the love of the worst. It is the worst, because it has separated from the Supreme, and altogether disagrees with Him; all the rest of the loves are intermediate, and with infinite variety relate themselves to the one or to the other; thus we more or less bear the effigy of the one or of the other. Those loves themselves are real essences which exist; if they were not real, their effigies would not in any wise be represented in us; for it is impossible for anything to exist, like to, or resembling that which is not. The type derives all that it has from the idea, according to which it is effigied; where there is no idea, no effigy also of an idea is possible. Without the Best and the worst, or good and evil, really existing, there would be no perception of good and evil, still less sensation, consequently no understanding of what is true and false, and no will of what is good and evil; in a word, no mind, consequently no existence of what is our own, and of the things thence flowing; thus we should not be shades and ideas, but altogether nothing.

5 the love is. As she said these words, our first-born kissed the hand of his wisdom, which she then elevated, perhaps excited by her ardor, that she might signify her meaning by gestures; at the same time he expressed his satisfaction with her speech by the flame of exulting life and with a favoring glance, which being perceived by the wisdom, I now clearly see, said she, that thy love is our love; it sparkles from the countenance, and especially from the rays of thine eye, for the very iris darts lightning; since according to the desires and joys of the mind, the ministering organs also exult, the sight especially sparkles from the love itself; for there is nothing in the body but what is impelled and leaps towards motions and habits similar to those of the love; hence thy suavity, and the cheerfulness and pleasing lightning of thy sight; for love rules the mind, and the mind the body, and thus life and nature, fighting under the same standard, act as one cause. To the intent that we may recall these things into our minds, as often as we abide in Helicon, that sacred hearth is in the court, living and burning with its perpetual fire,[1] that it may continually give light to the counsels of our understanding, and moderate the ardors of our will. Didst thou not observe how the ceiling and roof of our court became refulgent from it, and what thick darkness and torpidity seizes us, when it is half

6 extinguished? *That fire* represents Love itself; *its torches and flames,* the sacred burnings of our desires; *the hearth around constructed of adamantine circles and garlands,* the truths, and their intelligences, which, like vestal nymphs, guard the fire; *the burnished gold with which the circles of the hearth were overspread,* goodnesses and their wisdoms, for we are the priestesses and sacred ministers of the nymphs of that vesta. *That that hearth by its flaming fire seemed molten, as it were, into adamantine gold,* signifies the transparency of goodness by truths, and hence the harmony and union of the

---

[1] This hearth, with its fire, apparatus, and radiation, was described above, no. 51, where it was promised that its symbolical meaning should be explained; here now the interpretation is given, wherefore let the reader, if he pleases, first consult that passage.

one and the other. *The irradiation of innumerable colors,* denotes the perceptions of truth from good, and of good by truth; wherefore also *these colors appear in every intelligence according to the position of the eye of every one;* for we intelligences and wisdoms are not exactly alike in face, nor are we clothed with like bodies, but by the society into which we are joined by love, we constitute one understanding and one will, and thus thy mind; for there is no one thing given in us, nor yet in the nature of things, which is not made one by the consent and concord of several things, that is, by unanimity, nor is there any unanimity except by love. From these considerations now it ought to appear evident, that without love there is no life, and that the life is of such a quality as the love is.

68. Since therefore we live the life of Love, and from it our own life; and since we wisdoms and intelligences, who compose thy mind, in the fibres and veins of our bodies possess not blood but love, infused and continued from Love itself,[m] it concerns us to know what, and of what quality, that Love is, at whose nod the orb

---

m It is said that wisdoms and intelligences, or what amounts to the same thing, our mind, which consists of understanding and will, possess no other blood or spirit in their veins and fibres, than love, or its life: this indeed is confirmed by the phenomena of all effects; but that the same may in some degree be made manifest by anatomy, it may be expedient to give some idea of the formation of our mind. No one is ignorant that all our organs, both of sensation and of motion, and also the viscera derive their contexture from fibres and blood-vessels. If we pursue these fibres which all and together compose the blood-vessels, even to their beginnings, or first origins, by a continual thread, it is rendered manifest that they all close in the cortical glands, in the cerebrum, the cerebellum, the medulla oblongata, or the spinal marrow, and thus derive their origin from these glands; wherefore those glands themselves, which are the beginnings of the fibres, are also the beginnings of all the operations which are excited and exercised by the fibres; consequently in them are the beginnings of our minds and the minds themselves, for to them proceed all sensations, and from them flow all the determinations of the will into its acts, nor is any end or origin elsewhere given; wherefore on the destruction of those glands, or on the cutting away of the fibres which lead to the sensory organs, or to the muscles, sensations and actions instantly perish. Wherefore if we now consider those glands or little 2 spheres as the beginnings of all the organic forms of our body, and of their faculties and operations, by calling to our aid the anatomy of the brain in general, also the doctrines of forms, of order, and of degrees, also of influxes and correspondences, we may attain to the knowledge how those beginnings are formed, or how they are composed of the purest

is ruled, which we believe to be our own; for there are infinite loves, but there is one which acts the principal part in every mind, and which, as supreme moderator, administers the chief government, and assigns to the rest their offices: and since they are so many in number, our distinct perceptions [of them] perish; for their infinity alone, especially when they also disagree, obscures the mind; this also is the reason why that, which is all in all, escapes our view more than the rest; so also the love, which is the all of all in our little world or body, and which, as a deity, or as the soul of our forces, rules its courses and fluctuations by various and unknown reins; this is one of the causes why we do not easily distinguish one love from

2 another. There is yet another cause, namely, that every love, like a pantomime, by its gesticulation, assumes an appearance of the Supreme or Best Love, and thus entangles minds in its snares. For one builds a Helicon like another, which also it calls Olympus; it likewise begets intelligences and wisdoms, and introduces them into it. The palaces, too, which it calls musæa and athenæa, it fills with parasites and servants, who may favor, flatter, and portray its sports by act and gesture: yea, what is more, it also adorns the hearth in the court, and proclaims festivals, and orders them, even disputing with them, to prepare for itself frankincense, oblation-cakes, and

---

fibres, or of fibres resembling those of the body; and indeed evidently to that knowledge, that those little stamina of extreme subtlety, resembling, as I said, the fibres of the body, or fibres by way of eminence, cannot admit such an essence, or such a fluid, as do the fibres derived from them; consequently they cannot admit the animal spirit, still less the red blood, such as is admitted by the vessels, or by the arteries and veins; but in the place of them they admit a certain one in which is life, consequently one which flows down from the very fountain of life, and to which the animal spirit, and lastly, the red blood in the body correspond, receiving from it also their life; this is the life which actuates and governs our mind itself, or the organic beginnings; wherefore it is said, *that wisdoms and intelligences, in the fibres and veins of their bodies, do not bear blood, but love, that is, its life infused and continued from Love itself.* These things are confirmed more fully and clearly by phenomena themselves and effects, than by the obscure and lengthy way of anatomy and philosophy; although by the aid of those doctrines of which mention was made above, the same things may be absolutely demonstrated, but not intelligibly, except to those who are skilled in anatomy and philosophy.

The Worship and Love of God

sacrifices, with other like things, altogether as in our Olympus. It also commands the attendants and guards, that they call it the 3 Best, and laugh at those as insane, who dare to say that anything is prior to itself, or better than the Best. It also instructs its servants, that if any other love, inimical to itself, should pretend to dominion, they should make every disturbance possible, vibrate all the torches of life which they carry about with them, set on fire each blood, stir up black bile from the gall-bladder below, and thus fill with fury the vessels of the whole kingdom. And when the love has thus instructed and principled its mind, then all things derive their secondary birth from those principles as from roots,[n] and push themselves forward in conformity with its life; thus it excites a certain idea of paradise, which it calls its heavenly paradise, from which it contemplates the earthly paradise as its effigy. Moreover 4 also it strictly enjoins that they should adorn the possessor of that mind as a prince, with a royal robe, distinguish him, when placed on a throne, with a sceptre and crown, subject all things to his law and government, and persuade him that he alone enjoys sovereignty, and may issue his imperial decrees as he pleases. Never, under pain of exile, do they whisper in his ear that he sits on that throne as an illustrious statue or an image adorned with gold and gems, but totally void of power. From this thou seest, of what great concern it is, and how much above every other concern, that every one should know his love; and since there are so many loves, and all of them like so many actors are desirous to personate the Best,

---

[n] All things whatsoever which arise from seed and soul, in general, in species and in part, derive a secondary origin from the roots, or their beginnings; for seeds first put forth their root, and by it finally is introduced all the juice into the stems, branches, and fruits. The case is similar also in things animate, in which from souls, as from seeds, beginnings are first excited, and afterwards from those beginnings all things are brought forth; our minds are said to be the beginnings of the operations of the body which depend on the will; but before they become minds or act intellectually, they are only beginnings of fibres. This is common throughout nature, that similar beginnings are excited by their first origins, and that afterwards further effects are produced by these [secondary origins].

[thou seest of what importance also it is] to make distinctions in this multitude; for hence we derive the auspices of our life, and all its conditions, fortunes, and destinies.

69. But I recollect that I lately gave no small offense to thy animus by the mere mention of more than one love, and that therefore thou brakest the thread of my discourse as soon as I began it. I see clearly and am sensible of the same thing also at this moment, for thou canst not dissemble; the pupil of thine eye does not sparkle with a glad flame, nor dost thou face me with a cheerful and placid look; but that I may turn the purplish hue of that fire into brightness I wish to explain to thee what thou art ignorant of, namely, the nature and quality of those loves. It is better to learn this from thine own wisdom, than from experiments and proofs in the thing itself; for that other, which is contrary to our own, is not love, but an enemy, who by singular cunning invents reasons to impose upon the innocent and to circumvent and make them his favorers under a pretence of friendship, ensnaring especially the more incautious by slight blandishments; and that he may prepare to spread out his webs and all his nets he first injects ignorance of himself, as if no such love existed; nor does he tie his knots more artfully than in the shade of our understandings; for thus he dims the heavenly light, and extinguishes the sacred fire, in hatred of which he interposes such a shade, that he may afterwards establish his sports; and therefore he is never more alive, and more securely so, than with those persons into whom he inspires a belief that he does not live at all. Therefore it concerns us that thou be instructed; for he is never perceivable by his own light, since he veils himself in a shade, nor can he be known but by our light. But to come to the point: there is but one only Love, the fountain of all goodnesses and truths; but there exists also another, which, inasmuch as it is the origin of all evils, is also the origin of all falsities, but as yet thou knowest not what evil is, and what falsity, O golden infancy! This Love would also escape us, because it conceals its nature from us, but we apprehend it only by hearing of it. It is no longer concealed from thee

2

that there is a heaven and a world or the nature of heaven and the nature of the world, and that those natures are distinct and differ from each other, as lights themselves, and heats themselves, of which so frequently above; wherefore our minds are the centres of both, and suffer themselves to be bent and turned towards one and the other, as if on joints. God, the architect of both, as well of heaven as of the world, to the intent that all things which are in lowests might go and return to his highests, and those which are in outmosts to his inmosts, which differ exceedingly from each other, and thus might go forth and return rightly in their order; and that the universal world, like heaven, with its uses and delights, might inflow to our love by each way, namely, from Himself, and at the same time directly, and thus he might arrange all and single things from the sacred fire of His Love, and the sanctuary of Intelligence and Wisdom, excited also a fountain of life, with its infinite streams, in the very nature of the world, for without such a spiritual fountain in the world itself, the most perfect order would not have been induced. This was the cause of the creation 3 of the many spirits and genii, or of the many essences which live here, and of one prince or leader of all, whom we call the fountain of that life, and the rest the streams of that fountain. This prince was made the god of the world, and his palace like a heavenly palace; he has also his chiefs and governors, whom he appoints over provinces, and likewise his intelligences and wisdoms, as he calls them, together with infinite ministries, as the amplitude of that kingdom requires; but its whole control is his; for he possesses a great empire, as extensive namely as this universe, which lies before our open eyes. The nature itself of the world is void of life, and only made to be subservient to spiritual essences or living minds, as an instrumental or organic cause, for there is nothing in the universe but what tends to the use of minds. Nevertheless our Supreme created the whole universe, both heaven and the world, not for the sake of those essences or minds, but only for the sake of His own Love, or Only-begotten Son; wherefore all spiritual essences, and all living minds, are nothing but mediators of life, and thus again instrumental causes, consequently the whole is only a system of mediations, that the Love of the Supreme might be all in all, and 4 by it heavenly things be joined with earthly ones. For this end, this Emperor of such extensive dominion was created; but whereas so great authority and administration was decreed to him by our Supreme, he became so elated with his immense faculties (*animis ingentibus*), and so insolent, that he wished to seize heaven also, and to appropriate the power of our Love; for when left to himself, he considered no one as being above himself; therefore he entirely revolted from the Supreme by rebellious commotions against the Only-begotten: hence the empires or universes were divided; still he lives from the rays of the life of the Supreme, for thence is the life of all living things, yet not at the same time from the life of his Love, but from the dry fire of his own proper love; and moreover although he has revolted, he is bound under that necessity, as by curbs and chains, to execute obsequiously all the commands of our Deity; for that was the cause of his existence, and to continue the same he is rigidly restrained from being destroyed by the torments of his hatred arising from disaffection; also from telling any tales of his own world; but by lies he would disturb all knowledge of truth had not the Supreme known all and single things before the creation of the world from Himself, and what would come to pass by infinite other ways. From this it is now evident, that there are two loves which rule in the universe, namely, the Love of the Best, from the nature of his own Love that heavenly things may be united with earthly ones, and the love of the worst from the nature of hatred, and thus from the love of the disjunction of those things. From this one origin so many innumerable loves arise, for an infinite multitude is born from the revolt alone of one.

70. But whereas thou livest in thy golden innocence, and art ignorant of these destinies of the universe, I am willing to explain myself farther on the subject, lest perhaps thou shouldst think that I am telling thee tales, so let us descend only by a few steps of

our ladder into the court of this palace, and with thine own eyes thou shalt take a view of his cave, and of himself; also thou shalt contemplate an idea of the universe, the type of which we carry about with us. For our soul represents the Supreme creative Mind of the universe, since she also in like manner, like the goddess of her little world, or a vicarious deity, resides in supreme and inmost principles, and in her own sanctuary, from which she governs her little universe; to her also is granted a similar kind of Omnipresence, of Omniscience, and of Omnipotence, but within the limits of her own kingdom. Nothing also has its life therein, except from her life; for she has constructed, and, as it were, built all things from her own fibres, as from rays derived from the fountain of her life; yet she has not done this herself, but our Supreme, with His Love, by means of her. But thy mind, with thine understanding and will, 2 represents Love itself, or the Only-begotten of the Supreme, whose image it bears; for the soul first of all begat that mind, as its one only offspring, and afterwards by ideas and truths introduced into its sacristy, formed and produced intelligences and wisdoms, and thus constituted an Olympus altogether like to, and resembling that, which, being subject to the Only-begotten of the Supreme, is seen in the very heaven itself. *o* But the inferior or lowest mind, which is also called the animus, with its genii, represents that great prince of the world, to whom so great power has been allotted by

---

o That the soul has, as it were, built the whole body, by fibres produced from herself, and that first of all she conceived that mind which is called intellectual as her only-begotten, and constructed its Olympus, and presently introduced into it intelligences and wisdoms; and that she has delivered to it the rule of her own empire, and has reserved to herself, for the sake of gratifying it, only the nature of that kingdom, with several things besides which necessarily accompany the government of the universe, you may see explained above, with sufficient comprehensiveness and clearness; for such an affinity, not to say, relationship, subsists between them, that he who is in the knowledge of the one, is also in the knowledge of the other. That the ancients discerned more clearly than the moderns or Christians, that our body resembles the universe, is owing to the blindness of the minds of the latter caused by the prince of that shade, to prevent his own hell from being clearly contemplated, and still more the heaven of God.

the Supreme. Nevertheless these are not mere representations, but we really here live and walk as little universes, and carry both heaven and the world, consequently the kingdom of God in ourselves. The Supreme Deity, our Most Holy Father, is actually in our souls with His life; His Only-begotten, or our Love, is actually in the mind 3 itself which we inhabit. And that prince of the world is actually with his life in the animus, or in this lowest mind, but without disturbance, because he is bound and fettered by our Love, who like a doorkeeper possesses thy mind; consequently he is humble, officious, and civil; nor has he there any burning desire to touch our heaven, even with his little finger, because he dare not; in like manner, as thou seest, he is enjoined to make us acquainted with whatsoever befalls his little world, and to execute everything which we sanction and decree. Here thou seest, says she, the place of residence of those who first receive from the external senses all the images and modes of the visible world, and either bring them to our ears, or represent them to our sight; here again, is the residence of those who convey our commands by fibres to the muscles, and thus determine our decrees into acts. If thou art disposed to see the experiment, I will remove either the latter or the former, and thou wilt perceive the truth of the matter. We, in our sacristy, regard only ends, and arrange means, which, being next committed to the will, are delivered to that prince, that by his servants they may be brought forth into effects, so as to become uses designed by our heaven, that is, of our Love. The will itself, by itself, is nothing but an endeavor to act, from which nothing exists without the aid of ministries. But that animus or the prætor of our court, because he lies chained by our Love, lives under the necessity of obsequiously executing our decrees, for thus he sits bound to the rudder, and derives his life from our soul, or through it, from the Supreme; this also you may be convinced of by inspection alone. That he leads a life altogether different from ours, is evident from the power left to us, that we can will, and yet either bring things into act, or check them; also that we can keep watch, and remove ourselves from the animus and withdraw our whole mind from its delights and cupidities; for while we are intent, by the views of truth and of good, on preventing anything of the lumen issuing from its torches from overshadowing our light, so long we close those gates with bars.

71. But although this servant of ours, because he is chained, presents himself to us under so humane and peaceable a character, still he is the most outrageous enemy to our Love, and never can entirely discard his insown hatred. He is cunning, and has a genius adapted to fraud; nor does he desire and strive more for anything than to excite civil commotions among all his crew, and to pour them forth, when arranged under his standards, into the palaces of thy mind, so as to cast out us wisdoms from thy Olympus. The openings by which he can introduce himself are several, all of which I have already pointed out to thee; but as thou well knowest, there are only two ways of access to thy mind, namely, from above, and from beneath. The way from above is through the soul ^{p} and its sanctuary. This way is sacred, and to him altogether impervious, and indeed so narrow, that he cannot even insert his little finger through its windings, having a body so large and fat. This way is open only to the Lord of light, and to His Love. But the latter, or inferior way, is the only one through which the servant can creep and ascend; for this way is open, even from the gates of the senses to the lumen and modes of his world, consequently to images turned into

---

p Namely, where the soul is in its super-celestial form, consequently where it is in the beginnings of the operations of its body, concerning which above; for our animal kingdom is divided into three spheres, namely, into the sphere of principles, into the sphere of causes, and into the sphere of effects. The sphere of principles is in things supreme, where also are the beginnings of all fibres, and it comprehends in itself the soul, where it resides in its super-celestial form also the intellectual mind, and also the animus; for these being subordinate to each other act as principles of all the operations which exist in the inferior spheres. The sphere of causes is thence produced, the complex of which is the cerebrum, especially the medullary [portion], with the cerebellum, the medulla oblongata and spinalis; which therefore is separated and discriminated from the lowest sphere by bones and the vertebræ, as by walls. This last sphere, or the sphere of effects, is everything else which is properly called the body, with its organs, viscera, limbs, and muscles. The case is similar in the universe, in which also are given three spheres, namely, of principles, of causes, and of effects.

ideas, and also towards the walls, which are coated with muscles as with coats of mail, by or through which our ends burst forth into acts, and which are open into his world. But because he, by the ingenuity of his deceptions, knows how to employ every artifice, we have there prudently arranged our guards. Come along with me, says the wisdom, and recognize them; and then she led him to all the narrow gates and passages, and opened to his view all the shortest paths which could afford him admission; and at the same time she continued for a long time to discourse upon the artifices.

72. But we are in port and will no longer dwell on the enumeration of his tricks, which are infinite, and exceed all calculation. Nevertheless, the state of rule, which he induces on the subdued and vanquished mind, ought to be described. For when with delusive arts he has enticed to his side, or rather to his entanglements, the intelligences of the lowest sort of any mind, displaying before their eyes the badges and purple ensigns of his power, instantly the gates are opened by them, and his chains are removed; and immediately he arranges his genii under standards, and invades the court and sacristy with the torches and lamps of nature, expelling the intelligences and wisdoms inaugurated by our Love, which, because they are innocences, and thus gentle, and act only from love, betake themselves to flight, like doves at the sight of a kite, and entering into the sanctuary of their mother, as into a kind of asylum, they seal up the gate, and there see clearly all the disturbance which he excites; for from a superior station, as from a watchtower on a rock, all things which are taking place beneath are distinctly viewed, but not *vice versa.* I will however relate what has been told me: They say, that he imposes on the vanquished mind a similar state of government to that which he had intended to impose on heaven, and similar to the court which he holds in his own universe. For a subjugated mind he calls his Olympus or heaven, and as this is an effigy of the kingdom of our Love he is induced to believe that he has invaded and possessed heaven itself while he invades and possesses its type, and that in its place he holds the sceptre of the

whole; for he plays the same game in small things which he wished to play in great. Hence it may clearly appear, what would have been the state of the universe, if he had taken to himself the reins of government, for into this little heaven he altogether transcribes an effigy of himself. Hear therefore the order and the form which he 3 introduces; he absolutely procures to himself, in imitation of heavenly rule, intelligences and wisdoms, on each of which he impresses an image of himself; but which ought rather to be called insanities, as being born and produced from his truths, which are nothing but falsities and malignities. For he divides and compounds ideas themselves into whatsoever forms he pleases, inasmuch as forms derive all their nature from determination, and from nature their faculty and mode of acting. For every idea, however stupid, suffers itself to be adapted to, and, as it were, grafted into every form, as every color in every painting, or as every word in every division of a speech. From those insane intelligences, which live by lights and tapers, and dwell in dusky caverns, he forms that mind, and thus an image of himself; here he establishes his heaven, from which he governs all things below. But the rule of his government, such as 4 he keeps possession of in the world, as I said, he does not establish in that mind, where he resides as the governor of Olympus, but in the court itself, where are his genii with their affections, over whom he appoints a leader, whom he also calls animus; to these he grants all power of acting, according to their motions and instincts of nature. The animus itself he declares lord of the universe, and delivers up to it all the sceptres which he has obtained in his own world, and substitutes it in place of himself, while he proclaims himself among his own as a god; and moreover, he gives it the power of choosing whatsoever loves it pleases, and yet no others than what relate to the body and the world; hence arise so many phalanxes of loves, that, unless they are divided into genera and species, it is hardly possible to distinguish them from each other; for from the genii of that animus, which are now made, not servants and drudges, but princes of the world, there continually burst forth, as from a furnace, flames of cupidities. They also derive from their nature, that they have no taste for any other goodnesses than the harmonies and beauties of nature; nor for any other happinesses than the delights of the body and its senses; nor for any other desires than appetites and cupidities. They swear also by their deity, or by the conscience of their mind, that there are no such things as higher goodnesses and gratifications, which therefore they reject as phantoms or the dreams of Morpheus. The sycophant himself, residing in that Olympus, weaves also no other knots, or is employed about no other ends, than such as gratify that animus, and favor its genii; and by his wisdoms, as he calls them, he arranges all means, and does not subdue their lusts, or bind them to superior uses, as we do; but sets them on fire, giving reins to the will, that all things may rush headlong into act according to its blind impulses. He provides also, with the utmost solicitude and circumspection, lest anything from on high should insinuate itself, and bring with it any superior light, which he instantly extinguishes by means of his burning torches. For the most part also he joins prudence to wickedness, as I lately told thee, for by his well-planned deceptions he knows how to employ every artifice. The friends of that light he leads astray through many paths and labyrinthian windings, transforming himself also, like Vertumnus, into various and even heavenly images, and by specious representations eluding discovery, until he has transcribed them into his forms, and associated them with his intelligences; and in the meantime, by his genii, he inspires every sense of natural delights and the liberty of enjoying them. But what a liberty! While the mind is reduced under the yoke of slavery! For nothing can be truly called ours, but the intellectual mind and its will; hence we are named men, and are distinguished from the brutes: [It is necessary therefore that] this intellectual mind should draw its knowledges and forms of reasons from heaven and its light, and by the order above described should rule the animus, and by it call forth ideas from the world, and inoculate them when called forth with the shoots of the seeds of our love. For if it be governed

The Worship and Love of God

by slaves set at liberty, it is all over with the human principle and with ours, since in such case inferior things inflow into superior, and the whole order is inverted.

73. But still that villain does not lay aside fear, dreading every murmur and whisper. He attentively recognizes the guards set on both sides, for what alarms does not the consciousness of wickedness excite! Audacity is still restrained by fear, for a cold and lurid tremor always runs through the fibres, while he is struck with perpetual horror at the thought that the wisdoms of our Love have betaken themselves into the maternal sanctuary. Therefore he pricks up his ears with attention, in the hope that he may possibly perceive their discourses with their intelligences, for he well knows that they, although innocences, are still at the same time the highest intelligences and prudences, and that one truth proclaimed from their mouth disperses into the air a thousand of his fallacies, and that one spark of their light extinguishes a thousand of his lamps; wherefore he also instructs his nymphs by no means to lay open his machinations and plots, but constantly to make a pretence of being governed by our veriest loves, and never to appear in public, unless adorned with bright and heavenly clothing. Yet sometimes 2 the heavenly wisdoms privately rebuke the audacity of those intelligences, especially those that they know have revolted from their side and have suffered themselves to be transcribed into his forms; and they recall to their mind their former state from which they have fallen, and also their present and future condition. They then, it is said, are suffused with blushes, begin to be tormented, and to beat their bosoms through inward grief, and to suffer extreme pangs, and thus excite disturbances; and to turn the opening of their mind upwards, that something of lightning from heavenly light may burst in upon their companions, in consequence of which the terrified crew fly away to their dusky caves and dark hiding-places, not being able to endure the rays of that light. This also is said to be perceived in the court itself, for it penetrates like lightning into the cells, not through chinks, but through the gates

themselves, which stand open day and night; hence come deep and mournful sighs, which are called remorse of conscience. But that enemy, now calling together all his forces, and opening the treasures of his universal world, and not only setting his slaves at liberty, but also gratifying them with the hope of licentious freedom and dominion, assaults those intelligences which have excited the disturbance, and either casts them into exile, or secures them with chains. Thus all access to the sanctuary of the soul is closed up by strong bars; the gate also of the mind is thus fastened to the post, so that it cannot any longer be turned upwards. These things having been accomplished, he governs all things in greater security according to lust, and institutes votive sports and pastimes, especially of Apollo, in honor of the serpent Python; and adorns each nymph with laurel, the reward of victory, and creates queens, and calls them Olympiades and Heliconides; but each of the lower crew he calls his Parnassides, or also Aganippides, from that fountain, which the hoof of his victorious horse has burst open;[q] and thus he inflames all with new desires, and blinds all by his allurements.

74. But it is of concern to know what is the quality of their life, for they believe that they themselves lead a bright and super-celestial life, and that we lead an obscure life, much inferior to theirs; for

---

[q] The fables of the ancients concerning Pallas, the Muses, the fountain of Parnassus, the winged horse or Pegasus, with several other things, are mere significative representations of things similar to heavenly ones. The words [of the fables] become living representations, by which, as was shown above, they express at the same time several series of things. Thus the human understanding is figured by horses furnished with trappings, according to its various qualities; the sciences and intelligences by nymphs, and their supreme by a queen or Pallas; experiences by men, to whom those nymphs were married; and their leader by Apollo; clearness of intellect by waters, especially those of a fountain; and its obscurity, and various difficulties and disturbances thence arising, by turbulent waters; thoughts by birds of different genera, colors, and beauties, whence the Parnassides are so often said to be changed into birds, and *vice versa;* hence also they were denominated Pierides; not to mention several other cases of a similar kind, from which it is allowable to conclude that the fables of the ancients were mere representations derived from heaven; consequently that their minds were nearer to heaven than ours, which do not even know that such representations exist, still less that they signify such things.

from that vertigo they view all things inversely; wherefore I am not disposed to conceal, because it is worth relating, what I have heard and seen; for I was once associated in company with those heavenly wisdoms which occasionally traverse the whole globe that they may explore the disturbances and rebellious commotions which that tyrant continually foments and stirs up to act in his own world. Once in this company we met a herd of these intelligences, who walked in the market-place, clothed in bright and heavenly garments, strutting spiritedly about with arms akimbo, and who formerly had stood on the side of our Love, but afterwards suffered themselves to be enlisted into the number of stipendiaries of the other company; the celestials call them their friends, but we their sisters. When the Divine wisdoms saw at a distance those intelli- 2 gences, taking the shortest way to meet them, they approached with a friendly aspect, lest possibly they might run away, asking them, how it came to pass that they were so well dressed? They, at first sight casting their eyes to the ground, and blushing with shame, but afterwards recovering from their fear through their own audacity and the friendly question which was proposed, replied that they came from their sports, and indeed from the Apollinarian or Pythian ones, and at the same time assumed an appearance of cheerfulness, as if their minds (*animis*) were still delighted with those spectacles. But the heavenly wisdoms, who are not to be imposed upon by deceitful appearances, but look inwardly into the secret haunts of minds, having expressed their astonishment by a circular motion of the fore finger, exclaimed: O how dusky and funereal does your countenance appear! Where is the splendor of life, with which we not long ago saw you enlightened like so many stars? Whence comes that unlovely cloud and soot which now overspread your face? At 3 these words they were amazed, and looking at each other, they replied: Do you not observe how full of life our faces are? And with what a fire our eyes sparkle, and how our blood leaps from inmost joys? Why then are ye disposed to be jocose? Look also at our garments whiter than snow! But the heavenly wisdoms thus rejoined:

Ah, our friends, if you would contemplate yourselves with the gaze of our eyes, as we entreat you to do, ye would see yourselves altogether otherwise! Allow us then only to engage a moment of your time, that we may talk together familiarly as we used to do. We are aware that ye are fully persuaded that ye not only enjoy life, but even the supreme, and the heavenly life itself. That love, of which ye are images, produces also this belief, for it induces that *glaucoma**
4 upon your sight. But because ye are persuaded that ye are intelligences, ye cannot possibly be ignorant that life is two-fold, heavenly and natural; and that each is life, because each is spiritual; nor can ye be ignorant that this prior or heavenly life flows straight into our minds from no other source than heaven. The other life indeed is also from heaven, but not directly, coming through another channel, thus mediately, as also into the animi of wild beasts. Since now the door of your minds opens not into heaven, but only into the world; or since the hinge of that door is so fastened to the post that the mind can only look downwards; and since there is not even the smallest chink, through which a passage may be given for the entrance of heavenly light, whence then is your life? Or, through what gate do you admit the rays of your life? Ye will say perhaps, through that common way, or through the ear and eye. But whence then comes so dark a shade as to heavenly things? And whence come the shudderings and waverings between two opinions at the mere mention of superior life? Whence is your faith so unsteady, and, if ye consult the inmost principles of your lives, so null, respecting our Love, his Heaven, respecting a future state of the soul, and its eternity? All these things would be as pellucid as the clearest gem,
5 if the other door stood unlocked. Since therefore those things which are most essential of all, lie buried in so dark a shade of ignorance, and in so intense cold, from what fountain then do ye derive the streams of your life? Must it not be from that in which there is more of shade than of light, more of cold than of heat, that is, more

---

* A disorder of the eye, producing dimness of sight. (TR.)

of death than of life? Confess now, for ye are capable of feeling, whether this can be called living. Recall to your minds, although 6 perhaps ye have rejected all belief in such things, that it has been so ordained by our Supreme, that the Life of heaven ought to inflow into the nature of the world, by means of His only Love, which is with Him in inmost and supreme principles, so that not only light, but also spiritual heat, may excite the lives of our minds, and thus of our bodies. It is also known that another fountain of life was also made by our Supreme, whereby the life of our Love, with its universal heaven, might inflow into the nature of the world, and thus celestial things might be conjoined with terrestrial. This inferior 7 fountain of life was made a bond, or means of spiritual connection, to the intent, not only that all things might be held together, but also that they might proceed and return in their order from highest things to lowest, and from lowest to highest; without it, it would be impossible for our bodies to live in conjunction with their minds, for our animus is the bond of their union. When now that bond was rent, or the spiritual connection was broken between our Love and the fountain of that life, or the prince of the world, what life then remains? Is it not that which emanates from him [the prince of the world] alone? For it is known that there is no life without love and that the life is such as the love is. When now no life is any longer derived from the Love of heaven, tell me, in such case, what life do you lead? Does it not resemble death rather than life? But 8 attend a little further; possibly ye reject these things till to-morrow, that ye may involve the above brightness in shades; for I see clearly, that these things do not penetrate the soot of your minds, which we contemplate as covered over with pitch; that blackness itself devours and absorbs the rays of this light, and hides them in its black pores and crypts, so that not the least ray of light thence reflected appears. Let us pass therefore to those things which enter from beneath, through those large gates, into the inferior region of your minds. Tell me what is life? Is it not to understand what is 9 true, and to be wise in what is good? What then are your goodnesses, by which ye procure to yourselves the power of being wise, and finally of understanding, or *vice versa*. Are they not mere hallucinations of the senses, which apperceive all their objects most obscurely, and not even one part of the many myriads of those things which are contained in nature herself? [r] These most dark objects also your animus introduces as ideas into the minds, in which the prince of that world resides, as in his Olympus, and disposes and arranges those ideas according to the desires and pleasures of the animus and of its genii; hence are formed, and, as it were, begotten truths, which are your parents, O my intelligences; and when no Light from above, or from heaven, is admitted into these forms, tell me what understanding of truth, and will of good, in such case is thence born, or what truths and goodnesses thence arise? Can they be any other than mere fallacies and vanities? I will return therefore now to the subject with which I began; if the life of our mind be the understanding of truth and the wisdom of good, what vein of life in such case is in the intelligence of what is false, and in the wisdom of what is vain? Must it not be something contrary to the very life of heaven? Tell me now by what title, or by what name ye can mark this contrary something? Will any other title or name suit it than that which is called shadow, and a species of death? But still I see clearly, that not even this truth penetrates deeply, for the prince of

---

r That the discernment of our external senses is so obtuse as not to apperceive even a single part of the many myriads of things contained in nature, may appear clearly from the phenomena of sight, which yet is more acute than the rest of the senses; for the naked eye, unarmed with glasses, sometimes views a heap of living insects as some least visual point, or a kind of shadow; yet by the aid of optical glasses it is discovered that they are innumerable living animalculæ; and by the aid of still finer glasses, they are each of them seen to be furnished not only with members and limbs, but also with muscles, viscera, organs of the senses, eyes, brains, marrows, etc., most distinct. If glasses of a still minuter scope could be applied, new wonderful forms would be further discovered in each part before invisible; and hence it may be manifest how obtuse is the sense of our sight; but that the hearing, and especially the touch is still more obtuse, may be confirmed by innumerable things. Wherefore the light of the senses is so obscure and indistinct, that it may be rather likened to shade; yet from this spring ideas, and from ideas are formed truths, and from these finally understanding.

The Worship and Love of God

your court or the animus instantly involves these things in his shades and folds them up, when he has so involved them, in the smoke of his coals, into divers forms, in consequence of which no other medium and refuge remains for the confirmation of what we have said, and for the sealing of your faith, than that ye contemplate yourselves in mirrors, and thus by a light reflected into your eyes; for we carry along with us little mirrors, by virtue whereof, when applied to the sight, ye may be able to view, not your bodies, but your minds themselves in their own effigy, or according to the quality in which ye appear to the life to us, who are heavenly wisdoms. Having applied therefore those mirrors, they said, Look now, 11 and direct your eyes to all parts, and see now what is your quality, whether ye be Venuses or Pallases, and what is the quality of your bright polish, and of your heavenly dyes. Instantly they seemed to themselves like chimney-sweeps, or as a crew which stands continually at furnaces burning with sulphur, altogether like lamps covered over with black rust, and no longer as intelligences, but as insanities and madnesses; and unless they had moved their limbs, as in perpetual agony, you would say, they were not the effigies of life, but of death. They indeed attempted to remove their sight from that heavenly mirror, but still the image remained deeply impressed on their minds (*animis*). But, said the wisdoms, we will also accomplish this effect, that your animus with its genii shall delight you. Instantly they vibrated the light of their mirror, and at the same time opened the gates, that that disorderly crowd, after their accustomed manner, might rush in, with their torches, into the chambers of their minds, saying, Enjoy also this spectacle. And instantly all the genii appeared to them as snakes twining and hissing around their heads, and pouring their poison into the veins of their bodies, through ways opened by biting;[s] and they seemed to themselves to be so

---

[s] That the causes of all diseases, or affections of the body, flow originally from the diseases or passions of the animus, while, by inverted order, it rushes-in into the rational

many Gorgon faces. Being terrified, they wished to run away, but the motion of their bodies made those infernal locks to beat upon their bosoms and faces. Hence they became, as it were, congealed, and the frigid blood ceased to flow. Then said the wisdoms: Behold now your loves and your ardors! Believe us when we assure you, that your spiritual life, which awaits you, will be altogether like this, with infinite variety. For the activities of minds separate from the body exist, not like those of bodies by actions, through the medium of muscles and thus of flesh and bones, but by actual representations of their states, or by mere similar actualities represented to the life. Come now, and perceive with your eyes, consequently with your senses, in which ye have so much confidence, that ye carry about you the fatal images, not of life, but of death; for in proportion to the number of snakes, is the number of fires, and at length of the furies of your spiritual life, in consequence of which, pestiferous spumes are even communicated to the blood, while ye live here, and are so many causes productive of death. Begone, now, O beautiful flowers! together with that venom so sweet, which ye conceal in your fibres.

75. These furies, whom I can no longer call intelligences, escaped by devious and shady paths to their own hovels, but I am sure they could not escape from themselves. Learn hence what is the

---

mind, when the government is delivered up to the prince of the world, appears sufficiently clear from the animus being effigied in the countenance, in the eyes, in the actions, gestures, speech, respiration, etc.; but especially from its continual influx into the fluids of our fibres and vessels; concerning which influx, let us be instructed here from only one of its affections, viz., from anger which is also called wrath (*excandescentia*). For while a free course is opened to that affection, so that it can pour itself forth into the body, it instantly manifests itself by an ungovernable heat and fire. Since the blood burns, bursting forth into the smallest vessels from the great ones; the viscera are heated even to the marrow; the membranes are inflamed, the respiration is exasperated, the tone of the voice is harsh, the arteries swell, the senses are disturbed, the external as well as the internal; the grosser juices also are forcibly extracted from their places, and are injected as ferments into the humors. For instance, the black bile from its receptacle, the fæces, *ramenta,* and hard parts of which, as so many stimuli, together with the feverish heat, tend to harden the softer

quality of the state which is introduced by inverted order, while that charioteer of the world directs human minds by his reins, and drives them like horses foaming at the mouth, into such a variety of downward courses. In such case, since the world and heaven are confounded, since light is converted into shade, heat into cold, and all things are so turned upside down, that those which ought to look upwards look downwards; not unlike the trunk of a body without a head, which is beaten and bruised, inverted to the earth, with the feet and its well-shod and unwashed soles lifted up on high. I have been told by the heavenly wisdoms, that those minds in their bodies are also represented upside down in heaven, for the heavenly sphere, which human minds inhabit, and which belongs to the Grand Prince of heaven, with His wisdoms, loves, and concords, is invaded, and is ruled by the prince of the world, with his insanities, hatreds, and discords, to whom the sphere proximately inferior or natural, has been granted by our Supreme. Thus, where order is inverted, inferior things mix themselves with superior, or natural things with heavenly; hence comes ignorance of all things; truths betake themselves to flight and are to be investigated through infinite windings, and through the courses and clefts of several sciences, but still to no purpose; and although they are investigated, yet, not only is all their splendor wiped away and decayed, but in

---

blood and cause it to boil and burn; not only the precordia palpitate, but also the arteries; yea, fever itself, with its frenzy, represents itself in a kind of image so that there is not a single part of the body, even the smallest, which is void of anger and heat. Such is the correspondence of the animus and the body, and of the affections or passions of each; wherefore if we are disposed to investigate the very origin of the diseases of the body, we must recur to the animus itself, or the prince of the world, who rules the animus. Tell me, I pray, of a single disease, which does not spring from intemperance and the predominance of the animus, either in the parent or in the heir, and thou shalt appear as a great Apollo to me. Nor are even those diseases to be excepted which exist from fortuitous accidents, for those accidents would have been avoided, if men had not been under the power of that prince. Hence it is clear, that there are as many diseases of the body as there are lusts or cupidities of the animus set at liberty, also as many as there are mixtures of affections, as is clearly evident from fevers and all species of fevers, and other [disorders], as from

addition, they themselves are overspread with Cimmerian dark-
2 ness; thus a two-fold image of night succeeds. For which reason
the schools of those sciences are called sports; for the more they are
sported with, the more clouds are induced, or the more dense becomes
the darkness, insomuch that the light sparkling from heaven itself
is extinguished at the very threshold: yea, heaven itself is covered
with so terrible and thick darkness that it is unknown, not only
what heaven is, but also what the soul is, what the rational mind,
and what the animus; whether they are distinct from each other,
especially whether they disagree; how far human minds (*mens*) differ
from the minds (*animi*) of brutes: also whether life be anything else
than nature. For intelligence appears to them as madness, wisdom
as a spectre: gold is turned into dust, and a diamond into mud.
But so far is that deluder from loving the mind which is enslaved
to him, that he infects it with his venom, rends it in pieces by
hatred, and thus consigns it to his styx. For whatsoever he does, he
does from hatred against our Love, and still he continually makes
a show of heaven. Therefore, according to attempts commenced
from the beginning, and in which he is ever urgent, by his hostil-
ity he perpetually invades and subdues those minds which should
be the bonds of things heavenly and earthly, and by which alone
ways are open in a straight direction from things highest to things

---

burning or caustic, nervous, slow, wasting, malignant, intermittent fevers, from diseases of
insanity, of melancholy, hypochondria, etc. To consider only the deliriums of fevers, in
which the patients have a perverse sensation and perception of all things, dreaming as if they
were awake, and seeing things not seen, hearing things not spoken, acting from no cause
as from a cause, gathering feathers and locks as if they were present, separating wool, dreading their friends as furies, viewing children as giants, and all things which present them-
-selves as spectres, etc., etc. In a word, all the affections of the animus form types of
themselves in the diseases of the body. It would have been altogether otherwise if the animus had been kept bound, and under the rule of the mind, that is, of the Love of heaven.
The cause therefore of death ought to be judged of from the causes of diseases, for as many
as are the causes of diseases, so many are the causes of the destruction of the life of the
body. Hence it appears how that enemy, who presents himself to us under so friendly an
aspect, infects with poison the whole body, as well as the mind, and by discords bursts all
its connections.

The Worship and Love of God

lowest, and from these again to things highest. Hence by this way he constantly presses his ancient attempt; but in those minds, the gate leading to the inmost of heaven is shut, and secured by strong bolts, lest that inmost also should be invaded.

76. That so many innumerable loves, as they are called, could spring out of the rending of one, is clear from the snakes which those Medusean heads carried; for every one represents one torch of life, or one lust, consequently one love. When one also is cut off another springs in its place; and according to the number of the drops of their blood, which is poison, are the seeds of new ones. Nevertheless that they are not loves but so many hatreds and disagreements, may be manifest from their discord in every subdued mind, for they not only wage destructive war with each other, and multiply slaughter, but also, among all such minds, there reign perpetual frenzies, injuries, and subversions, since they are at continual strife with each other, or murdering each other by abuse; and if the laws of order did not restrain them, they would so terrify each other by their bitter and wicked warfare as to exceed all [ordinary] hostile fury. The prince of the world himself attends the combat, excites the minds (*animi*) of the combatants, and thus arms his clients with the torches of furies for destruction; he stands at their side, and gives his orders for the funerals and funeral pile of each fallen foe, that all the crowd may still engage in deadly warfare without intermission. These are the sports of his loves; these are his delights and purple pomps. In proportion to the severity of the conflict, and the implacability of anger, that maker of mischief opens his jaws wider, and bursts with laughter: nevertheless he is most indignant if every one does not venerate these his Erichthons as loves.

77. These most deceitful loves, although they are infinite in number, have still only two leaders set over them, one of which is called the love of self, but the other the love of the world, whom the prince himself calls his nobles. To these however are subjected several leaders of less power, satraps, chiefs of plebeians, centurions, with innumerable lictors, altogether according to his idea of the

great empire in the universe whose form of government he every-where induces. The empires of their nobles, inasmuch as they are extensive, are distributed into kingdoms, principalities, provinces, and dominions of various kinds, every one of which still resembles some effigy of the world, or the universe, the limits of whose sphere are more extended or contracted according to the proximity exist-ing between it and its chief. Thus there exist superior and inferior

2 loves of this nature. Every mind constructs in effigy and, as it were, builds some orb and world, in like manner as the Supreme Mind, in which it performs all the courses of its life, for it takes a view of ends, and procures to itself from nature the means by which those ends may attain effect. This great world also is nothing else but a complex of means, that the ends and decrees of the Supreme may be brought into acts and uses. These mimic worlds constructed by minds, run similarly through their seasons, like those of the year and of the day. The former they call the *fates of their life,* for they emulate the spring, the summer, the autumn, and close in winter. But the latter they call their *fortunes* with reference also to their mornings, noons, evenings, and nights, and are in a perpetual vicis-situde. But the storms, and the serenity which succeeds when the clouds are dispersed, they call the *fluctuations of fortune,* and ascribe

3 to *chance.* They are altogether ignorant that those vicissitudes may be so tempered, as to produce in the mind a continual spring, or a perpetual flower of age; for the sources of their fates and of their fortunes appear to them so complex, that they may be compared to a mass of earth-worms, which, when heaped together, either hide their heads in the ground or enfold them in the heap. For they are altogether ignorant that the universe, consisting of infinite universes with all those little worlds and orbs of minds, stands under the auspices of one Deity or of our Supreme, and of His Love, and is constantly governed by His Providence. They assign indeed the government of the universe to some Supreme; but the care of particular things they know not how to submit to any Deity; therefore they adjudge it partly to their own providence, which they

call prudence, partly to fortune. For they are not aware that Divine Providence cannot be universal unless it be in the most particular things, and that from these latter things it alone derives the name of universal; or that what is universal derives its essence and actuality solely from the singular things from which it exists. Wherefore when they affirm the one, and deny the other, they destroy both; and that they may thus destroy both, all their loves persuade them, because their prince suggests it; to the intent that their minds may be led to believe that all things are either afloat under the impulse of a blind fate, or are carried on by an irresistible fatality without any respite. So he stops up every passage to happiness and delight; for he knows well that nothing exists fortuitously and by chance.

78. But I see clearly, that thy mind is solicitous, and that thou art wondering, why our Supreme, Who both knows the least particulars of things, and rules them by His Providence, and who alone has Omnipotence, has suffered this tyrant so direfully and cruelly to depopulate His world, or human minds and thus to induce in the universal orb so execrable a state, or to behold, with Omniscient eyes, the ruin of His heaven. But if thou wilt listen a little longer to my discourse, thou shalt hear things stupendous and heretofore unheard. Our Omnipotent one could destroy the universe, with all its universes, by a single nod of His will, and thus thrust down headlong that tyrant himself, with the minds subjected to him, into Tartarus and Orcus, where the images of that night and shade, together with the furies, perpetually reign. This also He ordained, because His justice itself persuaded and excited Him to it; for if He should recede from His justice, He would recede from Himself. Wherefore also He burned with the zeal of the justest anger, and armed Himself with His lightnings, that He might thunder not only upon the tyrant himself, but also upon that universal society. But hear now, while He stood in the very act of striking with His 2 lightning—wonderful to relate!—our Love, His Only-begotten, cast Himself headlong into the midst of that rage, or among the very furies of the devil, where the stroke of the lightning fell, and

embracing with His arms those human minds, suffered Himself to be almost torn in pieces and destroyed by that mad infernal dog. At sight of this our Supreme laid aside His lightnings, lest at the same time He should devote His Only-begotten to His most just anger, and when He entreated Him in vain to depart, the Only-begotten, burning with the fire of Love, refused, entreating that He would spare those ignorant and guiltless beings, or destroy Himself with them, saying, that He was willing to take upon Him the blame of the guilty, and to suffer the penalties of justice; adding to His supplication, that He might not be left alone in the world. On this occasion the Most Holy Parent was so affected that He not only abated the flame of His justice, but, before He departed, was compelled, out of Love, to promise, that for His sake alone He would indulge that world so long, until it had run through its ages, and being worn out of itself, should fall into its winter and night, like its mortal inhabitants; and at the same time He gave power to our Love, of binding and loosing, at pleasure, that tyrant, His enemy. Hence his power has been so diminished, that he who before had ruled over royal territories was now kept shut up within narrow boundaries. Hence also those mortals, from the union of their infants with our Love, derived a life naturally mixed with death.

79. On hearing these things our first-born, being at first astonished at the great danger to which the universe was exposed, was, as it were, struck dumb; but presently being melted by so stupendous an instance of Love, a secret delight was communicated to his inmost marrows, and therefore sinking into the bosom of his wisdom, he remained there a long time dissolved in tears, being made thoroughly sensible in himself of what true Love is, and what is its essence; but after he had fed with tears of joy on that very tender affection bursting forth from Love, reclining on his wisdom, he earnestly entreated her to retrace her footsteps a little to the point from whence she had digressed, and to explain to him in what manner a full opportunity might be given him of enjoying this his Love. He said that now he perceived that he had no

other desire than that he might become not his own, but His, and that this desire, in consequence of the contrariety and opposition of loves apperceived by him, had manifestly exalted itself to the highest degree; for in proportion as he dreaded the one, in the same proportion he now loved more the other, and, as it were, would die to possess it. It occurred also to his recollection (*animum*) what she had before told him, that the life which he lived inflowed from without; and this not only from the Supreme, the Fountain of all lives, into the soul, which is the power of all powers of his kingdom, and from the Supreme Love, or His Only-begotten, into his mind, but also from his enemy into his animus;[t] and that she pointed out his cave, and himself there, and thus lying proximately beneath his feet, at the doors of the palace.[u] Yet he rejoiced that he saw him bound hand and foot, and that he durst not touch the gate, unless he was ordered; nevertheless he dreaded to look in that direction, and therefore kept his sight turned another way.

To these remarks his wisdom replied, "I will explain what thou requirest; from the observations which I have above dropped into thy ear, I find that thou art now sufficiently convinced, that our powers, in order that they may live, must be excited by influent forces; also that no life is derivable, except from a common spiritual Fountain; consequently heavenly life from the love of the Supreme, but natural life from the prince of the world, who was made a fountain mediating and joining the life of nature. And since the natural soul is delivered over to him, all they who live his life, without the Love of heaven, live a natural life, which is appointed to death; consequently they who worship nature as their supreme deity, adore, by that worship, this most offensive enemy of heaven. But that this his very cave is in human minds *(animis)*, to the end that

---

[t] That everything in the animal body is excited to operation by an extrinsic influx, or that our organic forms are nothing but powers accommodated to forces which act into them by their influx, see above, article 58 and note *y* there.

[u] On this cf. also above, no. 70.

in like manner he may connect the nature of our corporeal world with celestial life, he himself indeed conceals, in order that he may more securely play his pranks in the shade of the understanding, or in its ignorance of his nearness and presence; and while keeping close watch at the doors of minds, may disperse all fears of himself. Yet this delights him, that some people, as it were, point at him, but yet do not touch him, namely, they who deny that he exists, but still substitute in his place their own animus, with its lusts and criminal inclinations. Nor is it apperceived that he resides in the animus itself, except by those who oppose him, and steer their course against his inverted order, and thus, as it were, spread their sails against the tempest. For they who are carried down the stream, are ignorant [of the moving force] of the torrent, but it is otherwise with those who strive against the current; these are sensible of its resistances, and if they attend diligently, they hear its manifest murmurs. For he excites perpetual combats, and presents a thousand delectations and fascinations, or a thousand thorns and miseries; and either swallows the very bones cast into his jaws, or throws them back again besmeared, as it were, with foam. These [who resist], I say, apperceive that he does not stand outside, and that at every turn of thought he injects into minds ideas proper to the animus. For he is the keeper of the ideas themselves, which, having their birth from the modes and images of the senses, are called material or imaginative. From this they also clearly conclude, that the human principle is divided, or that man is partitioned into superior and inferior, or into interior and exterior; for they are made very sensible that something is dictated from heaven, and is contradicted by nature. Hence it is plain, that every one, howsoever distinguished by integrity of life, carries this (subtle enemy) along with himself, wheresoever he goes, since he inhabits and constitutes that very sphere of life where our animus acts, together with its genii.

80. There are therefore three fountains of life, which excite and actuate our three powers by their influx, as the light excites and actuates the organ of our vision. For that which gives and acts is called

active force, but that which receives and is passive, is called power. From active force alone without power, as from power alone without active force, no effect results, consequently no use; but active forces adjoined to their passives, or principles to their organic or instrumental forms, or associated by influx, produce efficient causes, whence come effects. From this very union result the sensation of our goodnesses, namely, that we feel it in ourselves; because He who is the fountain of life, feels it in Himself, and from us by reaction; since whatsoever inflows from the agent into his compeer and passive companion is performed also in the latter, because in the former. This is altogether according to the essence of Love itself, which is the veriest affection of the union of the forces of each nature, or of the agents and their passive subjects; which Love, when it is ardent, desires nothing more vehemently, or seeks more intently, than such a connection of its nature, namely, that it may be another's not its own, and conceiving that only to be its own which is reflected from another into itself. Such a unity, and at the same time mutuality, are presented to view by the close embraces and sweet cordialities of two lovers; for by the ardor with which they press each other, they so burn and labor to be mutually conjoined, that when such conjunction is entirely accomplished, they lead one life, although distinguished into two. From all this now, added she, you may conclude how full an opportunity is given us of enjoying our Love. Since now such is the connection and conjunction of the influent forces with our powers, the former conclusion is again confirmed, that it is the life of our Love which we live, and that the life is of such a quality as the love is.

81. But the first-born, still trembling as with fear, continually lifted up his countenance to heaven, that he might turn away his eyes from the couch where that enemy was said to lie. On observing this the wisdom looking at him, said: Why is thy mind filled with solicitude, and why dost thou avert thy sight from Paradise? Lay aside all apprehension, because there is no reason why thou shouldest be terrified; if it please thee, thou thyself shalt see clearly how

humble, subject, and tractable he is, as long as this sacred hearth diffuses such glad flames, and by them a sign is given that our Love resides in the throne of this Olympus. For in such case the enemy lies prostrate on the ground, and as a most obsequious servant, is eager to obey His commands and wishes, consequently to perform all the offices of our life. He indeed is wont to change himself into a variety of forms, amounting in number to more than three or four hundred, as for example, at one time into a dreadful dragon, at another into a wolf and a large dog, at another into a panther and a bear, also into flame, and the like; nevertheless under every ferocious appearance which he assumes, he is not able to hurt even

2 our little finger, still less to inflict a wound. Let us prove it! says she; and instantly she dragged him, despite resistance, out of his cave, whilst he struggled to re-enter it, and she commanded this sentinel or enemy, to show himself transformed into his monsters, one after another. And when she saw him turned into a dreadful dog with a frightful countenance, the wisdom rubbed his ribs, and thrust her whole hand into his immense jaws, and taking him by the tongue, led him at her will, putting a collar also about his neck; and encouraging the first-born to come near with an undaunted mind, she presently compelled him, and also thrust his arm into the jaw, and even his head, and took it out unhurt. The Cerberus indeed swelled with gall and burned with desire to give a deadly bite, but his jaws were so restrained that he could not attempt anything. Afterwards she ordered him to assume the form of a lion, and then the wisdom stroked his mane, and played with his teeth and claws, applying them to her cheeks; she also gave command that he should hug the first-born with his shoulders and fore-feet, and let him go

3 again. Hence the first-born becoming fearless, in like manner as his wisdom, touched and counted his claws and teeth. But when he was changed from this monster into a dragon, the first-born, at his wisdom's command crept over his fore-feet and shoulders even to the top of his head, and with his crests, scaly spires, and foldings, covered like a helmet his forehead and his temples; not to mention

several other sports which he played with him. Being changed also into flame, it was so mild, that it did not even singe the smallest hair or the fibre of a cuticle. When all this was done, Thou seest now, says she, that he is not so horrible and formidable, so long as our Love governs his Olympus in us, for it is left to His power, as thou hast heard, to bind him at pleasure with chains, or to let him loose; nevertheless the dog cherishes a deadly wound, and burns not only with hatred, but now also with revenge; but at this time he is tortured and rent asunder, by his own sharp and virulent bile.

82. When the first-born recalled these threats, and, as it were, perils of the wild beasts, he could not help feeling a slight horror creeping through the fibres under his skin; especially at the idea that his wisdom had thrust his head into the throat of so fierce a monster, and that the dog Cerberus, at the very moment, had become so furious, that all his veins appeared swollen with black gall. Therefore he asked his wisdom, whether she really exposed him at that time to any great danger? If perchance, said he, at that moment, the fierce brute had closed his jaws, armed with so many rows of teeth, would it not have been all over with my life? For I do not well comprehend, said he, how such a powerful endeavor could have failed to act. To this the wisdom replied, There are, as thou knowest, three fountains of life by which our three powers are excited. To the intent that all things may proceed rightly according to instituted order, the life of one fountain must flow into another, or a superior one into an inferior, and so forth. For the Supreme never passes into the lower, except by its intermediates, which are, as it were, the ladders and steps by which descent is effected from heaven into nature, and ascent from nature into heaven. Conse- 2 quently our Love, with His celestial life, never passes into our nature except by that mediating life; for which end this spiritual fountain so frequently spoken of above, was made, and a natural soul given to it, into which both the life of heaven and the nature of the world can be introduced, and thereby each, as with a bridge between, can be connected and held together. But because that connection was

broken, and that bridge, as it were, carried away, our Love, as thou hast heard, cast Himself headlong into the midst of the furies, that He might claim human minds for heaven; wherefore also power was given Him by the Supreme to restrain and rule that enemy at pleasure. The same thing is also now and perpetually being done. For our Love, with the life of heaven, casts himself into that life of his, which is natural and appointed to death, and thus actually tames and subdues the very soul of that (lower) life, from which all its endeavors burst forth into act, consequently tames and subdues it wholly from inmost principles, so that not the least of fury can pour forth according to its violence and ardor. Hence all its endeavors are checked, and its insanities restrained, and at the same time this lower life is driven by a superior or interior Divine force to all its duties, to the performance of which it was bound from the beginning. By this method that connection is restored, and minds are claimed for heaven, so that our Love flows in with heavenly life into the universal nature of our body. By this Divine benefaction this enemy's soul is subdued, and thus his very head is bruised; and the trunk of his body, together with the other foes similarly affected, that is, his genii, is subjected as a footstool to the feet of our Love, who resides and reigns on the throne of His Olympus. In a similar effigy our Love is represented in the Olympus of our minds, when the animus is subjected, for we carry in ourselves an effigy of the whole heaven.

83. I will now also describe the services that this lower life performs. That he is serviceable as a spiritual copula between the heaven of our mind, and the world or nature of the body, I know is sufficiently manifest to thee from the discourses which we have already had on that subject. For he presides over all the fibres which are let down from us into the members and organs of the whole body; they are his reins, by which he rules this our world, and its nature: consequently also he presides over the spirit of the fibres, and likewise the blood. He therefore it is who receives with hospitality all the images and modes which creep to our Olympus from

this universal world, through the sensory organs, according to the fibres, and who, according to our decision, gives them their places, and arranges them into order; hence his operation and activity is called the imagination, and to this our pure thought corresponds, and presides over it. Therefore from this lower life result, and by him are related to us, all those delectations which are insinuated from this world through the doors of the senses, and are hatched by the force of his imagination. Hence it follows that all cupidities belong to it, likewise all appetites, which from their origin are called natural and corporeal; from these result various affections, motions, and passions, which are said to be of the animus; for they are so many changes of the state of the life of his loves, or cupidities. According to the nature of these latter, he transforms himself into those horrible forms which thou hast just now seen, for all spiritual essences, not clothed with a heavy body, actually represent their states by similar variations of form. Moreover also by subordinate fibres he determines into action, and executes our decrees.

84. But while he still lies prostrate at the feet of our Love, let us pursue further the account of his duties. For there are three spheres of our body, namely, the sphere of principles, of causes, and of effects. The Supreme with our Love governs the principles of our life; but the animus the principles of nature; and whereas it presides over the fibres, it presides over causes, consequently over the sphere of effects; wherefore it transcribes all things, which are intended in the supreme sphere as ends, and are commanded as decrees, into the world or nature of our body, where those ends, like so many souls, put on a kind of corporeal shape, and pour themselves forth into effects, or sensible acts; for the spiritual life of our mind consists in the intuition of ends, which intuition is introduced into our actions. Wherefore action is regarded from its end, but not from its motion or form of countenance; this latter is put on, while that life, by the mediation of the animus, is brought down through the sphere of causes into the sphere of effects. Such a correspondence also, and actual established harmony by influx,

exists between things spiritual and corporeal, or between things heavenly and natural, consequently between those things which are of the mind, and those things which are of the body; so that the one resembles the other as an idea, a type, and thus they afford mutual aid, and in turn assist each other. And that this correspondence may survive, the reins must be delivered up to our Love, who compels the bridled enemy to all his duties; and thus superior things inflow rightly into inferior, and effects are presented in which are the uses, 2 which answer to the ends. When therefore the life is derived from heaven, and the ends as uses are emitted into the gyre of nature, or into the body, then the most perfect acts exist therefrom; for they derive their inmost essence, consequently their form, from heaven itself. Then those goodnesses, of which thou hast an inmost perception, while they pass into nature, are expanded into so many pleasures; the forms themselves of goodnesses are turned into such beauties that they may be said to descend from heaven; the sacred fire of Love becomes torches heated with pure delights; yea, what is inmost in these gratifications so diffuses itself through the fibres that it is perceived by the very senses. The cupidities and desires of the animus which were made to be the cherishers and incitements of corporeal life then become innocent and promote their native uses and advantages. Consequently they do not break the connections but strengthen them; for they kindle the desires of our will with a gentle flame, and fill them with delight; since our Love is in nothing more interested and more earnest than in His intention, that while we enjoy the happiness of His heaven, we may also enjoy the delights of the whole world, since the world was created by the Supreme for the sake of heaven. Thou hast heard above, that our minds resemble a celestial paradise; so also our bodies resemble a terrestrial one. For, as was said, so long as that enemy lies subjugated in the animus by our Love, all things come to effect according to the order induced by the Supreme; and in every effect there is its genuine life and soul. But it is otherwise if the reins be delivered to the enemy, for then all things rush into contrariety; and all the effects, or acts, which come forth, are like their ends, that is, their souls, secluded from the life of heaven, and devoted to death.

85. Let us now, if you please, direct the course of our conversation to the very goal itself, for now it is within our view, namely, *how full opportunity may be given of enjoying our Love, and this forever.* All my discourse, scattered as it appears above, is aimed solely at this point, for this is the hinge on which everything turns, or the veriest essential, which ought to determine and construct all the forms of our life, and the only centre to which the circumferences of those forms converge; for to enjoy our Love is the veriest life itself; what is everything else but flying feathers, trifles, and dung! For into us He has transcribed Himself and His universal heaven, in like manner also the world, and even hell; and He has given us, as it were, the option of choosing the one or the other. But in what manner mortals, while they tend towards this goal itself, direct their course through devious and dark roads, sometimes backwards and sometimes forwards, I have seen with mine own eyes, while as a companion to heavenly wisdoms, I have taken a view also of the terrestrial orb; for they everywhere institute and celebrate sacred festivals in honor of the Supreme, or the Deity, but with infinite variety. Most frequently they set up a kind of goal elevated into the form of a pyramid or obelisk, but the plain itself, where the races, whether in chariots or on horses, or on foot, are to be performed, are cut into several paths. Some form these paths into winding labyrinths, and when the sound of the trumpet is given by the crier, the crowd, while they set out from the goal, and direct their course through those paths, for the most part lose their way, and when they think that they are going in a right line, and have even reached the goal, they apperceive that they have wandered entirely from that point. Some also with their eyes blinded, rushed on, chained together in a long row, over whom were set leaders, bearing in their hands immense maps and charts, in which the windings of the paths were marked by guide-posts and indices. The leaders themselves, with their eyes wide open, appeared like lynxes, but

they who were blinded by the love of self and of the world, seemed to us like those who labor under a disorder called by them a *gutta serena,* or *amaurosis,** and some of them appeared blear-eyed, looking 3 askew. A troop of lictors followed the crowd, to compel by whips and scourges those who had escaped from the ranks to return to the appointed order. There were some also who, having run over the whole length of the course, seemed to have the goal in sight, when first appeared in the interval, a deep whirlpool broken up from the jaws of the mountains. From its other bank was seen this column itself of the goal with its decorations and rewards. So they apperceived at length with regret that they had to return the whole of their way, in order that they might get into the right path, which, by reason of its narrowness, had not been seen, but passed by. But some, instead of directing their course to the goal, saw themselves introduced by the deluder of the human race and his ministers, into proud edifices and aërial palaces, where their senses were fascinated by all kinds of fallacious delights and delusive objects, not aware that these were called the sabbaths of that enemy. It was otherwise with others, yet frequently by roundabout paths, shady scenery, or valleys, they found themselves being led away into errors; but they were late in detecting this, if indeed they found it out at all.

86. But whereas the evening is now approaching, let us pause awhile, and resume the thread of this discourse some other day. For it is not the same as with thee and with us. We are not in the race; we are in the inmost goal, and there we enjoy ourselves. We possess and enjoy our Love. In proportion to the number of thine intelligences and wisdoms, is the number also of infancies and inno-cencies, consequently we are so many images of Him. We perfect thy mind; by means of us therefore thou thyself art His image. We behold thy Love with our eyes, and by means of us thou also look-est upon Him. As often as He Himself enters in and goes out, He

---

* A disorder of the eye. (TR.)

salutes thee by or through us; and lest we should ever be without Him, He has given command to His wisdoms and intelligences, of whom He Himself is the acting soul, that they should never depart from us; thus by their kindness we enjoy His perpetual presence and life. Let us therefore all be joined together by an eternal bond, and let us take up our social abode in thy mind; let no times or seasons break the covenant of our society. We pledge ourselves to thee. We will now enter thine Olympus, as brides enter the bridechamber; lo! I see our Love Himself holds the torch and His wisdoms utter applause. . . . Thus ended this scene, which was the fifth in order.

PART TWO

which discusses the marriage
of the first-born, or Adam;
and
the soul, the intellectual mind,
the state of integrity, and
the image of God

Part the Second
Concerning the Marriage
of the First-Born

87. THERE was a grove, distant some furlongs from the Paradise of the first-born, surrounded with winding streams, and divided into insular forms by meanderings derived from those streams; the whole likewise was an orchard, in the midst of which also was a most excellent tree, which by its size and beauty emulated the tree of life, or the maternal tree of the other grove. There was nothing of pleasantness and of beauty in one grove which did not exist effigied in the other, insomuch that if those two groves had been included in the same plot of ground, they might have been called consorts, or, as it were, conjugial partners.

The first-born, on a time, led by the winding of the paths, 2 arrived at the spot about twilight, and when he could not retrace his footsteps by reason of the shade of approaching night, he betook himself into the midst of this garden, and lay down under the branching shelter of the above-mentioned fruit-tree, on a bed and couch a little elevated by flowers which had been gathered together, for the sake of taking sleep and passing the night. When sudden sleep closely disposed his external limbs, and presently their interior fibres, instantly there appeared to him a nymph, most beautiful in face and body, at the sight of whom, from a sort of sympathetic warmth, he was so enkindled, that suddenly a soft flame glowed in all his relaxed fibres, and when he attempted to enfold the nymph in his arms, she, as it were, like a bright cloud, fled from him, seeming to elude his touch and endeavor. He, in consequence, being more vehemently inflamed, and attempting to catch her in her flight, so wounded the joints of his breast that one of his ribs seemed to him to leap out of its place, the nerves being so distended by the operation of the mind, and the blood in the breast being put in commotion by the heart; but after some struggle, he seemed to himself to catch her, when he gave her frequent kisses, which he repeatedly impressed mostly upon her lips and mouth. At this moment, when she appeared still more beautiful by reason of the sparkling of a new flame, he suddenly awoke, and perceived with grief, that she was only the apparition of a dream; not aware that that fruit-tree under which he rested, in like manner as his maternal one, carried a similar egg, from which his future consort was to be born; that it was for her, as represented in his sleep, that he had striven with so much love; that the branch at his breast, lying in his bosom, was what he embraced in his arms; and that the very egg itself was what he pressed with his lips and his kisses, and thus infused into it a vital soul from his own.

88. Much moved by these things, and wishing to retain the delights of his rest, by falling into new sleep, but always in vain, at the first glance of Aurora he raised himself from his bed, and retracing his steps, he arrived at his own garden of delights, or the grove of his birth, without missing his way; yet it occurred to his mind that he was driven thither by a Divine impulse, and that he saw something offered to him, the event of which he should afterwards know.

89. In the meantime, in this little egg thus impregnated, the soul, infused by the first-born in the ardor of sleep, began to weave its forms, from the first celestial forms to the ultimate natural ones, and thus from these first beginnings to clothe itself with a body, but of softer stamina; and after the periods of their formation, or the courses of primeval life, to bring the birth to maturity, and by a force acquired to itself to give it exit and admission thereby into

the vernal aura. The fœtus, also, when brought forth, was initiated into and passed through the same states as those of our first-born, whose life, but in itself distinct, it carried and continued. In like manner also it passed its infancy even to the first flower of age under the parental care of the celestials, under whose auspices it grew every day, as in intelligence, so also in elegance of form and beauty of countenance, even into an exemplar of the beauties and at the same time of the pleasantnesses of the human race. From her face shone forth, not only integrity, but also the veriest innocence, insomuch that she appeared like a sort of celestial grace under a human form. For the spiritual principle itself communicated its image to her corporeal form, namely, the animus with its affections and changes of state, influencing the very texture of the muscular fibres, which texture was most tender and best adapted to signify the ideas of every emotion; while the desires of the mind entered into the still more perfect and more interior forms of the same fibres, which seemed to take on as if painted by colors in all variations from white to purple every least change. Finally, the loves themselves, by similar rays of a kind of vital flame, entered into these forms, which flame darted forth from the eyes as from its centres and hearths, so that from the very face itself, as from a kind of written tablet, the meaning of all her ideas and thoughts might, at one view, be beautifully comprehended and read by the eyes of another. In so sound a state of the soul, the image of all the interior faculties must of necessity be produced in the form of the body, and especially in the countenance, which is also called an effigy of the animus or sensuous mind: for there was nothing intervening which could invert and disturb the characters of such transcription; since the sensuous mind lay altogether subject to the government of the higher or intellectual mind (*mens*), in which the Love itself of heaven reigned. For this reason this first pair, when they were about to enter upon conjugial life, were enabled long to converse together without the tongue as interpreter or the assistance of the ear.

90. This most beautiful damsel, when she was now in the age of laughter and play, and every delightful object readily filled her mind with gladness, chanced in walking to turn her steps to the water of a certain crystal-like fountain, transparent even to its opaque bottom. Casting her eyes down into the water she was amazed at seeing an image floating beneath its surface, and at times emerging when she put herself in motion, just as if it was alive; but presently, when she observed that the same form expressed similar little motions with herself, and looking nearer recognized her own bosom of ivory whiteness with its breasts, and her own arms and hands, she returned in astonishment into herself, as from shade into light, perceiving that this was a reflected image of herself. But when, from the pleasure of its novelty, she had awhile taken delight in this effigy of herself, another wonder struck her and arrested her shifting ideas, namely, that she recognized in the countenance whatsoever she revolved in her mind, even her astonishment itself. She even recognized her wandering ideas about it, wondering that thus all the inmost recesses of her mind stood open and unlocked. When she was unable to disperse this cloud of amazement, as she had done the former, she betook herself with a quick step to her celestial choirs, asking them to explain to her, if they would, whence it came to pass that in her countenance were represented all the little affections of her mind, and the series of ideas thence excited; for she said that she had discovered in the fountain, that her face indicated and revealed whatsoever she inwardly revolved; and that for this reason it was impossible for her to conceal anything.

2 In reply, one of the celestials, who led the chorus, said, If thou hadst known, my little daughter, in what manner the interior and exterior powers and faculties mutually succeed each other, and according to that order mutually act upon each other, thou wouldst have ceased to wonder; but in order that thou mayest know these things, I will briefly explain them.

3 Thy supreme and inmost power is the soul (*anima*) itself, which is all in all of thy body, for from it all the fibres derive their birth

and the beginning of their determination. A second power or faculty is called the intellectual mind (*mens*), first of all excited and begotten by the soul, as by its parent, wherefore it calls it its love and only-begotten. A third is the inferior mind which is also called the *animus*. From these three principles the fibres of the whole body, with the inclosed spirit, proceed, and from the fibres vessels are constructed which convey the blood; from these vessels, and their ramifications, all the organic webs whatever, which are visible in the compass of the body, and inclosed in that compass, and which are called sensories, muscles, viscera, or members, are formed and woven together; such is the composition of all things in general.

But let us now retrace our steps, by explaining in what manner 4 the one acts and inflows into the other. The soul, in its highest beginnings, is clothed with a form, which is called super-celestial, and receives its life from our Supreme Deity. But the mind called intellectual gained its form from the soul and from its rays of life, which resemble the most simple fibres. This form is called celestial, and derives its life, while from the Supreme, at the same time from His Love or Only-begotten. For those forms or substances are only the first or the organic powers, which derive living action from the rays of their life.

But the inferior mind or animus having gained its form, which 5 is called infra-celestial, or the supreme natural, from the former, derives its life from a certain spiritual fount, which was made the connection of heaven and the world.

From these three distinct forms, as from their beginnings, flow 6 forth now all the corporeal or material forms, which correspond to purely natural forms, and which constitute the inferior spheres, or the body itself, consequently also the operations of their forms, changes of state, and methods of acting. But as to the correspondence itself by the influx of the operation of one form into another, it is first to be known, that the parent or superior form is related to the next inferior form as to its offspring, consequently as to its image, there being no difference between them but in regard to simplicity and perfection. Hence there exists and flourishes such a harmony between the forms, by the mediation of active and living forces, that a change of the state of one, which is effected by a variation of form excites a like change in the other correspondently; for a perpetual agreement reigns by mediate active forces, between like forms, especially when all things flow rightly in their order, or when the supreme form, which is the most perfect of all, acts into the next inferior one, and this latter in like manner into the following one, and thus successively.

7   Then all those changes of state, which are excited in the two supreme forms, evidently present themselves, in their manner, by corresponding similar forms, in ultimates. This now is the reason why thy soul and mind transcribe themselves into the gestures, speech, and other external activities, but especially into the countenance; and why there is not the smallest particle in the whole body which does not undergo a change similar to their affection; for as those forms rule in supreme principles, they rule also in the inmost of all principles. It is also a mark of thine integrity and innocence that this beams forth so plainly from thy face.

8   The heavenly intelligence, by living representations, exhibited all these things so manifestly to view, that they fell like so many painted images into the sense of this damsel who was endowed with genius as perfectly as with beauty.

91. When the young damsel applied all the attention of her ears and her mind to these words, and collecting their scattered meanings into one, after the controlling method of association as in nature or *after the natural law of association,* viewed them in their own light, as she herself was wont to call it, she had some hesitation about what was said at the close, namely, that a representation of the affections of the mind in the countenance was a mark of integrity and innocence, not knowing as yet what *non-integrity* could mean; wherefore in humble prayer she entreated them not to desist from favoring her with instruction, and that they would proceed to place in her light, what and whence was *a state of integrity?*

The celestial instructor, rejoicing not a little at this inquiry, 2
replied as follows: From what has been lately told thee, I am sure
that it has entered into thy light that three faculties in us mutually succeed each other, and act mutually into each other, namely,
the soul, the intellectual mind with its will, and the animus or the
inferior mind; and that in like manner there are three fountains of
life, by which those faculties, or powers, are excited to their life,
one of which in like manner acts and inflows into the others, and
thus conjointly into the nature of thy little corporeal world, even
to its extremities. Such is the order which our Supreme foresaw
(*prospexit*) from eternity, and thus established from the beginning
of creation; and such an order He has marked and established in
thee, my daughter. We celestial ones judge of *integrity* by virtue of
order itself from things highest to things lowest, or if you prefer
it, from things inmost to things outmost, thus from things most
simple to those which are ultimately compounded. For our sight
does not dwell on the surface, but penetrates into the marrows of
things, and looks at the beginnings of beginnings, and from these
follows the continuous thread even to the outermost texture, and
hence we form conclusions concerning goodness and integrity.
For whatsoever is perfect in the extremes, is in no case derived
from any other beginning but that where Perfection itself is, nor
by any other order but that which the Supreme has derived from
Himself, and introduced into His own heaven and world, and in
like manner into thy microcosm. Let us unfold therefore this order 3
itself, from first to last and backwards. Our Supreme, to the intent
that from His most holy sanctuary and inmost heaven, consequently
from His throne, He might rule the universe by His nod, and from
His decision, as in first principles, so also in ultimate nature, and
might thus found a heavenly kingdom, begat from eternity, or before
the creation of the world, the first-begotten of all living things, His
only Love, by whom He might connect and unite with Himself
things spiritual and things corporeal, or things heavenly and things
natural, that is, things living and things void of life; for without

love nothing conspires to unity and concord, or lives and is acted upon continually by one spirit, and thus has a tendency to one end, but everything disagrees and falls to pieces. He therefore was born to be a Union and Medium between things superior and things inferior, or immediately between the Supreme, His Parent, and heaven itself, that is, the inhabitants of heaven; wherefore it is He alone by Whom all order is instituted and perfected, or by Whom a way is made from the Supreme to the ultimates of nature, and back again, thus forwards and backwards; but He, inasmuch as He is the Soul of the whole heaven, a Divine Essence and Life purely spiritual, could not descend immediately into nature void of life, without a bond again spiritual, or a mediating life, into which the nature of heaven and the nature of the world might enter and be connected; for what communion of life and nature can exist, except by such mediation? But this spiritual inferior life, in consequence of the disorderly heat of man's own proper love and ambition, broke the connection. Wherefore now man lives, not the life of heaven, but of nature; and does not breathe love, but hatred, consequently not union, but disagreement; nevertheless by him our Love will enter the nature of the world, or of our body, and by his Divine power, in order to prevent the lapse of all things, will connect again what had been broken and rendered unconnected, and will recall the world to heaven as to its containant. To bring this about, the enemy, the violator of the covenant, must be put by our Love under the yoke; his fierce assaults must be broken, his destructive forces must be dissipated, his mischievous life must be doomed to death, and thus all his acts must be restrained within the sphere of endeavors only, and by this method he must be driven by force to the discharge of the duties imposed on him. This now is the very order itself, according to which there may be a transition from the Supreme into nature.

4   A similar order is also inscribed on the faculties or powers of our life. Our soul is ruled by the Supreme Himself; the intellectual mind

with its will by the Love of the Supreme; but the animus by this lowest mediator. To the intent that all things may flow according to this order instituted by the Most Wise, the Love of the Supreme, who resides in our minds, as in His own Olympus, will arrange the mediums of all ends inflowing through Himself or through the soul, and will inspire and fill with the life of His own Love, and by the animus, or its mediating life, first subdued and brought into obedience as thou hast heard, will inflow into the nature of our bodies, namely, into the fibres and their spirit, and from this latter into the blood, in each of which nature is admitted into a partnership of life, consequently into our universal little animal world, as well without as within; for nothing essential is given in the whole body and its natures, but a vessel and fibre with its blood and spirit, according to the various determinations of which arise all organic forms, fabrications, or textures, furnished for every use, and necessity of life. Thus the Life of the Love of heaven inflows into the universal system of our body from highest principles to ultimates, and lives and reigns all in all therein. This now is the order by which we exist, and by which we subsist; and so long as we subsist by it, so long we perpetually exist, or as we are born, are perpetually re-born, or as we are made, are perpetually re-made, and as we are connected, are held together in connection; creation itself is continued in us, and is called perpetual conservation; or integrity a perpetual renewal of integrity. And thus we pass a perpetual spring, or live the flower of our age, since the Divine rules in our natural principle, and what is heavenly in our corporeal principle. For He who instituted and establishes this kingdom in us, is Perfection itself, because He is the Supreme, and is Union and Harmony itself, because He is the Love of the Supreme. The state therefore induced by this order is what is called *a state of integrity* conjoined with a state of infancy and innocence, consequently with a state of immortality.

92. But this subject of so great moment let us unfold from its beginnings even to the senses. For this purpose let us compare the

emissary rays themselves of the three principles* with the purest fibres, although they can only be called fibres by way of analogy or distinction. But for the sake of understanding, let us borrow common expressions when others do not answer; for a fibre of the body itself is born from these conglomerated fibres so called of principles, as their ultimate offspring; hence from the nature of affinity it may be allowed to signify one by the name of the other. Every fibre whatsoever, which reigns in the universal body, derives its birth from the soul, for the soul is by its fibre the soul of its universe, and present, powerful, conscious, provident, and living in all [its parts]; wherefore its ray or most eminent fibre is the only substantial principle in things compounded, or the only simple principle in things aggregate, that is, in the fabrications or organic forms of the body. Its form in supreme principles, or inmostly in the very beginnings of the fibres, is called super-celestial; its determination, or fluxion, according to the fibres, through the inmost principles of the body, everywhere also seeks a similar form; which form is of such purity and simplicity, that it bears in its bosom the supreme essence of life. For this super-eminent fibre, viewed in itself, is alone recipient of, or capable of receiving that living essence; wherefore also it is called the soul, the power of powers, or the form of forms. From these most simple rays, which resemble fibres, is produced another beginning of a fibre, by a wonderful mode of a kind of infinite circumgyration, the form of which in supreme principles, or the very beginnings of the fibres, is called celestial, which also is the form of our intellectual mind. Through the most subtle pore of this fibre (for in the whole animated body, from first principles to last, there is nothing but what can be poured through or breathed through), there flows again a certain purely spiritual essence, which is the life of heaven itself, or of the love of the Supreme, born in like manner as the fibre itself, from that prior or supreme fibre. From these is now produced a third beginning of a fibre, the form

---

* Namely: the *Anima, Mens,* and *Animus*—mentioned above. (TR.)

of which in highest beginnings is called infra-celestial, and the pore or canal of which fibre is alone pervious to that spiritual essence mediating between the life of heaven and the nature of the world.

These are the veriest essences and most real substances, for the derivatives from them, and those things which are at length the object of sense, derive all their actuality and reality from them and their connection with themselves. From these three principles thus connected together in their operation, is now produced every fibre, which flows down by the nerves into the provinces of the body, and conveys down the white and purer blood, commonly called the animal spirit. From these latter are ultimately compounded vessels, called arteries and veins, for the conveyance of the red and grosser blood, from which, and also from the said fibres, all the organs and viscera of the body are fabricated and live by the life of each blood inflowing from those principles, and the fibre being there threefold. From all this it may now be manifest what is the method of all composition, and what is the successive order itself in beginnings, and the simultaneous order in the fibres thence derived; also what is the influx according to that order.

93. But I see clearly, my little daughter, said she, that still a kind of little cloud is floating in thy light, which also thou desirest to be dispersed; for I observe that thou dost not yet thoroughly see what is the quality of those forms which act in each other according to that order. For the better clearing up of this subject, I will begin again and review it from supreme principles, or from the first stamen.

Those forms, which are actual substances, and by changes of state perform their wonderful functions when mutually subordinate to each other, are circumstanced as follows: The first form of all proper to our soul is called *super-celestial:* but the second, which is of the intellectual mind, is named *celestial:* the third, which is of the inferior mind, or of the animus is called *infra-celestial.* To these now succeed forms purely natural, which, if they are to be denominated from the nature of their fluxion, are to be named as follows; the first of them is to be called *spiral,* observable in the corporeal fibres themselves: the second, *circular* or *spherical,* observable in the blood-vessels: the third, *angular,* properly terrestrial and material, serving the fluids and the blood itself, and also the spirit of the fibres, for corporeity. But what the quality of the nature of each form is, must be learned from what is made evident to the understanding by the aid of the senses, consequently from the last, or from the angular and spherical forms. The former, or the angular, from the mutual opposition of all its essentials, derives this quality, that it is heavy and inert matter, of itself unadapted to all motion. The other or spherical, is more perfect than the former in this, that its surface resembles an infinite angle, and relates to only one fixed point, opposite to all the points of the surface, which is called the centre; it is therefore accommodated to motion and variations of form. The third, or spiral, from its determination, derives still superior perfection, for it again puts on a kind of perpetuity or infinity, since its radii, inasmuch as they are spires, press circularly, not immediately to any fixed centre, but to the surface of a certain sphere which takes the place of its centre; thus it is still more accommodated than the former to motion, and to variations of form. The fourth, or infra-celestial, derives still superior perfection from a kind of new perpetuity or infinity; for its spires, like a vortex, flow into such gyres, that by them are marked greater and lesser circles with poles, as in the great sphere of the world; and the flexure and inflexure of its spires have respect to the spires of the foregoing form as the points of its perpetual centre; hence its power of varying itself, or of changing states, increases immensely above the other. The fifth, or celestial, puts on a new perpetuity or infinity above the rest, for this again regards, as its relative centre, the infra-celestial form, and all its determinable points; wherefore the resulting ideas of its fluxion are indescribable by lines and words; in the same infinite ratio, its faculty of changing states rises eminently above the foregoing. But in the sixth form, or the super-celestial, there is nothing but what is Perpetual, Infinite, Eternal, Incomprehensible, the Order, Law, Idea of the universe, and the Essence of all essences.

Such now is the ascent and descent of forms or substances in 4 the greatest, and in our least universe; similar also is the ascent and descent of all forces and powers which flow from them. But all their perfection consists in the possibility and virtue of varying themselves, or of changing states, which possibility increases according to their elevations, thus by multiplication into itself by infinities, so that in number it exceeds all the series of calculations unfolded or still to be unfolded by human minds; which infinities finally all become what is Infinite in the Supreme. Our ideas are mere progressions by variations of form, and thus by actual changes of state.

94. If thou couldst discern, my Beloved, how distinctly and in what order these forms are arranged and connected with each other, and according to their connection act and inflow into each other, from the mere aspect and infinity of so many wonderful things conspiring into one, thou wouldst fall down, from an inmost impulse, of sacred astonishment, and pious joy, in loving adoration before such a Maker. I will only briefly and simply reveal in what manner those forms cohere in the little type of thy world, or microcosm. For they all of them cöexist and cöoperate in every smallest particle which falls under the observation of the senses, exactly according to the order in which they press and follow each other. Since there is nothing simultaneously in any texture or effect which was not successively introduced; and everything is therein, according as order itself introduces it; wherefore simultaneous order derives its birth, nature, and perfection from successive orders, and the former is only rendered perspicuous and plain by the latter. Hence we Celestial ones judge of states of perfections, whether they be beauties, or goodnesses, or pleasantnesses. In order that this may be rendered still clearer, it is to be observed, that what is supreme in things successive takes the inmost place in things simultaneous; thus things superior in order fold around them things inferior, and wrap them together, that these latter may become exterior things in the same order. By this method first principles, which are also called simple, unfold themselves, and involve themselves in things

posterior or compound; wherefore every perfection of what is outermost flows forth from inmost principles in their series. Hence thy beauty, my daughter, the only parent of which is Order itself! But now let us return to the before-mentioned forms, and show in what order in thy microcosm these mutually follow each other and at length are gathered into one.

95. To the intent, my Darling, that thou mayest enjoy with me this curious and delightful spectacle, I will open to thee my bosom, and from the body will bring forth arguments of experience; this is to me not difficult, for I assume the human FORM* when I please, and *again lay it aside.*

2   Behold now, said she, this *nerve* alone, consisting of infinite parts, may serve for a mirror. Thou seest it girded with a double, yea a triple zone, and inclosed in a form almost the last, or the spherical form, and thus brought to its last or outermost forms. But I will remove now this thin covering that I may unfold the forms involved in their order. Having drawn aside therefore the zones or little coats, behold, says she, the fascicular composition of this nerve, which thou seest is made up of little nerves, and these again of fibres adjoined to each of them. These fibres, being disjoined from their bonds, are folded into spiral flexures, and are permeable to a kind of lymph, which is called the animal spirit, into which is infused life from its principles, which life it conveys into the streets and towns of the whole kingdom, and sprinkles on the blood itself. But lest the sight of so many things may render the distinct ideas confused, let us simply examine only a single fibre which admits its lymph, separate from connection with the neighboring fibres; and this fibre, according to my art, I will show thee in an enlarged form.

3   Look now, said she, and see by how many permeable fibres this little capillary tube (*canaliculus*) is encompassed, and in what manner these fibres are again and again encompassed by others, into

---

* Swedenborg in his theological works uniformly teaches that when angels appear to man it is by the opening of the man's spiritual eyes. (TR.)

each of which inflows distinctly its own life from first principles; such is the compagination. But to the intent that we may examine the forms themselves, and the connection of one with another, and finally the influx of one into another, let us pursue this fibre thus circumscribed, pressed gently with the finger, and set at liberty from its companions, even to its beginnings, which are observable in the compass or crown of the hemispheres of the brain and at the same time in the marrows of its axes. These are called glands, and from their situation are named cortical, and from their color cineritious. They are spherules of an oval figure, in the bosom of which is stored up not only whatsoever is in the fibre, but also whatsoever is acted and felt by the fibre. Wherefore, to prevent the rays of our vision from being scattered among several objects, let us look only at one spherule selected from the society, and unlocked in order from outermost principles to inmost.

Having withdrawn therefore the softest membranes, the first object presented to view was a kind of new brain, but in a diminutive form, again with infinite spherules, or little spheres, arranged into the infra-celestial form, all of which had a fixed relation and view to greater and lesser circles, and to their poles altogether as in the great sphere of the world. It was also rendered visible, in what manner this form taken from little spheres, by the variations of itself and changes of state, produced ideas called material; and in what manner each little sphere sent forth a diminutive fibre with its little duct and covered it with a small coat; and how natural life was infused into it from the lowest spiritual fountain which inhabits that sphere with its genii, and excites its organic principles; also in what manner all these fibrils, permeated by this vital essence, by circumgyrating spires, formed together a common fibre, or the nervous fibre of the body. Having examined these things, she next unclosed and opened one of these little spheres, and inwardly in it she again brought forth to view innumerable new little vortices, the highly adorned dwellings, as it were, of so many intelligences and wisdoms winding into a celestial form, which little vortices, by their infinite windings and circles, and most becoming order of them all, represented in a little effigy a kind of Olympus, or the Heaven of our Love. She showed also in what manner the Olympiades, the inhabitants of this heaven, by the variations of that form, or changes of state, conceived and directed the ideas of our intellectual mind; also in what manner each wove a most pure stamen emulous of a fibre, and infused into its little pore heavenly life, or the life of our Love; and from stamina as numerous as were the little vortices or the small habitations of the intelligences, contrived the superficies of the above-mentioned fibril, which is permeable to natural life. Again, one of these little vortices or little stars being laid open, there appeared the supreme of all forms, called the super-celestial, from which darted those rays, or fibres by supereminence, which being permeable to the life of the Supreme penetrated into Olympus.

This now is the inmost Heaven, says she, or the sanctuary of our soul, from which all things that live, act, and that are, and thus exist in that little corporeal world, derive their being (*Esse*). For from, as it were, infinite points of infinite purity arranged into the supercelestial form, radiate and shoot forth continually infinite lines of the same purity, from which are woven together the first of all things permeable to and animated by the supreme life, which being transcribed into a celestial form, conceive that emulous beginning of stamens produced in the second heaven from the woofs of the Heliconides. From these permeable forms is prepared that beginning of a fibre, which is inspired with heavenly life, or the life of Love, and is brought forth to form the third beginning of a fibre; from which last principle, in which the prior principles dwell together, the corporeal fibre is made up; being drawn into a spiral form. From this latter at length, flowing round into a spherical form, is unfolded the last channel, or blood-vessel, in which all things now exist together in a simultaneous series. Such is the generation of the organic forms of the body, from which, as in a mirror, the Order itself instituted by the Supreme is presented for contemplation. This Order is in our Supreme Himself, and at the same time in the Rays of His Life, from Himself, and is produced from Himself; for, as thou mayest recollect, the Supreme Form, in itself, has regard to those which follow in order, even to the last; wherefore the essential Order which thence comes forth, and is, as it were, unfolded, is of infinite perfection, because it is of the Infinite Himself. That these things are so, thou, my daughter, who art born into this very order, and the light of its life, although thou art still a damsel, yet, as I see, thou clearly comprehendest; but it is otherwise with those whose wisdom is grounded only in the fatuous lumen of nature; they allow themselves to be persuaded by nothing but the testimony of the external senses; and what is wonderful, they reject from their belief the most evident actions and effects, unless they see them also in a substance; wherefore when they regard truths from this connection and order, the chain snaps asunder, at its very first link, and thus their view remains fixed in mere earthly objects, or in matters which are born from the ultimate form.

96. But do not yet withdraw thy attention; again employ thy light, and look into the common centre of this little sphere, which, being placed at the top of the fibre, is its active principle and head; in its centre, as thou seest, is a little fountain, into which all those lives, through their little veins, continually and beautifully flow in the same order; here thou seest the fountains themselves, which, as being very minute, can only be viewed by the pupil of the eye alone, while the too abundant and wandering light is shut out from it by the eyebrows. This little fountain is called the fountain of life, for its lymph, thence called animal and spirit, being animated by these essences of life, flows down as a little stream into the containing fibre, even to its boundaries. But what is still more wonderful, those vital essences abide together in every smallest part of this lymph, being joined altogether in that society, in which they mutually succeed each other, uniting with themselves at length, from the circumfluent world, the most simple elements introduced by emissaries. These things I see clearly with my eyes, wherefore from what is seen by me I relate them to thee. For in

greatest things so also in least nothing is perfected but from the same order. This alone is the determination, which, by varying the form, varies the cause, and thus the effect, correspondently with its end or use. This spiritual lymph, conveyed down through its little channel, is at length brought into the blood itself and its globules, and finishes therein its last gyre; but to the intent that ultimate things may return to first principles, this blood is resolved, and through its little fountain of life is conveyed back into the fibres, and thus performs a perpetual orbit; from the continual breaking of these connections, hunger and thirst, or the want of refreshment by food and chyle, are produced.

97. These forms being viewed in their substance and order of succession, let us now take into consideration their mutual influx into each other, and the very essential order of the action thence resulting. But whereas that order penetrates, like lightning, from the highest citadel of heaven to the very bottom of nature, and, like an orbit in rapid motion, carries along with it the rays of vision itself, and draws discriminations into what is continuous, so that there exists only one and the same perpetual image, therefore thy mind must so stand upon its pivot that its view may be open at the same time into each nature, namely, of heaven and of the world. Having so said, she opened the doors, and while the damsel was looking around, Behold now, said she, in what manner the forms mutually excite each other to action, the first its second, the second the third, and the third the inferior ones, even to the last, almost as an axis excites a wheel, and the wheel its powers, even to the last, which bring into effect the exertions of all, and this with such unanimity, that everything successive unites in one general conformity, although each, by its own agitation, exercises its proper functions. But as the soul employs its states, so the superior mind, because alive, from itself exercises its activities, and from this again the inferior mind, and so forth, with perpetual condescension, determined by conformity itself, and at the same time by the method of connection and of influx; for every one was born and made to be obedient to

its next superior, thus all to compliance with the Supreme, which is the only source of the action of all.

98. This now is the order, says she, established by the Supreme, and determined by His Love into act, in which there is nothing but what is Divine, Perpetual, and Infinite; for such as it is in the Supreme Himself, and in His Only-begotten, such it is in its orbit, which flows and reflows in an eternal gyre from first principles to last, and from last to first; and because GOD is in it as in Himself, this Order resembles GOD Himself. All those infinities of respects, which, as thou hast heard, concentrate themselves in forms, being unfolded into this Order, so conspire to an only end, as perpetual circles to the centre of their centres. Wherefore there is nothing in it which is not full of Deity, and everything glitters from This as from a Sun, and puts on heavenly life; even nature herself is thence resplendent, and being, as it were, animated, becomes alive; for through her there is a path to the ultimates of ends, and from these the first is looked back upon.

As the damsel, from an infinite delight, was intent for a long time on these things, something like lightning glanced upon the sacred light of her mind, and gliding as it were by its influence into an interior heaven, she there beheld in their idea itself all things which she had heretofore viewed in a type.

99. When this new inhabitant of heaven had for some time fed the inmost principles of her mind with rapturous delights, suddenly relapsing, as it were, she briskly wiped her eyes with her finger, that her mind might recover its former ken, and thus again looking upon her celestial companion:

Proceed, I pray, says she, and instruct me by your skilful eloquence, whether or no this order presents itself clearly in an effigy; for as it descends from the centre into perpetual spirals, and in its descent expands itself and grows, and infolds and unfolds itself in the ultimate forms of nature, so possibly it unfolds itself with such clearness as to become wholly manifest to sense.

To this the goddess, touched with the love of this desire, If you please, says she, these your wishes also shall be granted: Look at my face, or, in the water of thy fountain, look at thy own; both thy face and mine carry that order in effigy; for whatever is the subject of thy mind's interior consideration, and whatever ideas are conceived and brought forth by thy desires, or are the objects of thy love, we read them all as copied out in thy countenance. We celestial ones discern this clearly, as just now, in what manner this discourse of ours excites thy delight and approbation. For those forms, just now unfolded in the beginnings of the fibres, in each fibril of thy countenance, one within the other, vary their states so beautifully, as even to instruct of themselves those who are ignorant of this order, as to what they inwardly mean, and in what manner they inflow into each other. Let us therefore unswathe them in their order, that thou mayest more clearly comprehend the signs of the changes of state.

The outmost form, or the common form of thy face, is, as it were, a tablet, on which are written the indications of the other forms, and it corresponds to that form which is called spherical. But the other, or the superior natural form, called spiral, from the wonderful orb of the fluxion of the motor or muscular fibres about the lips of thy mouth, and the lids of each eye, by the variation of connections and situations,[a] delineates conspicuously every progression of thy gladness as it unfolds itself into pleasure in that plane,

---

a In order that it may be seen clearly in what manner the motor fibres, or muscles of the face, shape their countenances, and mark the affections of their animus, it is necessary that we examine, not only their situation and connection, but also the general respect of all, and the particular respect of each, to their centres, and according to that respect, their direction to their centres. *That the orbit of their fluxion is performed around the lips of the mouth, and the eye-lids of each eye,* may be manifest from the following short description of them. If we wish to examine the muscles of the face according to their directions, that muscular flesh is to be considered as divided into three regions; the *first* of which descends from the upper part of the forehead even to the eye-lashes of the upper eyelids, the muscles of which are the frontal, the corrugators of the eye-brows, the pyramidal of the nose, the constrictor orbiculars of the upper eye-lids, and the elevators of the same. The *second* commences from the eye-lashes of the lower eye-lids, and closes in the orbicular of the

and at the same time unfolds that pleasure into laughter. But the third form, called the higher natural or infra-celestial, proper to the animus, and its genii, which immediately rules the fibres, and by these the vessels mediately, makes and declares itself evident by the purple and white and intermediate tinctures with which it paints, as with colors, those variegated webs; for it brings the blood into brighter textures, in agreement with its delight, and thus presents to the view something spiritual mixed with what is natural. But the fourth form, or the celestial, which is that of our mind, and of its loves, insinuates inwardly into these colorings the rays of a kind of flame, and elevates and kindles the picture with a kind of heavenly and spiritual fire, insomuch that the gladness, from the abundance of desire, is so livingly brilliant, that every one grasps it at first view, without the teaching of science. Into these [lower forms] the supreme form, or that of our soul, infuses supercelestial light,

---

upper lip, the muscles of which are called elevators of the upper lip, vulgarly, the laughing muscles, the incisors, the canine, the zygomatic, the myrtiform, which is ascribed to the nose, also the buccinator, and further, the semi-orbicular of the upper lip. The *third* takes its beginning from the semi-orbicular of the lower lip, to which are added the triangular muscle and the quadrate; not to mention the lesser muscles discovered by various writers, and which may be discovered every day, inasmuch as the face of one man never has muscles similar as to situation, magnitude, quantity, direction, to that of another, by reason that there are as many countenances as there are animi, and as many animi as there are heads, or men. That there are three regions, appears from this circumstance, that the muscles of one region can be excited to motion, or contracted and expanded, separately without the muscles of another, as may be clearly seen in a mirror, and thus known from experiment. The muscles of the first region are common, less common, particular, and most particular, arranged altogether for use, according to the rules of the doctrine of order, of degrees, and of society. For their most common muscles are the frontal, the less common are the corrugators of the eye-brows, which latter arise from the pyramidal muscle of the nose. So that those three muscles are subordinate to the most general frontal muscles, with which also they communicate, being connected by fibres. To the corrugators of the eye-brows are subject the orbicular or semi-orbicular muscles of the upper eye-lids; but to these are subject or subordinate the elevators of the upper eye-lids; all these muscles are allotted principally to the bringing of external aid to the eyes, and thus assisting the sight, for they are all determined towards the upper eye-lid. That the muscles of the middle region conspire to the aid of the inferior eye-lid, and at the same time to the superior lip, every one may discover on making the experiment in a mirror by a living act of sight.

that is, life; or vivifies or illuminates with life all the little points of thy face with its light, whilst the second [form] impresses and communicates to it spiritual heat, and the third adjoins nature to life, and altogether according to the vibration of that flame, beautifully tinges the face, as a flower, with red and white. But the fourth [form] draws and designs the lines themselves; whilst the fifth brings out to view all these conformities, as in a veil. Look now from this mirror, and see what is the quality of Order itself, and in what manner the spiritual principle shines forth from the natural, and the Divine from the corporeal, consequently the whole of Order; and since this resembles our Supreme and His Love, therefore we celestial ones, who are His images, whilst we are clothed with a body, cannot assume any other than a human face like unto thine; for from this we are acknowledged as to our origin. All these things relate to fibres, for whatever is done in the fibres manifestly imbues the countenance, and unfolds itself in that order in which it exists in the beginnings of the fibres, and finally in the fibres themselves, namely:

The life of the Supreme from inmost principles;

Heavenly Life, or the life of His Love, from principles proximate to them; also

Mediating or natural life; finally

Nature herself, who carries that order in herself, consequently in effigy; thus altogether according to the series of the folding together of the fibre we have been examining, and of the involution of its beginnings.

Hence also it is evident how, according to that order, prior things infold themselves in posterior, and again infold themselves from these latter; and thus in what manner they establish their gyre from first principles to last, and from last to first; for first principles infold themselves in things posterior, as centres in circumferences, or as the inmost principles of a nut in the husk and shell; and then and in like manner they unfold themselves, but backwards, as if removing their swaddling-clothes that they may return from things outmost to things inmost. Thus, and not otherwise, the gyre provided from eternity and established at first creation, is perfected.

100. But this Order, viewed in substance and in its effigy, that is, in the face, is called beauty and handsomeness, the perfection of which results from the agreement of all essentials, from inmost principles to outmost, that is, from the correspondence of life with its spiritual heat or fire; of the thence arising coloring tincture, by which the flaming principle itself becomes pellucid; and lastly, of this flower of beauty whose lines are drawn by the fibres according to the laws of nature's harmonies. At last all these appear upon a surface of beautiful curves. But the agreement of all these things cannot possibly exist without a spiritual principle of union, or Love, in the veriest rays of Life; from that principle alone beauty derives its harmony, its bloom and reality; and life, its day-dawn and vernal freshness; wherefore love itself shining forth from grace of form, by its hidden and insown virtue, elicits mutual love, and as an index reveals the vein of beauty.

101. While the damsel caught these words with an eager ear, and, as it were, absorbed them with her whole mind, she retired a little into herself to reflect, for she began to consider and to weave together some of these newly conceived ideas; and whilst she in some degree restrained her respiration lest it should interrupt her mental revolvings by too deep reciprocations, she again, with a soul, as it were, set at liberty, gently accosted her celestial companion in these words:

I will tell you of an idea which has crept into my mind, in consequence of what you have been saying about the beauty of the face arising from that order of the Supreme, and being only a perfection of the body; but I see clearly, that a perfection still more illustrious and more excellent flows from the same order, namely, the perfection of the life itself, which properly or principally involves the state of that integrity, concerning which you so kindly promised to instruct me. I entreat you therefore to add one favor to another, by instructing me, what and of what quality is *perfection of life?*

To this question the celestial intelligence replied as follows: I perceive, says she, that our ideas, thine and mine, like consociate sisters, tend to the same point; for my discourse of itself already runs into the subject of thine inquiry, since one perfection involves another, for another and another is born from the same Order. The perfection of the body is the perfection of form in its substance, from which, as from its subject, springs forth the perfection of forces and of life; for nothing predicable exists which does not take its actuality from this circumstance, that it subsists, that is, from its substance. From what is not something it is impossible that anything can emanate; the very forces and changes of life become efficient, because they flow from a substance. Wherefore a similar order has place in thy forces and modes of forces, as in thy fibres, regarded as substances. Hence it follows, that the perfection of life makes itself visible in the perfection of the body as its effigy. And because perfection of body, especially beauty, is an object of sense, but perfection of life, like a mist, shuns human ken, unless it be viewed from a sublime principle, therefore I wished to present a mirror of the latter in the former, for the sake of gratifying thy desire.

102. But lest our ideas should wander and like things scattered have to be gathered up again and brought back to our main subject I wish to explain simply, at the outset, what perfection of life is, that it may appear perfectly plain to the understanding.

Every one, while he lives his life, lives the order of his life; for life itself is nothing but the order which is lived. Nevertheless amongst the infinite orders which mortals live, there is only One which leads to Life; the rest go away in different directions, and incline to what is contrary to life. That only Order is the Order which the Most Wise, Who alone Is and Lives, has prescribed and instituted from Himself, such as it is in Himself. This Order reigns both universally, and most singularly, in thy and my little world of life, insomuch that not even the smallest particle belongs to thy body on which that Order is not inscribed from its first principle to its last; as thou lately sawest in the little fibre, the small head of its beginning, and in the individual [parts] of the lymph which runs through the little fibre, and in the rest of the things which enter into and compose any texture. Hence also this Order is in the universals of singulars, for the greatest things, as things compounded from their parts, derive their order, consequently all the laws of their order and of their form, from their least things. Since now this Order is in all those things which constitute substance, it is also in those things which thence result as acts; wherefore this Order lives its life, and rules in thy least actions as in the greatest; for it continually produces an effigy of itself, as through so many mirrors, from things least to things greatest; therefore such as the Order is, such is all that which in act is lived, and in life is acted. But now to state the matter briefly: The above Order is such, that super-celestial life inflows into heavenly life, and this latter, by a mediating life, into the sphere of nature, even to its boundaries, from the last of which it revolves back again to its first principle by acts of putting off, as in its descent by acts of putting on. Super-celestial Life is the life of the Supreme Himself. Heavenly Life is the life of His Only-begotten or Love. Mediating life is the life of him, who, being made the connecting medium of life and nature, afterwards revolted; but nature is what has no life. In this single and simple mirror, look at that single and simple Order, and refer to it, as to an exemplar, all the orders whatsoever which flow about and revolve in the breasts of mortals.

103. To the intent that thou mayest perceive the above order in thyself, my daughter, thou needest to be taught what each power, in the little world of thine own life, is intended to do. The soul, which lives the super-celestial life, regards ends; but the rational mind, which lives the heavenly life, arranges means that ends may be turned into uses; while the natural mind or the animus, which leads an animal and mediating life, brings into effects the means of uses, which effects may correspond exactly with ends. Thus ends

are the souls of all effects, and effects, which uses mediate, are the bodies of all ends. In this manner the Divine, from the highest, in its descent clothes itself continually with the forms of nature, almost as a centre with orbicular spires, even to the last boundary of nature, on which, then, all things remain most fittingly inscribed. Such now is every smallest motion of thy body, which derives and obtains its animal life from effects, its heavenly life from uses, and its supercelestial life from the ends of uses; whence that least motion puts on a human habit, and is called action; in the least principles of which action, as in the greatest, dwells thy mind and also inmostly the soul in its order, renewing and perfecting the state of the mind.

104. But this semi-gyration, to the intent that it may perform an entire gyre, as it involves itself from the first principles of life to the last of nature, so it must continually again revolve itself from the ultimates of nature to the first principles of life, that is, it must put off the forms of its body and of nature, and sliding back into the interiors of itself, must put on heavenly forms, together with the super-celestial, in which forms alone dwells the Life of this Order. For heaven can enter into nature, but never can nature enter into heaven; death has no access to life, nor shade to light; unless death and shade are separated there is no possibility of enjoying heaven. Wherefore in thy body, the ultimate effects of nature, let in through the doors of the senses, are given over to the care of mediating life, which has a natural soul under the appearance of ideas. In this their custody, under the view of the intellectual mind, they do not appear as effects turned into ideas, but as uses, without the clothing of nature; for it is contrary to this order, that anything clothed with body shall enter from beneath into the sphere of uses, or the heavenly sphere. Finally, these uses, under the view of the soul, are not looked upon as uses, but purely as ends, which being thus gifted with the veriest life itself, tend together to that One Only End, or to the glory of the Supreme. Thus, and not otherwise, what is last flows back to its first principle, and nature back to its Life.

The Worship and Love of God

105. But summing up these scattered remarks into one conclusion, I would observe that the gyre of this Order is thus described, namely, from the Supreme, who is the veriest Life Itself, through His only Love, and thus through heavenly life, and from this through natural life into nature herself; and then back again from nature, through the same natural life to heavenly life, but by continual puttings-off, and thus through the only Love to the Supreme or to the veriest Life itself. Thus the hinge of all things is turned, and the door is opened from Life and to Life, and the gyre of this order is perpetuated by the only Love, or Only-begotten of the Supreme, by Whom, and for the sake of Whom, are all things.

106. But before I close this general observation, I wish to adjoin, in the way of a concluding remark, a description of the happy life of those who live this order. For they live the same life with us, the inhabitants of heaven, but a human life, because they are clothed with a body. Thus they are sent into the earth that they may enjoy the gratifications of the ultimate world, while at the same time they taste the satisfactions of heaven itself: and the two together beget a fulness of delight, and reveal the pleasantness of the whole order to all the senses. For with their soul they are wise in Divine Ends, and with their minds they know uses, and with their bodies they know effects. But they perceive only the pleasure of effects in the goodness of uses, and the goodness of uses in the happiness of ends; for they live thus in the body in order that minds may live under the appearance of a body. With the inhabitants of heaven, or with us, they hold perpetual consort, for we associate with them in mutual discourse; we are to them oracles, while we are consulted, and deliver to them plain messages from heaven. In fine, they live in a light which no shade interrupts, into which light nothing but truths descend, which beget the understanding proper to their minds; and into the rays of which light nothing but goodnesses enter, which excite the voluntary principle of their minds; thus they act under perpetual inspiration. For the supreme way stands unobstructed in them, from the soul into the mind, and *vice versa,* from the mind

into the soul, through the Love of heaven, and is continually open to the light of its intelligence, and to the fire of its wisdom. But the other, or inferior, way from the animus into the mind, is so barred and shut, that no entrance is open for nature, even the smallest. For that door from the mind is only turned outwards, to the intent that heavenly light may inflow into natural light, and natural light may never flow back, and thus be mixed with heavenly. For in them the intelligence of truth and the wisdom of good, flow down into nature from their fountain, through one only and pure vein; but they never return from nature to the same vein, and thus to their fountain, unless purged from all defilement.

107. But directly contrary is the lot of those who in practice do not follow this Order, which is of Life, but the inverted order, which is of death; these, in outmost principles, appear indeed to have bodies with human faces, but when viewed with our eyes within the bark and external covering of nature, they resemble the inferior animals in countenance; for they live the life of their animus, that is, an animal life, or the life of the body, in other words, natural life, and not at the same time the mediating or celestial life, which conjoins the life of the Supreme to natural life. Wherefore all genii, who also influence the inferior animals, burst forth from their work-houses into the sphere of their mind, and put to flight the human genii, by nature heavenly, or thrust them down into their prisons. Thus they wholly invert order; wild and fierce slaves, set at liberty, seize upon the sceptre of the kingdom; the prince of the world, the most incensed enemy of heaven, who is in the animus, and presides over the body, with the torches of his nature, and the phalanx of his loves, rushes into heaven, and there displays his conquering troops, and thus confounds highest things with lowest. Hence so dark a shade[b] spreads itself over the

---

[b] In what manner a shade is induced on the intellectual mind, when order is inverted, may be shown to apprehension from the principles explained above, no. 95; for, as is there maintained, there are three forms, which succeed each other, one above or within the

sphere of their mind, that their lives are living dreams, and like persons asleep, they are in deep ignorance of what heaven is, what the soul, what the intellectual mind, and what the animus, consequently what Order is. For lower things thus mix themselves with higher, like mire with waters of the clearest fountain, with which they make eye salve and anoint their eyes, so that they see all things but understand nothing. Wherefore they fly about like owls which hate the light, and wander like an ignis fatuus from fen to fen. Concerning the Love of heaven, concerning us, the intelligences, concerning Heavenly Life and its Mediation, concerning Divine Inspiration, and concerning the double way into the mind, in a word, concerning all things above nature and its life, they prattle like parrots without understanding, and act coldly because without any will. For by inverted order they take nature for their inmost life, and reject Divine things to the circumference; wherefore also in their public and private engagements, they pretend to be governed by the love of heaven, and regard the Supreme as the end of all they

---

other, namely, inmostly the super-celestial, intermediately the celestial, and exteriorly the infra-celestial, or the supreme natural; all of which, according to the description, conceive and produce fibres, so called to distinguish them; from the connection of which together is composed the corporeal fibre, which conveys the lymph called the animal spirit; for the corporeal or nervous fibre cannot derive its origin from other than those purest sources which are purer essences than such as is the animal spirit; which essences can be no other than the vital ones, from which that spirit itself derives its life; those vital essences must also of necessity be as many in number as are the faculties of life itself, which are the soul, the intellectual mind [*mens*], and the mind [*animus*]; and yet all derive their life from the Supreme, who is the life of all living things; they also roll in the circles of their order, and re-roll, according to the manner of influx and of the correspondence of its life; besides many other things, which may be drawn more plainly from the description itself. Conceive now that the infra-celestial form, or the outermost form of life, in the principles above explained, is proper to our mind [*animus*]; and the interior or middle form, is proper to the intellectual mind [*mens*]; and that one is excited by the other to the changes of its state. If now the interior or celestial form, that is, the intellectual mind [*mens*] excites to the operations of its functions the exterior or infra-celestial form, which is of the mind [*animus*], in such case all things succeed according to order; but if the exterior form excites to operation the interior or superior, in this case the order is inverted, for thus what is more imperfect acts upon what is more perfect, that is, natural life upon celestial. Hence

think and do, while inwardly, as at the centre, they conceal the love of self and of the world; and fearful above all things lest these latter loves should burst forth from their covering, they assume deceitful countenances. Because they are aware that the life which they live is that of inverted Order, in other words, that ultimate effects are their uses, and these uses are their ends, and their ends begin in nature; and when they have performed a certain gyre, their ends close also in nature, consequently in the shade of its night, and the cold of its winter, and thus in those habitations below which are called Erebus and Orcus.

108. From this representation of order now in both its effigies, it may plainly appear to thee what *perfection of life* is, for such as order is such is life, as well in its most minute principles as in the compounds of all most minute principles. That Order of ours, which is Divine, Infinite, and Immortal, like the brightest light, is never transparent, unless it be viewed as to its quality from that

---

it comes to pass, that those little vortexes, which are called the diminutive habitations of wisdoms, and constitute that form, are absolutely jumbled together, and become almost evanescent; for on the flight of celestial life, by which they are animated, they fall away and perish; hence all communication is destroyed between the supreme life and natural life; and the changes of state, or the intellectual ideas, become of a nature so imperfect and gross, as to correspond only to the changes of the state of the inferior form, or to material ideas and their sports, or to genii or minds [*animus*]; the consequence of which is, that mere shade takes the place of light in things purely spiritual or celestial; a similar state also occupies the universal fibre, resulting from these three principles, and at the same time its essential spirit; for a fibre derives from its principles all the conditions and nature of its life. That fibril, so called by way of distinction, which conveys celestial life, becomes, as it were, a half-dead and impervious tendril, because it is without support in itself, and thus natural life alone reigns, in which nevertheless is the life of the Supreme, but without mediation. This now is the veil which is interposed, so that what is celestial cannot at all manifest itself; and hence results a similar perverted order, as well in the smallest as in the greatest exercises of life, because it is in all the fibres, from which, as substances, all forces, modes of forces, or actions, are derived; altogether as was related above. By these means the superior way is closed, which effect takes place when the inferior way is open inwards, or the gate of nature thither opens. Effects themselves confirm this truth with such perspicuity, that every one who is endowed with any power of genius, and any spark of experience, cannot but acknowledge it; for truth, when published, manifests itself by its own light.

other order, which is natural, finite, and mortal; in like manner, as thy image, in the limpid water of a fountain, is never seen as to its quality, unless it be reflected to thy sight by the opacity of the bottom of the fountain; from the aspects of opposites, both the one and the other is discerned, nor does truth itself appear, unless in the mirror of what is false; thus neither does our lucid and bright Order appear, except from the above shady and dusky order, which therefore I was desirous to present to thy view, to the intent that thou mightest learn what is meant by what is Perfect and Entire.*c* The Order of this Life, or the Life of this Order, induces that state which is called the *state of integrity.* And because that Order in itself, is of such a quality as it is in the Supreme Himself, therefore whosoever lives in accordance with that Order bears *His image.* Receive now the key, by which, if thou openest the gates, thou mayest both view and enter the sacristies of heaven itself.

109. But thou, my daughter, art the only one, who with him who is alone with thee in this world lives this order, and bears its image. That only one is not far off from thee; he stands in the centre of thy grove, and looks at thee with longing gaze. We observe him, but he is ignorant of it; do not turn thy countenance in that direction, but let him come to thee, and court thee with humble entreaty. Thou art to be the consort of his life, and the consort of his bed, for he is assigned to thee by heaven.

This also is the day appointed for your marriage, and the hour is at hand in which you are to be united.

Instantly the heavenly bridesmaids tied up into a smooth knot her hair, which covered her neck in ringlets, and inserted it in a

---

c Concerning this order, more may be seen in our first part concerning the worship and love of god (nos. 62 to 67, and 74, 75). Also further considerations respecting forms, and the three faculties of our life; as respecting the soul (nos. 34 to 38, and 41, 70); respecting the intellectual mind [*mens*] (nos. 46 to 53); respecting the mind [*animus*] (nos. 70, 79, 83, 84); respecting natural life, and its fountain of life, or the prince of the world; respecting the cause of his existence, his function, and revolt (nos. 69, 70, 74, 75); also respecting mediation between Divine life and natural life (nos. 78 to 83).

golden circlet; and at the same time they fastened with their fingers a crown of diamonds set on her head. Thus they adorned her as a bride for the coming of her husband, adding ornaments to her native simplicity and beauty. The damsel, still ignorant of her fate, and of what was meant by marriage, and by partnership of the bed, while the heavenly attendants were thus employed, and possibly while, by turning her eyes in that direction, she at the same time got a glimpse of him, had such a suffusion on her cheeks, that life sparkled from the inmost principles of her face as into a flame of love, and this flame assumed a purple hue, which beautifully tinged her, like a rose. Thus she was changed, as it were, into the image of a naked heavenly grace.

110. While the first-born led a solitary paradisiacal life, and fed his mind at ease with the delights of the visible world, he recollected a thousand times that most beautiful nymph, who, during his sleep, appeared to him in this grove; wherefore a thousand times he retraced his steps thither, but always in vain; the idea of her, which was in consequence excited, kindled such a fire as to inflame his very marrows, and thus to turn his tranquillity into anxious cares. This ardor increased even to this day, in which it was Divinely appointed that his wound, which then lurked in his inmost veins, should be healed by the fruition of his desire. Wherefore while he now again wandered along the same path, he came even to the entrance of this grove, which was the only entrance, without mistaking his way; rejoicing intensely at this circumstance, he hastened instantly to the midst of it, to the very tree, under which he had once so deliciously rested; and seeing the couch there, the vision of his sleep so revived, that he spied, as with his eyes, her very face. And while he was wholly intent on her image, and extended his sight a little further, lo! he saw and recognized the nymph herself, in the midst of the choir of intelligences. At this sight he was in such emotion, and so filled with love, that he doubted a long time whether his sight did not deceive him; but presently, when the crowd of his thoughts was a little dispersed, it occurred to his mind, that he was brought

hither of the Divine Providence, and that this was the event of which previous notice was given him in sleep; and that she it was whom heaven had marked out for him as a bride and a conjugial partner. I see clearly, said he, that she is mine, for she is from my own bosom, and from my own life. But we must proceed according to Order, that what is Divine may be in what is honorable, and what is honorable in its form, or in decorum; she must therefore be wooed and courted with entreaty. While he was intent on these and several other things, the celestial intelligence beckoned to him with a nod to come near; and while he was leading the bride by the hand, this scene was ended, which was the sixth in the theatre of the orb.

PART THREE

which discusses the marriage of the
first-born pair;
and
the sun of life,
the spiritual and natural borders, and
the degrees of the mind and of forms

Part the Third
The Married Life of the First-Born Pair

111. WHEN now she was left alone to her only one, in order that they might pass pleasantly the intermediate time until evening, for the sun was still equidistant from its rising and its setting, the bride led about her bridegroom by the hand through her natal grove and its magnificent palestra and scenes, for it was like the most pleasant theatre of the orb. They met nothing which did not fill all the senses with the pleasantness of beauty, and at the same time everything gave opportunity for conversation and turned this first experience of their lives into intimacy; from which the youth could not but turn the conversation to the testification of his love. For all things were in vernal flower and genial sport, and as it were enticed the pledges of union with the love which burned to hasten the unition of the associate mind. Everything was auspicious, heaven itself favoring; wherefore no delay interposed until the bride also burned with a like torch of mutual love and declared herself as favorable and pleased at the coming of her bridegroom, for which favor he humbly gave thanks and declared her to be his one only delight in the world, the beauty and the crown of his life which, placed upon his head by the heavenly ones, he accepted as a bond to his fidelity. Thus there was consent by both, and a covenant, which they also confirmed by mutual kisses. The love thence conceived and born grew and slowly became a flame. For in that most perfect

state of their minds' life a pure innocence with delights most sweet and affecting to this new born infancy nourished and incited this love. From these auspicious beginnings a new condition of life, distinct from the former and not hitherto perceived, entered into both; namely, nothing presented to sense smiled upon and was pleasing to one which did not also affect the mind of the other; and thus from consent their gladness was united and exalted; so that the vein of all delights inflowed into a heart as it were united, but divided into two chambers. There it joined itself into a common stream [each part of] which did not sweetly taste its own pleasure without at the same time tasting also that of the other.

112. In the early morn, when Aurora sent forth on high into the hemisphere of heaven the rays of the rising sun, like arrows tinged with gold, they both awoke at the same time from a most sweet sleep in the conjugial couch which they had shared; for a kind of heavenly lightning glanced over their eyes, driving away rest and drawing the attention of both away from each other and to itself. There appeared something in a middle region of heaven which was to display and signify the universe with its destinies and inmost certainties; this presented itself to the sight of both as in clear daylight.

FIRST: There shone forth a Centre of Dazzling Light, of such infinite brightness that the solar flames, radiated from Aurora, retired into shade, and the glowing torches of the constellations immediately disappeared. Thence also the eyes of both began to blink so that they were altogether compelled to close them with their lids; but nevertheless the splendor shone so clearly that it flashed through to the purest points of the fibres. This Centre so poured forth Its Light through the universe that its terminations or ends vanished from the sight, and then, because of the incomprehensibility, a blackish stupor was poured forth into the spheres of all the senses.

SECONDLY: Round about this Most Bright and Spacious Centre there appeared to be produced a Border, purple from brilliancy, but flamy, glittering with a transparent beauty, tinged with a Tyrian hue, a circle of gems. This was flowing about into perpetual orbits, in number like those of an endless Meander. The orbits gyrated in perennial courses and revolved their ends from firsts to lasts and when they had revolved insinuated them again in firsts. The gyres were constant, but because they entered into and receded from each other, the sight following them was led astray, although the revolutions of all flowed and reflowed most uniformly. This border and its meandering banks were crowned by most beautiful faces and forms of bodies the foreheads of which were encircled by gems like little stars, which were also surrounded by a yellow border. All the forms resembled the first-born and his most beautiful companion and represented loves like them in the beautiful couch in which they reclined.

THIRDLY: When both had fixed their gaze with unspeakable delight upon all these images of themselves, this lovely border was surrounded by a circle which presently changed into a brazen and iron color and turned and wreathed itself like a heart. That fiery river, like a vortex, establishing perpetual orbits and continually progressing and rolling itself about in similar orbits enclosed the interior border in a surrounding wall. But, as in the hollow of the heart, there appeared a twofold way, one for the influx and circumgyration of the flame of the interior border, the other for this black and arid encircling fiery vortex. The rivers, properly mixed in the middle of the hollow, broke forth through one gate, but presently being again divided, after having made a circuit, they returned into their veins.

FOURTHLY: In these two belts produced round about the Most Bright Centre there appeared heaped together an immense mass of innumerable eggs which surrounded the zones. Into these little eggs, from the heart mentioned above, innumerable rivulets, like the veins with their branches in the body, arose most distinctly and inflowed determinately, from which rivulets those eggs having been animated and made alive brought forth offspring (fœtus) of which those which were touched by the flame of the interior border, put on human forms; but those which were scorched by the fire of the exterior circle acquired animal and brutish countenances; and, what was wonderful to see, every offspring of the eggs performed its orbit; but the human forms inclined inwards, while the brutish forms continually inclined outwards. By these perpetual windings and whirlings the throngs of these human forms parted from each other, which parting left an immense space and a steep cleft.

FIFTHLY: This universal orbit was encircled and enclosed in a circuit, clear as crystal, through which there appeared whatever had hitherto been seen openly before the sight. And then the skilfully adjusted and arranged order of all things, as of a sphere [consisting of] innumerable lesser spheres, and these of least, was moved around harmonically into inflections through orbicular gyres.

SIXTHLY: This great circuit resembled an egg, which, rotating about its centre, involved multiplex bands. The last gyre having completed its revolution and while the bands still held it confined although loosened, there rose up from the centre a Human Body. Under its feet the bands not yet unloosed involved themselves again in spirals. On these being again unloosed by unfolding, that Human Form was raised up on high and was swept up (*evolavit*) into heaven. The circuit itself was then unfolded, the interior border being separated from the exterior fiery one. Its circumferences wound round about a certain globe, into new orbits, by which elevating itself on high through gyrating spires, it attenuated itself into the form of a cone.

FINALLY: The spire being continued from the apex of this pyramid, it flowed about into new spires, which having again revolved stretched themselves forth pointedly into helices, and so on and on.

113. Amazed by these sights they again contemplated each other, and each wished as it were to read from the face of the other what was the interior thought concerning these things. Both of their minds reasoned similarly and framed a series from firsts to lasts; and as the thing itself, so also the faces of both were liberated from shadows and brought into light. The youth, noticing this in the face of his consort, touched her cheeks with the palm of his hand

The Worship and Love of God

and gently asked her to begin from the sanctuary of her mind to explain what she knew to be the interpretation of this heavenly phenomenon and to open to his bosom the secrets of the destiny that was seen, as she believed them to have evolved themselves. For, said he, from the connection of the things which followed each other from beginning to end we clearly see that the vision portrays the universe with its destinies and in most certainties, and therefore it has presented itself to our view in a middle region between heaven and earth on this the first wedding-morning of the parents of the future human race.

But his companion, having been given the opportunity of speech by this short argument, modestly replied that she considered things so deeply hidden in the arcana of heaven and involved in the progressive evolutions of so many events, as they appeared in the vision, to be of so high an import, that, as regarding them, she did not dare to open her mind, which ran over the surfaces of things so lightly and cursorily; but she wished, if he would only regard her desire favorably, to depend upon his statement in these and similar matters, for he had examined such subjects more thoroughly, because more slowly and maturely, and had explored them more sharply in their interior chains of connection. I indeed perceive that, said she, but by a certain favoring consent, which I received from thy face, which reveals the ideas of thy mind to me, [I know] that the whole universe, including heaven and the world and whatever steadfastly pursues its life after its own fashion constitute a great series and an immense complex of means to a certain ultimate and most holy end, for the sake of which there are the creations of so many uses and hence of so many effects, and on account of which from what was seen before I was made the consort of thy life and bed; for from the connections about the Central Light of infinite brightness, from the borders and circles, also from the animated eggs which were placed around, and from the circumvolution of the whole and finally from the pyramid which arose convoluted most beautifully in spires, it appeared that all things which had preceded tended only as evolutions to the building of their pyramidal goal. For this universe, which we behold, is only the complex of means and ends, tending and conspiring towards an only [End]. For the Supreme Mind, or the Architect of the things of the universe,—who sees most minute things, even those of the future, as present together in Himself, and thus in His Own Clearest Light,—foresaw and provided Ends, before times and spaces arose, thus from eternity, which should continually flow forth from the First Itself to ultimates and from these flow back again to the First Itself; therefore He established and instituted a great orbit, or He founded the universe, heaven as well as the world, according to such a design that Ends foreseen and provided might exist in act and thus put on the reason of uses and the form of effects and so revolve in their gyres. Therefore these actual intuitions of Ends and their determinations into the nature of the world by the mediation of heaven are sent forth and so clothed that they appear to the senses to constitute that which is called the great orbit of the universe. This consists of perpetually smaller and thus of least orbits, so chained together that they flow into each other and flow in such order into the great orbit that no accidents whatever occur.[a] For the Infinite sees nothing in our finite things except the Infinite. For all the orbits which we speak of are only designs from His Ends as from centres, and, as was said, determinations to uses and the forms of uses and thus centres of centres arranged as it were into fluent circumferences. Hence is the consent and the harmony of all things; for the ultimate end of the First, or the first end of the ultimate

---

a That the Supreme Mind, according to the intuitions (*Intuitiones*) of Ends from eternity, established the universe, which was to be a complex of ends or means, we may contemplate in our own minds as it were in mirrors, or rather as in types. We also, before the origin and existence of means, regard and intend some end, for which, in order that it may exist in act, we seek means, or mediate ends, which shall all promote the first and relate to it, or as it were portend its image. For we as it were see the principal end joined with the mediate ends, which is the reason why we embrace the means with as great a love as the end itself. These means, taken together, constitute a certain world, in which all the

The Worship and Love of God

end, rules and disposes the middle ends, and these, whithersoever they turn, bear in their bosoms or faces, as in a mirror, the image of that only End. Since therefore there is nothing in the universe which does not derive its being (*esse*), its ability (*posse*), its action (*agere*), and its life (*vivere*) from Him who alone Is, it follows that not even a point or a line can be made except from Him and by Him, according to the reason of the means designed to that end. The thought that anything might by chance fall out of The Orbit of End is repugnant to the attributes of the Divine Essence, although our minds, which are most finite and in shadows, by a gross view of things separated from their connection and by a vague regard of means most remote from the end, and also by regarding a few things only, may fall into error and their ideas be easily taken away.

My mind likewise, while I know that those various infinite things adapt themselves harmoniously and most beautifully to the gyres of order and finally to the last gyre, flies through them lightly and cursorily; wherefore I ask this first favor of thee, my dearest consort, that thou deign to disclose to me from the Divine Oracle, that most deeply hidden response which was given concerning the ultimate destinies of things in the heavenly phenomenon that appeared to us. For I know that there are as many responses sent to thee from

---

mediate ends are called uses, and all uses existing in act are called effects; thence is our moral world. Such little worlds, which are a complex of means, every rational mind establishes; and whatsoever does not tend and conspire as a means to its first end it discharges from its little worlds, or rejects and proscribes as vile. Since our finite minds, wrapped in nothing but shades, design such things, what shall not the Infinite Mind in which there is no shade, but which sees most particular things in the clearest day and to which Omniscience, as also Omnipotence, are adjoined that the results of ends may be provided! The life and essence of all minds consist in the intuition of ends, and at the same time in their disposition to some ultimate ends, which, because it was also the first, reigns as it were alone in all and each of the means. From this very life the excellence of human minds should be judged, which, if they regard the love of self or a similar love as an end, will also attribute a kind of previdence and providence to themselves, so that they strive to appear as deities and deduce all the courses of ends from themselves and lead them to themselves; but of what quality their providence or prudence is, will be, God willing, disclosed in what follows.

heaven as there are objects represented before thy senses,* and that thou dost not allow the intuitions of thy mind to be drawn away from the regard of singular things into deviations while thou art constantly reducing scattered things into their series and finally joinest together these series into the most universal series of all, upon which thou dost fix thy gaze. Since, therefore, my will, being subject, is obedient to thine, permit thou that the other faculty of my mind, which is called the understanding, also depend upon thine; for I pray that thou, who rulest the one, wilt also instruct the other. To these words she added the sweet enticements of love, and so mightily enforced her prayers and desires.

114. From this discourse of his young bride, so elegant and full of wisdom, concerning the Divine Providence of singulars in the universals of the universe and at the same time from her showing by means of love, her desire of knowing and drawing forth the things which are deeply enfolded in minds, and also those more deeply hidden, of heaven itself, the first-born was aroused by a certain delightful amazement, which, the tinder of his love having been kindled by beauty, poured into him a certain purer fire and at the same time a sense of pleasantness from this partnership in his very life. When, from these first-fruits of delights, he came into the distinct perception of the pleasures born thence, he in return thanked her with an ardor equal to that with which she had earnestly solicited him to tell her, and promised her that he would unfold those secrets, which heaven had opened to both by means of a picture, in so far as there had been a revelation to him of those things. For there was nothing that was for her sake that he did not will and regard as a duty.

115. Before I begin my interpretation of that heavenly wonder which predicted the fate of the orbit of the universe, according to the parts which arose successively and were seen distinctly, I wish,

---

* Compare, Introd. to *Principia*: "Man in His State of Integrity," part I, p. 38. (F. S.)

The Worship and Love of God

if thou, my beloved, wilt permit, to further continue the thread of the web which thou hast so skilfully woven, and to exhibit that very End itself which the mediate ends, or the universe, which is the complex of them, regard as their Coronis or Last [goal]. It may be manifest to everyone that the world with its earth, and this with its triple kingdom, does not exist on its own account, but for the sake of an end prior and superior to itself, namely, for the sake of heaven, and this on account of the Glory of the Most Wise Creator, wherefore all the orders of the universe conspire to that Order, and from it as their First, they derive their origins and beginnings, and to it as to their Last and at the same time their First they return with this crown of all ends, that is, with His Glory (thus fulfilled). Wherefore, there is nothing in the heavens nor in the worlds which does not bear His Glory as it were in effigy; for all mediate ends, as they regard, so they also declare, the Last. But in order that His Glory might be declared in the most holy manner, He so established all things and constituted them by creation, that from human minds, and according to their human quality, there might be formed a heavenly kingdom, or a certain holy society, of which, as of one body He might move the soul, and His Only-begotten or Only Love, the mind, which in our bodies from understanding and will is called rational. That human body, last represented to us, and finally hatched from the grand egg, signified this heavenly kingdom or holy society.

116. But let us examine the singular things in the series in which they appeared, and as we evolve them, let us determine the connection of the things which followed with those that preceded, and thus behold the order; and finally, from the End of ends, the wonderful progression and correspondence of the intermediate causes; for only in the ultimate which crowns the work is seen the relation of the things which preceded and only here the provided agreement of apparent disagreements shines forth. Thus are dissipated obscurities, which have arisen from an unconnected series of perceptions and hence from a prejudged Order of the things of

the universe, as of a machine composed of parts, some of which are not yet prepared or seen.

I

117. FIRST: *The Centre of Dazzling Light, of such Infinite Brightness, shone forth, so that the solar flames, radiated from Aurora, retired into the shade and the glowing torches of the constellations suddenly disappeared.* In order that we might by means of an effigy of nature behold heavenly forms, the Supreme Life of Minds was willing to represent Itself by a Dazzling Light, which poured itself forth from a spacious centre, as if from a Sun, into the ends of the universe. Thence Heaven took its origin and thence the world, Heaven mediating. That Light, or Life, shone forth from the Sun of Life of all things, or of the Intelligence, Wisdom, Justice and Glory of all things: for there are as many determining forms of truth, whence is intelligence, as there are rays flashing forth from that Light or Life; there are as many Goodnesses (*Bonitates*), whence is Wisdom, as there are Sacred Torches within the rays. The Order thence flowing is called Justice, whence are the Laws by which the universal orbit is ruled. The splendor of this Life, or of Intelligence and Wisdom, and of Justice from these, is called Glory, which because it includes all those in itself, is, as was said, the End of all ends; and its Splendor of such Infinite brightness that everything must appear as shadow in its presence, even the Intelligence and Wisdom of human minds, yea of heavenly ones; wherefore the solar flames, radiated from Aurora, are said to have retired into the shade, and the glowing torches of the constellations to have departed and vanished.

118. *Thence also the eyes of both began to blink, so that they were altogether compelled to close them with their lids.* The Supreme Life of Intelligence and Wisdom, represented by that most bright Light, and the Glory appearing in Splendor from the most holy Sanctuary of Its Justice as lightning, is so supereminent because Infinite; and if the Infinite were to inflow into human minds without the mediation of Heavenly Life radiating from His Only-begotten, it

would reduce their life and sight into the shade of death, as if the solar splendor were to dazzle our unveiled eyes. There is no communion of the Infinite with finite things, except through Him, who mediates; wherefore life without Him is not life, but the image of death and shade. Therefore it was that our eyes began to blink so that they were altogether compelled to close themselves with their lids, before there appeared to be born around this most brilliant Centre the Border, ruddy or flamy from the brightness. It would be as if some one dared to look into the most Holy shrine of that Wisdom, or enter the court of Its Justice, and there search into and unfold the Laws decreed from eternity; he would be immediately punished for the temerity of such daring; for such a vertigo would seize the sight of his mind, and shade would blind it, as would befall the sight of the eye of him who gazed steadily at the sun, the pupil of his eye not being protected; on account of this danger there arose our blinking and the veiling of our eyes by their lids.

119. *Nevertheless the splendor shone so clearly that it flashed through to the purest points of the fibres.* The Divine Life signified by this Light is the only Life of living things; they are only rays of the Light of this Sun, or streams of the Life of this fountain, which, modified as it were into various forms, attributes to the sight of our minds its light, that is to say its life which is Intelligence and Wisdom and which consists in the Knowledge of truth and in the perception of good. This Light penetrates our luminaries (*lumina*) whatever be the veils that cover them: for whatever of light there is in the luminaries of the universe or whatever of life there is in souls, minds or animi, and in the senses and actions of their body, is derived from that alone; but where it is without the mediating Light, Life and Justice of Its Only-begotten, there is not light but shade, not life but death, for there is not Justice but the punishments of Justice on account of injustice. Our soul, which does not live its life from itself, but from that Only Life, is in all the beginnings of the fibres of its body, not only as the reason of their existence, but

also as giving them birth; for organic or compounded things are nothing but beginnings or simple things, determined into various forms according to uses. This also was the reason that the Splendor of that Light, the veil not hindering, shone so brightly that it flashed through to the purest points of the fibres. Thence it also appears that nothing can be so skilfully covered over in outmosts, or so artfully concealed in inmosts, which the Omniscient will not see through most clearly in Himself or in His Light.

120. *This Centre so poured forth its Light through the universe that Its terminations or ends vanished from the sight.* In this Light, or Life, there is nothing but the Infinite. Our sight or understanding, which is circumscribed by most finite boundaries, either falls into delirium, or into a swoon, or perishes as a sailor in a great ocean, if it dares to behold and still more if it dares to examine the infinities of the Infinite. From heavenly Light itself, from which is the sight of our minds, or the understanding of truth and good, we may clearly see that the shrine of His Wisdom, consequently of His Providence, by which He rules the universe which is the complex of ends, or of means, from end to end, is altogether inaccessible; therefore, the terminations of that Light, poured forth through the universe, to our sight appeared to vanish, and for this reason also *a blackish stupor, because of this incomprehensibility, appeared to be poured into the spheres of all our senses.*

II

121. *Round about this most bright and spacious Centre there appeared to be born a Border, purple from brightness, but flamy.* The splendor of that Light, or the Glory of that Life, which poured itself forth to the ends of the universe, that is, through ages of ages, from eternity to eternity, could not be communicated to our minds, and still less to the other or lower powers of our lives, without manifest danger of death. For what else would result from a communion of the Infinite with finite beings, or of the Most Holy and Just, with us who live from the dust and in it, but that we would be accused

of impurity by Its Holiness, condemned by Justice and sentenced to death; therefore, He begot His Image, or Son, from Eternity, through Whom or through Whose Life He might inflow mediately into the faculties of the life of our body; Who, because He was born the mediation and the one Only Love of the Supreme, it is His Life, which is signified by the Flamy Border purple in its brilliancy, which appeared round about this most bright and spacious Centre. This is the Life which is properly called Heavenly and which excites the understanding and will of our minds. For Life is twofold, one is heavenly and the other is natural, but both are derived from the only Life of the Supreme. Natural life without the mediation of the heavenly is, as was just said, not life but spiritual death in the likeness of life; for there is no mediating Love, Holiness or Justice, and from this separation between the Divine Life and the natural life of man perpetual combats arise.

122. *Glittering with a transparent beauty, tinged with a Tyrian hue, a circle of gems.* That Heavenly Life, represented by the Flamy Border, not only pours Divine Light into our minds, which live it, and thus transforms them into intelligences, but it also pours in the Flame, purple from brilliancy, from which the intelligences also become wisdoms. For it is the Divine Life, from which is the intelligence of truth, represented by the brilliant Light, and joined to Love, effigied by the purple Flame, which causes intelligence to become wise, namely, that it not only perceives from truth what good is, but also from good what truth is; and thus from truths and at the same time from goods, he worships and loves the Best, that is, the Supreme;[b] wherefore without an interceding or mediating

---

[b] To understand and to be wise are two altogether distinct things, for we may understand and still not be wise; but one leads us to the other, namely, science to the cognition of truth (*veri*), and truth (*veritas*) to the cognition of good, and it is the good which is sought for. But in order that we may be wise, it is necessary, not only that we should know and thus understand what truth and good are, but that we should also be affected with the love of them. Therefore, in the degree that there is good or the truly useful in the objects

Life of that Flame or Love, the Best or Supreme could not at all be approached because not conjoined by Love, for APPROACH BY WORSHIP IS SUCH AS IS CONJUNCTION BY LOVE; this Intelligence together with Wisdom, it was, which glittered with a transparent beauty, tinged with a Tyrian hue, a circle of gems.

---

of our minds' intuition, which objects we embrace and consequently pursue as an end, in that degree we are wise. This we may clearly see from the operations of our minds, or from the series of their progression, which is this:

First, by way of the senses, which is called the posterior way, we either immediately seize that which will be a help or instrumental cause leading to the knowledge of things, or we take it from the memory, into which the objects of the senses are brought under the appearance of material ideas.

Second, we take that which is perceived by our inmost sense, or laid up in the memory, and as it were introduce it into our intuitive or rational mind and there turn it about and rationally discuss it, although we ought to view it only from above and thus revolve our intellectual ideas above it; this is called thought.

Third, these ideas, or thought, frames its reasons into a series and thus forms a certain analytic equation, or a chain entwined by reasons, which is called judgment or the formation of judgments from the objects of thought.

Fourth, under these, as in calculations, we draw a line and from them we argue as in logic. But these, which have hitherto been turned about in the sphere of the mind, are mere inquiries of truths, and by means of these inquiries, or their series, inquiries of goods. But in themselves they are bare cognitions and pertain to the first faculty of the mind or the understanding, that is, to intelligence. But here the hinge as it were turns, for this first scene of the operations of the mind is immediately succeeded by another, namely,

Fifth, to choose from the calculations and conclusions of judgment that which will regard the end or use, is called the choice of good, and

Sixth, this is finally brought to a certain principle of actions called the will, within which are all those things which preceded and were chosen. For, as all the essentials of motion are within the conatus, so all the essentials of action are within the will, so that the will is a certain living effort (*conatus*) into which are brought those essentials produced in their series from the understanding.

Seventh, it is this which may now be called Wisdom; for in the degree that the good or the truly useful is within the thoughts, judgments, conclusions and selections, that is, in the will where they all are together, and in the degree that this is produced in act, in that degree we are said to be wise.

Eighth, but it will be seen below that within the will there is a certain life, which flows from the love of the end in view and which reigns generally in the whole series of operations and which especially determines, as the principal active force, that part which is called choice and thus excites the will also into act. Such then is the circle of operations of the rational mind which begins from the sphere of sensation and is terminated in the active sphere over which the will rules. Hence now there is an ultimate Good which is to

123. *This Border was flowing about into perpetual orbits.* The universe, which contains in itself both heaven and the world, consists of several forms, each of which constitutes its own sphere. The supreme form is called the super-celestial, the second is called the celestial, and that which follows the infra-celestial. There exist as many forms and spheres in our bodies as in the universe; they succeed each other and correspond. That supreme one, which is called the super-celestial, is proper to our soul; the second, or celestial, is of our intellectual mind; and the third, or the infra-celestial, is of the animus or the lower mind. I know that thou didst lately see demonstrated before thine eyes by the heavenly intelligence the wonderful gyres of the circumfluxions of these [forms] in the beginnings of our fibres, and how the celestial form, which is of our intellectual

---

choose and to pursue the Best to the end that we may enjoy it. Wherefore all the things which precede are mediating causes and like servants and attendants, some of who bear the key of the court, others that of the temple itself and still others that of the inmost shrine where Wisdom dwells on her throne. For what are truths without an ultimate regard for goodness! Or what is the understanding of the mind, or intelligence, unless to know how to choose the Good, to prefer the Better, and finally, to will the Best! To this nature herself impels our minds, that is ourselves, for everyone desires and pursues happiness; neither is happiness given except in Good, consequently neither the greatest happiness except in the Best; nor does Good flow except from the Best and indeed by mediation. Wherefore to know much and also to understand, and not to be wise, is to rave in the midst of the sciences, or like Tantalus to be surrounded by water, but never to drink a drop; for it is Wisdom which completes and crowns intelligence and effects that intelligence may understand. But what is the Best? All truths promptly disclose it with one consent, namely, that the Best is that which is the first Origin of all goods and truths, or from which, as from an inexhaustible and perennial Fountain, all goods flow as streams; or, more simply, it is the First, for this is also the Supreme or Highest, whence it follows, that it is God, or that it is in God. From the consent of all truths, yea, from the dictation of goodnesses, we may perceive that because all happinesses derive their origin from this Best they also derive their inmost essence from It; for the nearer we approach the more deeply are our very wills filled with gladness for [even] the infinite solicitudes themselves eagerly desire these joys.* From the concordant suffrages of truths we may also know that we are born to enjoy these inmost delights of the will. From all these things it follows as a conclusion that the highest of all cognitions is to know how to approach God, in Whom

* The MS. here is obscure. (TR.)

mind, by infinite windings and circles and their most regular order, represented in a small effigy a certain Olympus, or the heaven of our Love, altogether like this Border which appeared to flow about into such perpetual orbits.[c]

124. *In number like an endless Meander;* which orbits wind about in endless turnings and having run through their allotted courses flow back again into their sources. If we diligently investigate, with an interior keenness of vision, our minds and their modes of turning, we will see meanderings of a similar fluxion, such as in this most beautiful Border, which represents in an effigy the Heavenly Life, and the Heaven of our Love, or the Only Begotten of the

---

is the Best, and also the Greatest Happiness. But, to *approach* in spiritual things is to be *conjoined,* while to recede is to be disjoined. Conjunction, however, is only given by Love, for Love is union itself of spiritual connection, for by its conjunction even disjoined things are connected. Love also is the soul of all happinesses, for we only enjoy that which we love. Love is also the very Life of our minds, for if you remove the loves, our minds grow torpid and as it were die, but such as is the love such is their life. Thence now it follows that as the highest of all intelligence is to know how to approach God, in Whom is the Best, and also the Greatest Happiness, so the highest of all wisdom is *to be conjoined to God by love;* this now is that which was said, *that such is the approach by worship as is the conjunction by love.* But although we have explored what the Best and the Greatest Happiness are, still, nevertheless, innumerable things, which break through by the inferior way, or that of the senses, fly about in our minds and represent themselves as the best things, consequently as deities; and with them, innumerable loves, surrounded by spurious truths, which with their flatteries and allurements persuade to the same delusion, especially when we live in darkness regarding those spiritual things in which our very Life is and so natural things feign that light. Wherefore unless Heavenly Light with its Love inflowed into the sphere of our minds through the superior way we could not at all understand what truth is, consequently neither what is truly good, still less be wise. For those loves are so many torches, and those spurious truths are so many fatuous lights (*lumina*) which endeavor to extinguish the love of the Best and the Light of that flame or Love; and the Love of the Supreme receding, or the superior way being closed, they actually extinguish them, so that instead of understanding they rave and instead of being wise they are insane, or what is the same thing, spiritual shade and death succeed and occupy the mind, in which natural things should have no place but only be as it were seen from heaven under the feet. For that spiritual mind is created in order that we should live a purely spiritual life by means of it, but the animus, which is the lower mind, is spiritual as well as natural, so that by means of it power may be given to descend from the spiritual into the natural.

c We have fully treated of these forms in part II on the *Marriage of the First-born,* nos. 90, 93, 95, 99, 102, 103; also here and there in part I.

Supreme.[d] For such is their substantial form, by whose variations, or changes of state, are formed and produced those rational series, by means of which ends are defined as uses, and these determined into acts. For human minds are little effigies of the great Heaven, that is, they are so formed that they both can and should live the Heavenly Life; for when they are led by the Heavenly Life, they perceive truths, which are the objects of their sight; and it is the spiritual Flame, or Love, which so leads them, for Love alone excites the lives of minds to action. From these things it may be known of what quality are the gyres of the celestial form in the grand body of the universe, here effigied by the meanderings infinite in number which flow around in endless windings and having run through their allotted courses flow back again into their sources. In general it must be maintained, that the Supreme has transcribed into us, as into small types, the ideas (*ideas*) as well of His Heaven as of the world,[e] in order that the gyres of His Ends and Means, from firsts to lasts and from lasts to firsts might go forth and return through us.

125. *he gyres were constant, but because they entered into and receded from each other, the sight following them was led astray.* Human

---

d That the ideas of our intellectual mind exist by means of actual variations of form, or changes of state, may be seen in parts I and II where it is very often pointed out and demonstrated.

e That human bodies with all the faculties of their life are created types, and thus forms and powers, in correspondence with the active forces which are in the universe, may be seen demonstrated here and there in parts I and II. But in order that these things may be presented in clearer light, it is of importance that in progressing from part to part, this truth be kept in sight. It is manifest to every one, that the organs of our senses are altogether made or fashioned according to the nature of the atmospheres of the world. The ears with their drums, entrances, little canals and windings are fashioned altogether according to the nature of the modifications of the air, which is fully shown by the science of acoustics and by that of music. The eye with its tunics and humors, and finally with its retina, is an organ or instrument plainly formed according to the modifications of the ether, or to its variations of light and shade, which is shown by optics; the eye also, when taken out of its orbit, resembles a *camera obscura,* as it is called. Wherefore if we will industriously examine the structure of the eye it will be manifest to us, by the help of the sciences, of what quality is the ether and its modification. From these things it is now evident, that these two organic forms or powers are altogether made according to the nature

societies, which, as I foresee will form that grand body under the auspices of Heaven, will perform these gyres from the first to the last and from the last to the first; and accomplish their courses, as in a plane, to that pyramidal goal which was finally seen. For as minds, according to intuitions of ends, rule their bodies, so Heaven, which presides over the life of our minds, rules those societies as the grand body of the universe, according to the will and decisions of the Supreme, or according to His Ends foreseen and provided from eternity. These ends by heaven are similarly defined as uses, and determined into acts, and thus, under a constant government and an order designated beforehand, they are borne to the Crown of ends which is the Glory of the Supreme Deity. It is this providence of particular things in things universal, which performs such constant gyres. But we, who look at superior things from lowest ones, see the successive series of ends from some intermediates which are bent down as far as possible into the narrow orbit of our own life. For we behold that which is a simultaneous outgrowth of innumerable

---

of the active forces of the air and ether, that is, of the atmospheres of the world; and those atmospheres exert their active forces when the organs themselves exert their passive and instrumental forces. These atmospheres, therefore, are what properly constitute the active world, the quality of whose nature is manifested by modifications. That there is nothing of life in the atmospheres every one may conclude without any other demonstrating arguments than the phenomena which are before the eyes and have been collected. The remaining organs of the external senses, as powers, similarly correspond to these atmospheres, but as the two former powers corresponded to their active forces so do these latter correspond to their forces of inertia. The organ of smell perceives the figures of the parts which are heavy or inert, and the effluent exhalations which fly about in those two atmospheres; for according to their forms and the affections of that sense arising thence, that organ perceives them distinctly. The tongue perceives similar parts, but still heavier or more inert ones, which flow about in water or other liquids, especially such as are saline. The sense of touch perceives the very changes of state of the atmospheres and water, such as heat, cold and tempests, besides many other related things. In a word, the organs of the senses are made for a perception of all things which exist and occur in the spheres of the world. Since now the organs of the external senses are only powers made to correspond with the active forces of the world, properly so called, it follows, that the substantial forms of the internal senses are also in the same way powers to which correspond those forces in the universe in which there is Life. For they live more than the rest; since they perform the functions of their life even while the external senses are at rest and lie

The Worship and Love of God

successive things, regardless of any connection of things past with things to follow, and consequently we behold only in the greatest obscurity what from such a vast complex of means must be the ultimate destiny of the universe. So by our vague ideas we are led into error concerning the provided order of the universe. This is the reason why one gyre appeared to enter another, and a second one to recede from still another, which led the sight following them into errors, *although the revolutions of all flowed and reflowed most uniformly.*

126. *This border and its meandering banks were crowned by most beautiful faces and forms of bodies whose foreheads were encircled by gems like little stars, and these were also surrounded by a yellow border.* These are the inhabitants of Heaven, called Intelligences and Wisdoms, minds under a human form, servants and attendants of their Prince or the Only-begotten of the Supreme, who, because of Him, live in heavenly Light and pour a similar light into human minds. Thence also is their intelligence of truth and wisdom of

---

altogether deeply asleep in their shade. These internal sensories, which are also the beginnings of the external, as may be manifest from all phenomena, are three. The lowest, from its affections, is called the lower mind or animus, whose faculty of action is called imagination and whose component parts are material ideas. That this faculty is distinct from that of the rational mind, may appear from brute animals which enjoy similar affections and an almost similar faculty of imagination, and from innumerable other proofs, the mere enumeration of which would fill pages. See part I, nos. 70, 83, 84. This sense, which is the lowest of the interior ones, cannot but be excited to action, like the external senses, by its life or by its active or living force. This is the life which is properly called natural, or animal, because of the brutes which live it. Over it the prince of the world, or the devil, rules, for if there is a similar life there are also similar affections, natures and animi of life concerning which we have frequently treated in parts I and II, especially in nos. 74 and 77. Besides this lowest of the interior senses, there is a higher one, which from its proper affections and loves is called the intellectual mind, from its faculty of action called thought, to which the will also is adjoined; the parts of thought are the immaterial ideas. Its life is called celestial, because it altogether corresponds to the life of heaven over which the Only Love of the Supreme, or His Only-begotten, rules. This life is properly human for the brute animals altogether lack it. To its life, as to that of the other degrees, there must correspond a living force in the universe, whence it derives its activity and life and from whence it comes; this is called Heaven, wherefore the life which it is designed to live is called celestial. That this faculty or power (of the intellectual mind) is different from the

good. These are they who, under the auspices and at the will of their Prince, because they preside over human minds, govern the decisions and thus the destinies of that grand Body or of human societies. For he who rules minds rules also their bodies since these are obedient to the understanding and will of their mind. Wherefore it is Heaven by means of which the Supreme directs and leads the courses of His Orbit to the last goal of ends. The gems by which their foreheads were encircled are truths, which are similarly transparent from their clearness and on account of which the intelligences shine as little stars; but the yellow halo which surrounded them, signifies goodnesses, which, excited by the Love of the Supreme transforms intelligences into wisdoms.*f* Because these inhabitants of Heaven appeared to me to be similar to thee, my consort, I am persuaded that thou resemblest in an image a heavenly intelligence

---

lower mind, appears not only from its thought, which is distinct from imagination, and from its ideas, which are called immaterial, as distinct from the material ideas or those of the memory, but also from its loves or inclinations which are contrary or opposite to the loves and inclinations of the lower mind, called the passions of the animus. That the intellectual mind is also different from the soul is clear because it is not in the foetus nor in those recently born, but it makes a beginning and grows up with age. Also when its highly organic form is destroyed or injured, it is likely to become delirious and to grow insane, which is not the case with the soul itself which still rules its body according to the laws of order.

But the supreme power is called the soul, from which everything in the body derives its life, concerning which also much has been said above, and also that the soul itself is excited by the Life of the Supreme. From these things it now appears that we are types of the universe, and that we carry about heaven and the world like small universes in ourselves in a certain effigy, but only as powers (see part I, no. 58; note *y* there; and no. 59); for unless there flowed in as many forces and lives, as there exist faculties or powers in us distinguished in degree, one degree could not live a life different from the others and properly its own. Thence it is evident, that from our very selves, if we will only distinctly examine our faculties, we may clearly see of what quality the universe is, as well Heaven as the world. These things, although they are the marrow and essence of the Sciences, are nevertheless more deeply hidden in shade than anything else, and nothing is less cared for than to know our spiritual lives; which carelessness is to be attributed to no other cause than that we do not live the Heavenly Life, whence is the light of intelligence, but a natural life, or only in the senses, the body and the world, which life only involves all things in shade.

f Cf. part I, no. 67 near the end.

and wisdom and at the same time their Love, not only in thy face but also in thy mind!

127. It is thus established most wisely by our Supreme that there be perpetual causes and mediums of life which succeed each other in such an order that the things which are pleasing to Him and preëstablished may flow undeviatingly into effects. Even as in our bodies, which are small types of the universe and for that reason are also called microcosms, in which is the soul inspired by the Supreme Deity, which has so fabricated and furnished its little orb, called the body, that its ends, determined by means, exist in act and effect. Wherefore He began first of all to design and found a certain image of Heaven, or a certain Olympus which He delivered to her intellectual mind (*menti*) to be ruled by intelligences and wisdom; afterwards also a lower and mediating life, and so forth, so that she might descend as by continual mediations, as it were by ladders, into the ultimate nature of the world of her body. But all these things are for the sake of the intellectual mind, her only love, to whose government the administration of the whole was delivered and subjected,[g] altogether as in the grand body of the universe.

III

128. *This lovely Border was surrounded by a circle of pure fire.* Nothing is presented to the senses in the natural world, to which something in the spiritual heaven does not correspond. For nature exists for the sake of serving life, or the world for the sake of Heaven, in order that ends defined as uses may be exhibited as effects. These effects contain the reason of their existence in uses even as uses have the reason for their existence in ends. Wherefore in order that the secrets and wonders of a spiritual nature may reach our intellect they are represented before our senses by means of figures. Lights (*lumina*) signify lives, from which is understanding, but fires the

---

g These things were treated of in part I, no. 50, where there is a copious description.

loves of that life; wherefore intelligence is called spiritual light (*lux*) and its love, spiritual heat. As that lovely Border with its light and its flame, represented heavenly Life with its purest Love, so this fiery circle represented the infra-celestial life with its grosser love. This latter life because it is immediately set over and adjoined to nature is called natural, and on account of the brute animals which it properly vivifies it is called animal. The faculty or power in us in which it lives is called the lower mind or the animus from its loves or affections, which are also called the lusts and passions of the animus. Because these derive their ardor especially from nature and wave their torches immediately into nature, that life is effigied by an arid or glowing fire: and as heavenly life is ruled by its Prince by means of spiritual essences, which were called intelligences and wisdoms, so also this infra-celestial or natural life is ruled by its own Prince, called the Prince of the world, who presides over nature and by means of his genii, in whom, as in himself, there is a similar natural life, he excites our animus to action. This life is so distinct from the heavenly life that the one may be lived and not at the same time the other, for natural life without the heavenly is actually lived by the brute animals while by us the heavenly is lived together with the natural which is subjugated and is obedient to the heavenly.

129. *Which circle was presently changed into a brazen and iron color.* This Prince of the world from whom this life, called natural or animal, emanates as from a general fountain and from whose genii as from the streams of that fountain, was made and called into existence to the end that he might serve as a connecting medium between Heaven and the world, or between life purely spiritual and nature devoid of life; for there is no communion of purely spiritual life with nature, as there is none of light with shade, nor of a living thing with a dead one, except by a mediating life with which the soul or natural life is endowed. Without its service neither brute animals nor our lower minds or animi would be excited to the performance of the functions of their life, for we are powers,

or if you prefer it, faculties of life, which are constantly excited to action by a force inflowing extrinsically; [h] wherefore without such an interceding life all communication between our minds, gifted with understanding and will, and their little corporeal world and its nature would be altogether intercepted; for our minds only regard ends and arrange means, and commit them to their will, from which they could not be determined into acts unless there were a life, with a corresponding power, presiding over the spirit of the fibres and the blood of the vessels, and immediately opening the gate into the nature of the body. The Prince of this life with his administering genii was made for the sake of this most excellent use, and set over the world, and joined to our Supreme by means of heavenly life or that of His Love. In the beginning, and from himself and his own nature he was most obsequiously obedient to all commands and performed the duties enjoined upon him; but afterwards, captivated and enticed by the unbridled love of self and the world and inflamed by the insane lust of arrogating even Heaven to himself (for from his nature he derived such a blindness and insanity) he altogether revolted from the Supreme and His Love. Heavenly life thereupon receding, the connecting medium between the Supreme and nature was torn away, and the life of that prince was turned into the image of death, and the light of that life into shade. Wherefore that purely fiery circle was observed to pass over into a brazen and an iron color.

130. *This circle turned and bent itself like a heart.* The organic forms of our bodies are altogether fabricated and furnished according to the nature or modification of active forces; for unless active forces and organic forms altogether corresponded to each other, no acts could be presented or effects determined. It is the ultimate form of the body which is produced and joined together by the vessels, called the arteries and veins, by their determinations, or

---

h That we are only powers, which, as organic forms, are excited to action by a force inflowing extrinsically, see above, part I, nos. 58, 59.

their acting force, called the blood and its circulations. These vessels with their blood flow together into a certain general receptacle called the heart, and by this, effect that the circle of ultimate life be continual and perennial. That natural life was effigied by that fiery circle because it presides over and rules its body and nature, especially its blood and vessels and by means of them the viscera, muscles, organs and the modes and actions flowing thence; hence, like the blood, so also this circle is said to have turned and bent itself like a heart. With its own fire also, that is, with the torch of its own desires, it especially inflames the blood and pours it out into the animus and its easily irritated genii. Hence it is that as the life of animals lacking reason consists in the blood, so also does that of those who live and follow a life not properly human, or a life of the passions of their animus, that is, a life properly animal.

131. *That fiery river, like a vortex, established perpetual orbits.* In order that the things here involved may be unfolded and fall clearly into the intellect, we will thoroughly examine those forms which by natural life as an active force are excited into act that they may perform their functions. The proper form of the natural life in the beginnings of the fibres, I know was also shown to thee, my Dearest, by the heavenly intelligence![i] The form called infra-celestial flows like a vortex into such gyres that by them are delineated greater and smaller circles with their poles, as in the great sphere of the world. By the variations of its form, or changes of state, that life produces our material ideas and determines the endeavors (*conamina*) of the will into act, not to mention the forms which are lower and proper to nature and which are actuated by the fibres with their spirit and the vessels with their blood, in all of which there is the same. . . .

[The remainder of the MS. has not been found.]

---

[i] Concerning the fluxion or determination of the essentials of this form, called the infra-celestial, see part II, nos. 93, 95, and also elsewhere.

APPENDIX

A few fragments of what seems to have been a continuance of the work have been found in manuscript, but no finished conclusion. Of these fragments as transcribed and translated by the Rev. Alfred Acton we include the following. The first fragment is of especial interest both as describing the origin of disease and also in its bearing on the period of the composition of this part of the work.

I
On the Origin of Disease

[112] "When that fiery circle was turned into one of copper and iron rust, that is, when the prince of natural life revolted from the Prince of celestial life, then, as was said, the bond between our Supreme and this life was intercepted; since love was turned into hatred and friendly correspondence to discord. Wherefore that prince, being unable to invade heaven itself, desired to intercept the communion of our Love with the world and its nature. On this account he invades human minds which present heaven in a little effigy, and conveys into them his torches and cupidities, and moreover, his shades; and thus he lays claim also to the heaven of those bodies. He continually attempts his daring deeds commenced from the beginning; and thus drives celestial life and the love of heaven wholly into flight and, with this, intelligence and wisdom and, with these, innocence. This is spoken of as 'shutting off the

inner Border as with an interjected barrier.' From his form in the beginning of the fibres it is also apparent how he invades our heaven or the intellectual mind. For since he is an active force, and by their changes of state produces material ideas and rules these according to his desires, that is, according to the desires of the world and of the body and its senses,—celestial life, which creates the interior and superior form, in the mean time fleeing away—he alone it is who rules also the changes of state in them. For those spherules which thou didst see were collapsed and empty because they react without being acted on by any intrinsic force. Hence they submit to their gross modifications, and thus induce shade in place of celestial light and insanities in place of wisdoms. Thus he scatters his hatred like poison in the beginnings of the fibres, and, from these, in the blood. Hence come all the passions of the animus and everywhere the image of death, because the cause of death."

II
Beginning of Vital Functions

[133] "If we make investigations into our brain it becomes evident that the cortical glands are not only the beginnings of the fibres, but also the beginnings of all the vital functions. For sensations stop only where the fibres stop and voluntary actions commence only where the fibre, whereby the active spirit is committed to the muscles, takes its beginning. Since this is in the beginnings of the fibres it follows that it is here that our animus and our intellectual mind by changes of state produce these ideas; and, consequently, that such cortical gland is in miniature a kind of brain within the brain; and that therein are similar spherules and substances which by variation of their form create those ideas such as now constitute the form. Respecting this we may be clearly instructed by the doctrine of Order and Degrees and also of Forms, illustrated by the form of the cortical glands in the brain.

"See part II, no. 107 note *b*."

OBSERVATIONS

On the Character and Purpose of This Work

The title of this remarkable work,—a work which is probably unique in the entire history of philosophic and psychologic writing,—enigmatic as it has seemed to the cursory reader,—will, when carefully considered in connection with a deeper knowledge of what the work contains, undoubtedly reveal better than any other solution its real meaning and purpose.

Its production marks the conclusion of the three distinct periods of the author's investigations previous to his illumination and seership, namely, the Scientific, embracing the early works in Geology, Physics, and Mechanics: the Philosophical, including the work on the *Infinite* and the Lesser and Larger *Principia:* the Anatomical, the Physiological and the Psychological, embracing the works on the *Animal Kingdom,* the *Economy of the Animal Kingdom,* and on the *Soul, or Rational Psychology.* In these works we have an account of the creation out of the Infinite of the physical universe as the habitation of the soul of man, and of the nature and operations of the soul in this its physical kingdom or realm. But it is in the work now before us that the generation and formation of the soul itself are described and so is reached the completion of the author's philosophical doctrine of creation.

The work is dramatic in form, being composed in a poetic style unlike that of the author's other writings (excepting the early poems), and the first two Parts present a succession of six Scenes or Acts. The principal impersonations in the drama are the Supreme Love or the Only Begotten; the heavenly Intelligences or guardians; the First-begotten, or Adam; the Mother Soul and her daughter Intelligences and Wisdoms; the Spouse of Adam; and the Prince of this World; all of which are represented as individuals participating in the development of the perfect human being.

The work was published in part by the author in 1745, two years after the opening of his spiritual vision and his introduction thereby into that higher and more real knowledge of the spiritual world and of the Divine Word, on which is based the entire series of his theological works. But it clearly embodies those conceptions which were, as he distinctly avers, the rational conclusions following the entire course of his own scientific and philosophical investigations thus far. In some of these conceptions, such as that of the Only Begotten, the Prince of this World, and the redemption of man from the power of the latter, the reader may find what seems discordant with the truths as afterward revealed. But it should be remembered that the symbolical form adopted, like that of the literal sense of the Holy Scripture, is capable of interpretation in harmony with those deeper spiritual truths into which the author was being providentially led. They were foreshadowings rather than contradictions of the sublimer truths to be revealed, and—what is of profound significance—the work, which was the last struggle of the unaided human intelligence to attain that goal constantly in view from the first—"a knowledge of the Soul,"—was left unfinished. The sacred recesses of knowledge to which he had aspired were still closed; but he has reached their threshold, and here in this great crisis of his career he kneels as in an act of adoration and offers up in humble confession and supplication this his work on *The Worship and Love of God.*

It is a confession of the inmost motive that has inspired all this writing hitherto, an acknowledgment of the insufficiency of human reason to survey Divine things except by Divine guidance and a supplication for this guidance into the higher knowledge. The author's mental attitude, as well as the intention of the book itself, is best described in his own language. In the posthumous work, the *Adversaria* or *Explicatio in Verbum Historicum Veteris Testamenti,* he says:

"In my treatise on *The Worship and Love of God,* Part the First, I have treated of the origin of the Earth, Paradise, its verdant bower and the birth of Adam, but still according to leading of the intellect or the thread of reason. Inasmuch, however, as human intelligence is in no wise to be trusted, unless it be inspired by God, it is of importance to truth that those things which have been taught in the little work just mentioned should be compared with the things revealed in the Sacred Codex and herein with the history of Creation revealed by God to Moses, and the point examined, in what way do they coincide? For what does not straightway coincide with what has been revealed must be openly declared as wholly false or as an aberration of our rational mind. With this end in view, I felt bound to premise a careful study of the first chapters of Genesis.

"Now when I had compared these things together with unremitting care I was amazed at their agreement; for the first thing treated of in our little work is the universal chaos or greatest Egg of the Universe which contained in itself the heaven and the earth according to the first verse of the first Chapter of Genesis, etc., etc."

Here is emphatically asserted the distinction between the knowledge obtained by reason and its philosophy and that obtained by revelation, and it is most plainly declared that the system here set forth has been arrived at by the philosophic process, with no claim to the authority of revelation.

Further, the relation of the philosophic and the theological knowledge is fully described in the following eloquent passage from the work on *The Economy of the Animal Kingdom,* part II, no. 266.

"For the mind which is within nature there is no path open beyond and above nature; consequently none by which philosophy can penetrate into the sanctuary of Theology.

"No human faculty or perception can possibly understand, of itself, its own essence or nature; much less the essence or nature of anything higher than itself.

"Thus no organ of the *senses* can understand what *perception* is; no organ of *perception* can understand what *intelligence* is; nor can *intelligence* in so far as it is merely natural, understand what *wisdom* is. It is the higher that must be the judge of the lower. Therefore the lower exists by favor and help of the higher."

"Wherefore, I beseech you, let us not seek to pass beyond the assigned limits, nor in the course of our reasonings rashly trespass upon things sacred. All that is allowed us to do is to touch with a kiss the threshold of things holy, that we may know there is a Deity, the sole Author and Upholder of the universe, who should be the object of our reverence, adoration, and love; and that the providence of our reason is respectively nothing whilst His providence is all in all.

"But what kind of being He is, in what manner He is to be worshipped, in what way we are to draw near to Him, this it has pleased Him (immortal glory be unto Him!) to reveal by means of His own holy Testaments and oracles. Only entreat Him earnestly for pardon, make use of the means He has given, weary Him with prayers, speak to Him from the soul, and not from a heart covetous of the world, and surer than certainty you will see laid open to your view the innermost sanctuaries of His Grace."

Finally, in the work itself, Part the First, Chapter Second, no. 30, after describing the earth as now at the "height of its creation with nothing wanting to any sense by which it might exalt its life and replenish the soul itself with joys," he continues:

"There was yet wanting that son of the earth, or that mind under a human form which from the paradise of earth might look into the paradise of heaven, and from this again into that of earth, and thus from an interior sight, could embrace and measure both together, and from the conjunction of both could be made sensible of pleasures to the full; consequently, who, from a kind of genuine fountain of gladness and of love could venerate and adore above everything the Bestower and Creator of all things. There was no object, not even the smallest, from which some resemblance of

Deity did not shine forth and which, in consequence, was not desirous to offer itself to the enjoyment of such a being as could *return immortal thanks to that Deity for himself and for everything!*

Is it not the purpose of this book to bring the tribute of the richest harvest of the author's scientific and philosophic labors and lay them, in the humble attitude of thankful adoration, on the threshold of those sacred recesses into which he could have access only by an act of Divine Grace, and which access was now to be granted in opening to his vision the reality and the order of the spiritual world and the wonderful depths of the *Arcana* or spiritual meaning of the Holy Scriptures?

As to that in the philosophic theory of creation here presented which will probably strike the scientific reader with the greatest amazement,—namely, the arboreal origin of man in place of birth from a lower animal form,—it may be permitted to suggest the co-ordination of this theory with the generally accepted theory of the evolution of the animal kingdom as a whole from the vegetable and the resultant inquiry whether the step of transition may not as reasonably have been immediate from the highest of the lower order to the highest of the higher as from the lowest to the lowest and thence upward by intermediate steps; and, further, that, as to the origin of human life, the science of the present day is by universal confession so far from having reached a finality that it can approach the theory here set forth with an open, if not an entirely unprejudiced mind. For the solution of this as of all other of the deep mysteries of being and of life every candid student will cherish with Swedenborg the inspiring trust: *Tempus venit quando illustratio.*

Frank Sewall
Washington, D.C., October, 1913